ANDERSON FAMILIES

Arms Matriculated in 1780 by
James Anderson

Anderson Families

of Westertown and the North East of Scotland,
their descendants and related families with
Armorial Bearings and historical notes on
contemporary events

Michael A. Anderson

Phillimore

1984

Published by
PHILLIMORE & CO. LTD.
Shopwyke Hall, Chichester, Sussex

ISBN 0 85033 555 8

Typeset in the United Kingdom by:
Fidelity Processes - Selsey - Sussex

Printed and bound in Great Britain by
THE CAMELOT PRESS LTD
Southampton, England

CONTENTS

LIST OF PLATES

(between pages 50 and 51)

Frontispiece: Arms of James Anderson, 1780
1. Anna Waugh, widow of Rev. John Anderson
2. Isabel Hay, wife of Rev. Alexander Anderson
3. Rev. Alexander Anderson
4. Margaret Anderson, daughter of Alexander and Isabel
5. Alexander MacPherson of Cluny
6. James Anderson
7. Alexander Anderson of Montrave
8. Lady Margaret Hampton, wife of Alexander Anderson of Montrave
9. Montrave House, *c.*1850
10. Alexander John Anderson of Montrave
11. Anna Eliza Jones, wife of Alexander John Anderson of Montrave
12. Alexander Arthur Anderson
13. Ada Catherine Seaton, wife of Alexander Arthur Anderson
14. Alexander William Anderson and Winifred Ann Pusill
15. Extract of Matriculation of the Arms of Michael Arthur Anderson
16. 'Grace Dieu', County Waterford
17. Henllys Hall, Beaumaris, Anglesey

LIST OF TEXT FIGURES AND FAMILY TREES

FOREWORD

by

The Rt. Hon. The Earl of Dundee, P.C., J.P., D.L.,
Hereditary Royal Standard Bearer for Scotland,
Hon. President of the Scottish Genealogy Society

During his visit to Glasgow in May 1982 Pope John Paul II pointed out that as the successor of St Peter he had come to Scottish soil in order to meet the spiritual descendants of St Andrew. Son of Andrew, or Anderson, when used as a patronym, has therefore direct relevance in Scotland, and it gives me great pleasure to write a few words here about Michael Anderson's account of the lives of his family.

In view of this patronym it is perhaps fitting that the family, although originating in Banff and Aberdeenshire, should come to settle later on in the area of St Andrews itself. And from the mid-16th century when the story begins, while Scotland was torn by the conflict of religious ideas, it is also interesting how the lives of several generations of Anderson ministers happen to illustrate so clearly the problems shared at the time by all Scottish sons of St Andrew, whether clergy or laity. For in Scotland the religious conflict was quite as much if not more, to do with the particular distinction between episcopacy and presbyterianism, as it was to do with the general differences between Roman Catholic and Protestant. The case between presbyterianism and episcopacy was, of course, closely linked to the development of a political balance in Scotland and in Britain after the Reformation. Thus we find that Alexander Anderson was an episcopalian and a monarchist, although he signed the 'Solemn League and Covenant' in 1643, whereas his son John remained a Presbyterian before and after the Revolution of 1688. But both men had the wholehearted loyalty and support of their parishioners at Auchtergaven, and as the family motto indicates, conscience was free from guilt.

In 1780 the arms were matriculated, and Michael Anderson proceeds to trace not only the main branch from which he descends, but also to give brief histories and biographies of other families connected by marriage. The appeal as well as the paradox of genealogy is that what appear to be branches are really main stems and what appear to be main stems are really branches. It all depends whether you have journeyed to 18th-century Scotland in order to look forward at 20th-century England or Canada, or whether you look back to the past from your own century. Thus from the 18th century we look forward and watch how the Andersons spread out from Fife over Britain and overseas, moving between the different careers of the Church, law, the East India Company, architecture, engineering and accountancy. Then from the present day we look back at the lives of Andersons alongside those connected to a particular father-in-law, son-in-law, or daughter-in-law of the 18th or 19th centuries, the Lindsays in Fife and Edinburgh, or the Hampton and Lewis families in North Wales.

Michael Anderson's research has been thorough and his presentation is objective and vivid. This account will be of great interest to all those who bear the name, and as a type of historical approach expressed through the lives of a particular family it will also give valuable insights to the student and general reader.

DUNDEE

Birkhill,
Cupar,
Fife.

ACKNOWLEDGEMENTS

My research for this book has been greatly helped by assistance and advice received from a number of people, in addition to the members of my family. I should like to thank:

The Earl of Dundee (formerly Lord Scrymgeour) for reading a draft of the book and for arranging for his father to write the Foreword. Regretfully, the 11th Earl of Dundee died in June 1983.

The Earl of Crawford and Balcarres for reviewing the history of the Lindsay family.

Malcolm R. Innes of Edingight, Lord Lyon King of Arms, for additional information used in compiling the chapter about Anderson Heraldic Links.

Sir John Gilmour, Bt. of Montrave in Fife for help with the chapters concerning Alexander Anderson of Montrave and his sons.

Sir David Baird, Bt. for advising on the descendants of the last Lord Blantyre.

John Peter J. Anderson for making available many of the papers of Sir Francis James Anderson and other more recent family information.

Barron C. Christie for providing information and papers concerning Charles Joseph Anderson and his descendants.

MICHAEL A. ANDERSON

PREFACE

A NUMBER OF ANDERSON FAMILIES appear to share the same origins from the north east of Scotland in the 15th and 16th centuries. Some of these families come from the Banffshire and Aberdeen region and in particular from Westertown. The known history of the Anderson families from Westertown starts from about the end of the 15th century. Although their origins before then have not yet been established, there are various theories concerning Anderson families from before that time. Two earlier books dealing with specific Anderson families are *The Andersons of Phingask and Their Descendants* by James Mackenzie Anderson Wood printed in 1910 and *Records of a Family of Andersons of Peterhead from the year 1560* by A. D. Ferguson and C. F. Anderson, printed in the 1930s.

In his book, J. M. A. Wood suggests that there are two main divisions of the Anderson family in Scotland. Those of Lowland Scottish descent and those having a Celtic origin. Quoting Wood, Ferguson and Anderson say he expressed the opinion that all the Andersons of Ross, Sutherland, Elgin, Banff and Aberdeen sprang from the same ancestor. They suggest that genealogists are trying to trace back the various Anderson families to the joint ancestor. At present, however, the records do not seem to go back much before A.D. 1500. It is generally supposed that he bore the name GILLE AINRIAS (servant of St Andrew), sometimes written GILLANDERS, and that he was the 1st Earl of Ross *c.*1157, who revolted against King Malcolm IV and was forfeited in 1160.

William Anderson in his three volume work on Scottish families *The Scottish Nation*, published in 1868, dealing with Anderson (the son of Andrew or St Andrew), writes that 'The Gaelic sept of Anderson are said to be an offshoot of the old potent stem of Clan Anrias from which sprang the MacAndrews, MacGillanders and the Gillanders'.

It is noteworthy that the two previous books dealing with Anderson families also covered the north east of Scotland. Phingask is a part of Fraserburgh and Peterhead is farther round the coast. Westertown is inland, near Huntly, on the borders of Aberdeenshire and Banffshire.

Whatever their origins, information currently available clearly indicates that the Anderson family being considered were firmly established in the north east of Scotland by the 16th century. This book was originally conceived to trace the history of one branch of that family. The volume of information discovered in the course of research for this project, however, is such that the scope of the book has been considerably extended. It now provides information not only about a number of Anderson families but also about a wide range of other families with whom they have associations. The book contains a substantial amount of historical and genealogical information which it is believed will be of significance to all who have an interest in Scottish and family history, or are engaged in specific studies into any of the families mentioned in the text or charts.

My interest in Scottish history and genealogy was aroused at an early age by my father's references to past members of the family who had lived in Scotland. Apart from some most valuable outline information contained in family papers, no detailed facts covering the family were available before the early part of the 19th century. Subsequent enquiries made over a number of years revealed, however, that a considerable amount of material was available which was both factual and descriptive. This source material includes references to members of the family in a whole range of published works. This book brings together much of that information and to it has been added the results of further research into original records to complete the links between different generations of the family. The whole project so far has occupied a great deal of 'spare time' spread over more than thirty years.

From a genealogical research point of view, it was extremely helpful that in 1780 arms had been matriculated by James Anderson. The supporting information, going back to the 16th century, provided an outline pedigree around which it has been possible to construct this fuller account which shows something of the lives of many members of the Anderson family and others to whom they are related by marriage. This development work was also greatly helped because a number of the earlier members of the family had been ministers in the Church of Scotland and therefore some records had been made concerning their lives. Conventionally, any genealogical study tends to follow the name through male descent. Whilst that practice is followed in this book, considerable attention has been given to the line of female descent, including the families of several of the wives and daughters, where information is available.

The records supporting the 1780 grant of arms refer to the family of Anderson as living at Westertown in the County of Banff in the 15th and early 16th centuries. Details of known or probable descendants from this family are given in the course of this book.[1] In this connection, a key heraldic reference is to be found in a book dealing with some of the burial grounds in the north east of Scotland written by Andrew Jervise in the 19th century.[2] At a place called Dunbennan, north of Huntly in Aberdeenshire, not far from Banff, he refers to an old burial stone dated 1627 on which the name Anderson appears. Jervise identifies certain initials as flanking a shield charged with the Anderson arms. These are described as being a saltire (St Andrews Cross) between three stars and a crescent in base. Later in this book full details are given of the arms which were matriculated in 1780.[3] It will be seen that the saltire has changed to a chevron but with the same three stars and a crescent in base.

Having noted the similarity in arms described by Jervise, it was an amazing coincidence to discover further sets of the arms incorporating a saltire. First in the Greyfriars burial ground at Perth, again associated with the name Anderson and dating from the 17th century. The latest discovery was when the arms were seen by my younger son in nearby Chester Cathedral. There the arms are displayed on a cenotaph which holds the book of names of 8,417 of all ranks of the 22nd (Cheshire) Regiment who fell in the Great War 1914–17. The inscription shows that the cenotaph 'was erected in memory of Lieutenant General Sir Warren Hastings Anderson, K.C.B., Quartermaster General to the forces, Colonel of the regiment from 1928 to 1930. And also of his father General David Anderson, Colonel of the regiment from 1894 to 1909'. The possibility that these Andersons were descended from the same line of Andersons from Banff and Aberdeenshire, suggested by this heraldic coincidence, has not yet been fully explored but is discussed later and any additional information on the origins of this family would be welcomed. These examples, however, illustrate the continuing value of heraldry as a form of identification, a theme which is further expanded in chapter thirteen.

From the north east of Scotland, one branch of the family moved south to Perthshire. Subsequently they moved to Fife and then to Edinburgh. These were the centres of activity for several hundred years as described in the following chapters. More recently, some members of the family moved to England and some overseas. It is to be hoped that in due course this drift away from Scotland will be reversed.

An attempt has been made to portray the lives of some of the main members of the family in their historical setting. No original historical research is involved here and grateful acknowledgement is given to the many sources that have been drawn upon which are detailed later.[4] It is hoped that the short outline historical explanation contained in the Introduction and referred to in the subsequent chapters, in particular regarding the battles which raged in church affairs, will be of interest and stimulate further reading into these aspects of Scotland's history. It is believed that it may be unusual to be able to show the role of several generations of the same family within the early turbulent history of the reformed Church of Scotland.

As explained in later chapters, one result of the research which has been undertaken has been the discovery of complete branches of the family, previously unknown to current members of my family. These discoveries alone would have justified the many hours of research involved. Help in correcting errors and omissions and with answers to some of the specific questions raised in the book will be gratefully received. In years to come, as more information becomes available, it may be there will be a case for an expanded edition. My experience is that genealogy and history are live and dynamic subjects, with fresh facts constantly being discovered. It is a question of discipline therefore to pause in research and record information in a form which makes it available to others.

INTRODUCTION

Ecclesiastical Events in Scotland during the 16th and 17th centuries

THE HISTORY OF SCOTLAND in the 16th and 17th centuries was dominated by the often violent conflicts which stemmed from differences in religious ideas. This period saw the impact of the Reformation in Scotland and the development of diverging concepts concerning the way the reformed church should be organised. An examination of these historical events helps to give an understanding of why the organisation of ecclesiastical affairs in the Scotland of today is so different to the position which prevails in England. The clash of religious doctrine in this period has also to be seen against the background of the political differences and alliances with both England and France at that time.

To appreciate something of the pressures and events leading to the Reformation, it is useful to briefly review the events from the time of James IV of Scotland. He married Margaret, the daughter of Henry VII of England, and for a time there was relative peace between Scotland and England. Henry VIII came to the throne in England in 1509 and relationships between the two countries deteriorated. At a time when England was at war with France, James IV led his army into England in 1513. The Scottish army was severely defeated on 9 September at the Battle of Flodden and the king himself was killed. The new King of Scotland was the two-year-old infant, James V.

When Henry VIII in England broke with the Church in Rome, James V in Scotland had no incentive to follow his uncle's example and so the country remained Catholic. His sons died as infants and he himself died in 1542 when he was only 30. He was succeeded by his infant daughter, Mary, who was only seven days old when she became the Queen of Scotland. Her mother, Mary of Guise, was French and therefore a Roman Catholic. Scotland had been firmly Roman Catholic since the reign of King David I, 1124-53. In the 16th century the pressures for religious change were mounting in Scotland, as elsewhere. In France, the pressure was resisted and she remained Roman Catholic. In England under the influence of the king, a dramatic change was taking place. In Scotland, the queen mother and her supporters favoured France and the Roman Church. A number of other Scots, however, were beginning to favour the new church ideas and a closer association with England.

The liberalisation of religious thinking received a severe check under the influence of Cardinal Beaton who took strong measures to try to stamp out the new ideas. A number of people were publicly executed for their heretical opinions. In 1546 Cardinal Beaton was himself murdered at St Andrews Castle. French military force was brought in to restore the position in 1547 so that the Roman Catholic faith was once again the prevailing influence. Henry VIII died in January 1547 but attempts were still made to bring the two countries closer together by a marriage between the new King Edward and Mary, the young Scottish queen. This did not suit those who favoured closer ties with France. Queen Mary was sent to France and in due course married the dauphin.

The queen mother exerted her influence to become Regent in Scotland. Her aim seemed to be directed at making Scotland a province of France. Many in Scotland were concerned at the increasing ties with France which were viewed with as much suspicion as the ties with England. Under the vigorous leadership of John Knox, the new Protestant movement was developing in Scotland. In England, Elizabeth came to the throne in 1558 and the new thinkers in Scotland tended to find Protestant England a more acceptable ally than Catholic France. Queen Mary returned to Scotland in 1561 and the events leading up to her forced abdication in 1567 in favour of her infant son, James VI, are well recorded elsewhere.[1]

During this time the Protestant Church had been developing in Scotland. The new Church of Scotland was ruled through meetings or General Assemblies. At these, leading ministers and laymen met to conduct the business of the church. The king and his advisers disliked the growing influence of the ministers. They favoured the system of Episcopacy which was the form of church organisation based on rule through bishops as opposed to being ruled and organised by the ministers and laymen themselves, meeting in Assemblies.

John Knox died in 1572 but the influence of the Presbyterian clergy continued to grow. As they saw it, faced with the ever present threat of the Roman Catholic Church and the preference of the king and others for the Episcopalian system, the ministers in the Presbyterian Church had to make extreme claims to save the system and faith they believed in. By 1580 the power of the General Assemblies of the Church of Scotland was very great. At this time, the Assembly met several times a year. The ministers had great influence over the people as they possessed the power of excommunication. At Dundee in July 1580, Episcopacy was formally condemned and all who held the office of bishop were ordered to resign. The Assembly of April 1581 established courts known as Presbyteries which became the distinctive feature of this form of the Church of Scotland.

The policy of James VI seems to have been dominated by his desire to rule England as well as Scotland which he did from 1603. Having obtained information about the way Episcopacy was organised in England, James VI sought to establish the same system in Scotland. In 1610 James VI contrived at an

Assembly in Glasgow to have an end declared to the Presbytery. The church from then was once again to be ruled by bishops. In 1617 King James again visited Scotland to try and model the Scottish Church even more closely on the lines of the English Church. For some years after this, there was great dissension in Scotland, especially concerning the form of the communion service. This period saw the start of conventicles whereby people left their normal churches to attend secret meetings organised by ministers who did not accept the imposed system. Although the changes King James made in the organisation of the church might have been accepted, the changes he tried to impose on the basic beliefs were not.

In 1625 King James died, to be succeeded by his son, Charles I. He had married a Catholic princess which had the effect of arousing the suspicions of a large section of the Scottish people. In fact, the new king continued to pursue the policy of developing the Episcopalian Church and imposed various measures to support this policy. As a revolt against the intrusion of the king into church affairs, in 1638, the Scottish nobles entered into a Bond or Covenant of mutual defence and common aims. This became known as the 'National League and Covenant'. The mass of the people supported this with great enthusiasm. It was the contention of the covenanters that the right of summoning Assemblies belonged to the church itself. An Assembly at this time rejected the changes which had offended the new church and in particular rejected the idea of bishops.

King Charles sought to reassert his authority by means of an armed invasion of Scotland. What became known as the first Bishops' War ended in a form of compromise under which Charles I had to concede practically every demand made by the covenanters. Further conflicts between the king and the covenanters continued until 1642. In 1643 the General Assembly met and drew up a bond of mutual defence and common action. This was to form the basis of an alliance with the English Parliament. The document was called the 'Solemn League and Covenant'. If King Charles I had only accepted the terms of the Solemn League and Covenant, the Scots would have continued to accept him as their king. However, he did not and this was one of the contributory factors leading to his execution on 30 January 1649.

The son of Charles I accepted the terms of the Solemn League and Covenant and was declared King of Scotland shortly after the death of his father. Cromwell made a special appeal to the clergy in Scotland but realised that only a military victory would overthrow the support for King Charles II. This he eventually achieved at the Battle of Dunbar in 1650 which he followed with further actions. This stopped Charles from becoming King of England as well as Scotland for another nine years.

For a period under Cromwell relative stability prevailed in the affairs of the church. In 1660 Charles II was restored not only to the Scottish but also to the English throne. The people of Scotland had supported the king, yet it had been

Cromwell who had brought some peace to the church. Charles II was now to prove an even greater disaster for the Presbyterian Church of Scotland than his father had been. By 1662 he had re-admitted bishops and made ministers dependent upon being appointed by them instead of their congregations. Practical examples of the effects of these changes will be given in the chapters which follow. Ministers were ejected from their churches if they failed to conform to Episcopacy. Conventicles were re-established by dissenting ministers and by 1670 they had become more numerous than ever. The authorities tried to stop conventicles by using soldiers to suppress them. Those who attended 'found the need to begin to carry weapons for protection as well as their bibles'. The king and his advisers became alarmed by the rise of armed conventicles and feared an uprising. Systematic coercion was applied against the people who would not accept the new church principles. Each year the measures taken against the Presbyterians increased in severity.

Over a number of years, so called indulgences were made available to persuade ministers who would accept Episcopacy to return to their churches. Although a number of ministers did accept, it was the ministers who did not accept the indulgences who gave character to this dark period in the history of Scotland.

> The period owes its character to that indomitable section of the Presbyterians whom neither concession nor relentless pursuit could persuade to palter with their consciences and accept a Government which, in their conception, existed to destroy every belief which they held most sacred.

Charles II died on 2 February 1685 and was succeeded by his brother, James. From 1685, even greater measures, including torture and persecution, were taken against all those who did not conform to the declared state view of the church. Most of the non-conforming ministers had to go into exile and the spirit of the Presbyterian Church in Scotland was very low, but not totally extinguished. The re-establishment of Roman Catholicism was proceeding under the new king. This was a matter of great concern to both Episcopalians and Presbyterians. An heir to the throne was born in June 1688 and seemed certain to seal the fate of all Protestants in England and Scotland. This led to the Revolution of 1688 and by the end of the year William of Orange and Mary were established on the throne in London. The Presbyterians welcomed this deliverance but the Episcopalians realised that William would not be likely to support them in Scotland. He came from Holland where there were no bishops and where many of the Presbyterian exiles had found refuge. It was now possible for the exiled Presbyterian ministers to return home.

One result of the Revolution was that in contrast to the extremes over recent years, it was now possible for a new spirit of moderation to be created in Scotland. Although the Presbyterians were now re-established, they could afford to exercise tolerance in their dealings with others. Never again were the religious conflicts in Scotland to completely outweigh the secular conduct of affairs.

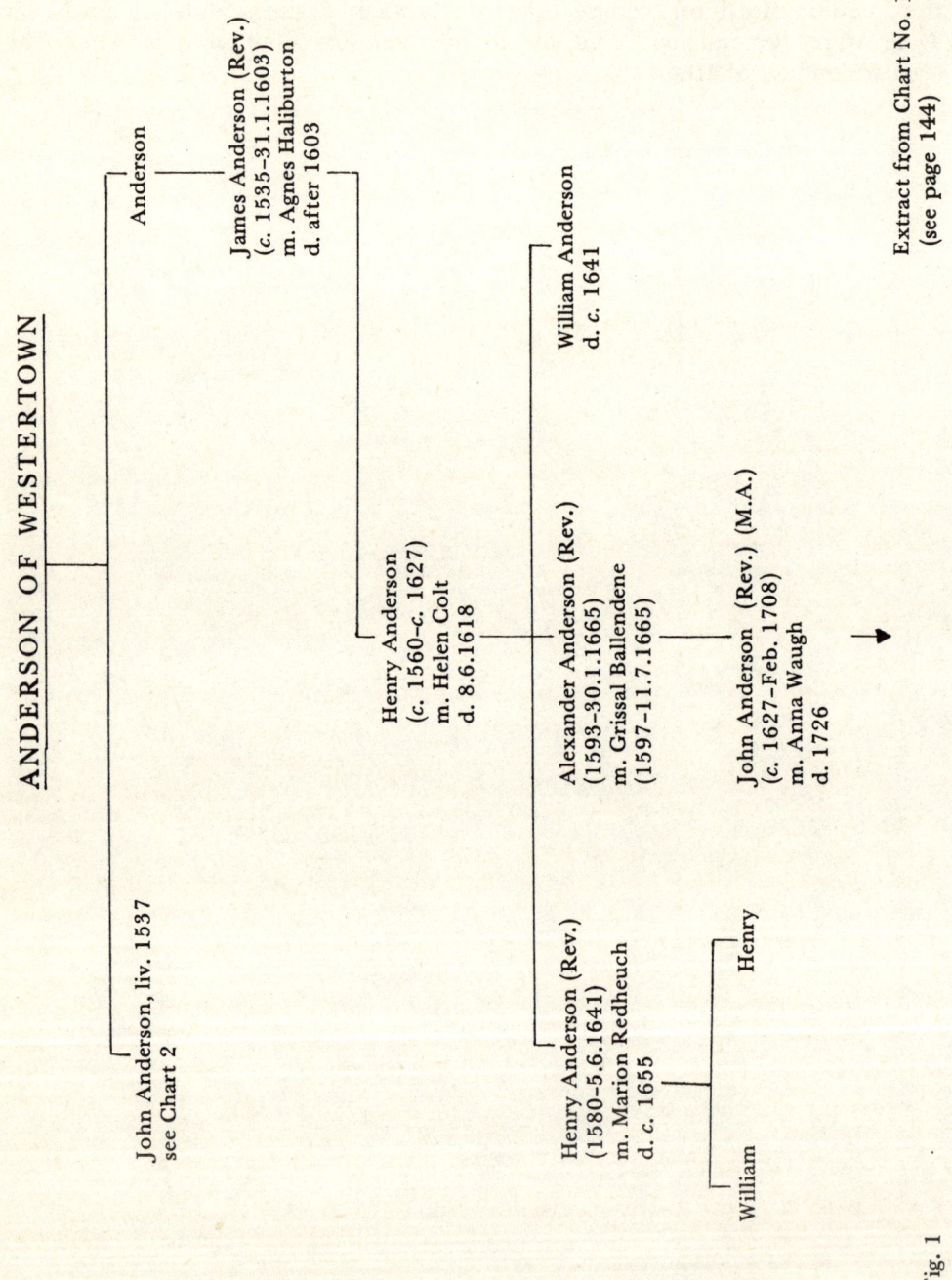

ANDERSON OF WESTERTOWN

John Anderson, liv. 1537
see Chart 2

Anderson

James Anderson (Rev.)
(c. 1535–31.1.1603)
m. Agnes Haliburton
d. after 1603

Henry Anderson
(c. 1560–c. 1627)
m. Helen Colt
d. 8.6.1618

William Anderson
d. c. 1641

Alexander Anderson (Rev.)
(1593–30.1.1665)
m. Grissal Ballendene
(1597–11.7.1665)

Henry Anderson (Rev.)
(1580–5.6.1641)
m. Marion Redheuch
d. c. 1655

Henry

William

John Anderson (Rev.) (M.A.)
(c. 1627–Feb. 1708)
m. Anna Waugh
d. 1726

Extract from Chart No. 1
(see page 144)

Fig. 1

CHAPTER ONE

James Anderson (*c.* 1535–31 January 1603)
Henry Anderson (*c.* 1560–1627)

JAMES ANDERSON, the first of the descendants from the Andersons of Westertown being considered, was probably born between 1535 and 1540. One can only speculate as to whether his parents still lived in the Banff and Aberdeen areas of Scotland and whether that is where he was brought up. It appears that his grandfather was a younger son of the Anderson family from Westertown. Although little is known about the early life of James, he must have received a suitable education for him to be trained to enter the church. He played a significant part in the Reformation period and was later described as being one of the reformers of religion in Scotland.[1]

In November 1569 James was appointed to be the minister of Bendochy and Kettins.[2] This appointment was made within the lifetime of John Knox who died in 1572. John Knox had blazed the trail for the new Church of Scotland and following his death there were many men, including James Anderson, willing to continue the reforming work which he had pioneered. The years following the death of Knox were very difficult years for ministers in the new church who could not even be sure of obtaining a stipend upon which to live. James Anderson's work during this time must have been recognised by others as on 2 December 1582 he was appointed to become the minister of Stirling. He then played an even more active role in the wider affairs of the church and was a member of the General Assemblies held in April and in October 1583.

In Scotland, even in 1583, a great number of people still supported the Roman Catholic Church. At about this time, having become established in the reforming movement of the church in Scotland, James Anderson wrote a poem which criticised the way the Roman Catholic Church had developed. This long poetic work has a long title:

Ane Godly treates about the First and Second coming of Christ, with the Tone of the Winters Nycht; shewing briefly our native Blindness, where in we were misled by Popery, and the clear light of the Gospel now manifested in our Days to the Glory of God, and the comfort of all them that hope for Salvation.

11

This long poem consisted of some sixteen pages octavo and was dedicated to John Erskine of Dunn. The work is quoted in McCrie's *Life of Melville*. McCrie includes the cryptic comment that the excellence of the work 'does not depend on poetry'. The date of the first edition is not certain but a copy was printed in Edinburgh in 1595 and the work was reprinted in 1851. An imperfect copy of the second or third edition is in the National Library of Scotland. This copy was printed in Edinburgh by Alexander Hart, perhaps in 1614, and is the Auchinteck copy sold at Sothebys on 23 June 1893.[3] An additional copy of the work is also held in the National Library of Scotland in Edinburgh.

In 1584, King James took measures to curb the growing power of the ministers in the new church. As a result of these measures, many ministers had to seek refuge in England. It is not certain whether James Anderson was one of them but he was a member of the General Assembly in May 1586. At this controversial Assembly, the king tried to have revoked the sentence of excommunication which had been passed by the Synod of Fife on the Archbishop of St Andrews. It was only by threats as well as promises at the Assembly that the king finally succeeded.

Queen Mary was executed in England on 8 February 1587 which doubtless had a marked effect on Catholic/Protestant relationships. A General Assembly was held in June 1587, and James Anderson was a member. He was also a member of the General Assemblies held in August 1588 and in 1590. In 1590 James was appointed to be the minister of Kettins. It is assumed that this was now a separate church from Bendochy where he had earlier been the minister. Such was the progress of the new Presbyterian church that by 1595 it was considered that the Catholic faith was no longer a 'formidable danger'.[4] The king, however, continued to strengthen Episcopacy which suited him much better. The conflict between the two forms of the Reformed Church was to form the basis of church problems in Scotland until 1688.

James Anderson attended his final meeting of the General Assembly in 1602. He died in January 1603, a short time before the death of Queen Elizabeth of England who died in March 1603. He therefore did not live to see the union of the two countries which had been the ambition of King James.

James Anderson had married Agnes Haliburton (or Halyburton) who survived him. The marriage probably took place between the years 1555 and 1560. The Haliburton family may well have been friends for some years with the Anderson family. A later chapter discusses another marriage between another James Anderson and another Agnes Haliburton some fifty years later than that of Rev. James Anderson. James and Agnes had at least one surviving son who, interestingly, was named Henry and was probably born in about 1560. One wonders whether the name chosen was in recognition of the Protestant progress made by the former English king.

Although there is a shortage of information about Henry Anderson, it is known that he became a burgess of Perth which seemed to have been the main centre of his, and his children's lives. In the entry about Rev. James Anderson, Hew Scott's *Fasti* shows that he had a son, Henry, who was a burgess of Perth. The same record shows that the father of both Henry Anderson, the minister of Monzievaird and Strowan, and Alexander Anderson, the minister of Auchtergaven, was Henry Anderson, a burgess of Perth. The records supporting the later matriculation of arms in 1780 (see Chapter 5) show Alexander Anderson, the minister of Auchtergaven, as being descended from James Anderson, although it does not refer to Henry Anderson. However despite this omission it seems reasonable to conclude that Henry Anderson, burgess of Perth, was the son of Rev. James Anderson and the father of Henry and Alexander Anderson and probably other children also.

Records concerning a Henry Anderson, burgess of Perth, can be found in the book of North Perthshire monumental inscriptions.[5] This records that in Block G of the Greyfriars burial ground in Perth is a tombstone which refers to the Anderson family, merchants and glover burgesses in Perth. There are references in the book to the Testament records, St Andrews Commissariat, concerning Mr. Henry Anderson, merchant burgess in Perth, and his wife, Helen Colt, who died on 8 June 1618 and was buried at Greyfriars. It appears likely that Henry Anderson died in 1627 as that was when his will was registered. There is also a reference to Catherine Sandeman, the wife of Mr. Anderson, who had eight children. However, she was possibly the wife of one of the sons of Henry Anderson, possibly William, who in turn also became a merchant burgess in Perth. It would be interesting to learn if there are any surviving descendants from these eight. However there is some evidence of another marriage between a member of the Sandeman family and an Anderson. In her book about writing a family history Margaret Stuart records that the Sandeman pedigree shows that David Sandeman married in 1716, Margaret, the daughter of David Ramsey of Baldene, Fife. Their daughter Catherine Sandeman who was born in 1717 and died in 1759 married in 1738 John Anderson a merchant in Perth. Their children were:

1. David Anderson, born 1739.
2. Thomas Anderson, born 1740 and married Sarah Rose, their children being:

   a. Rose Anderson, who married Thomas Hay Marshall.
   b. Catherine Ann Anderson.

3. Margaret Anderson.
4. Jane Anderson.
5. Catherine Anderson who married David Lindsay, their son was:

   a. Harry Lindsay, and he married Jane Sandeman. Their children were:

      i. William Sandeman Lindsay.
      ii. David Lindsay.

    iii. John Lindsay.
    iv. Catherine Lindsay.
    v. Mary Lindsay who married F. H. Ramsbotham, M.D.

It would be of great interest to discover whether the 18th-century Anderson family and the 18th-century Sandeman family were descended from the same line of each named family noted in the book of monumental inscriptions from the previous century.

Considering the religious turmoil of the time, it is perhaps not surprising that Henry Anderson did not follow the example of his father and enter the church. It appears, however, that at least two of his sons did and some information concerning their lives is contained in the next chapter.

CHAPTER TWO

Henry Anderson (1589 – 5 June 1641)
Alexander Anderson (1593 – 30 January 1665)

HENRY ANDERSON, the son of Henry Anderson of Perth and the first known grandson of James Anderson, was born in 1589. He was educated at St Andrews University, obtaining his degree as a Master of Arts in 1613. In 1623 he was admitted as a minister and became the minister at Monzievaird and Stowan.[1] He married Marion (who died between 1650 and 1660), the daughter of James Redheuch of Aberlednock, and they had two sons:

1. William, who died before 7 May 1670.
2. Henry, who was apprenticed 14 May 1645 to Robert Brown, a merchant in Edinburgh.

Rev. Henry Anderson died on 5 June 1641 and it would be interesting to discover if there were any descendants from his two sons.

It has earlier been explained how King James moulded the church so that by 1612 he had established the system he desired in Scotland with a Protestant Church ruled by bishops; in other words, an Episcopalian system as in England. In the same year, 1612, Alexander Anderson, the second known grandson of Rev. James Anderson, matriculated to enter St Salvators College at St Andrews University. He graduated in 1615 with the degree of Master of Arts. Alexander is stated to have been on exercise at Perth on 19 February 1623. He was admitted as a minister at Dowally in 1623.[2] During these years he must have been greatly involved in the arguments concerning the basic conflicts in belief at this time. On 10 February 1627 he was transferred and admitted as minister at Dunkeld and Dowally.

Following the changes in church organisation being made by King James, an enactment had been passed in 1617 that two of the parishes in north Perthshire should be combined. One of these was called Auchtergaven and the other called Logiebride. They lie between Perth and Dunkeld, the centre of Auchtergaven being Bankfoot, near the main Perth to Inverness road. However, ignoring the

15

enactment, the Bishop of Dunkeld in 1628 resolved that the parishes should continue to be served each by its own minister. With the advice of the Presbytery, Alexander Anderson was translated from Dunkeld to become minister of Auchtergaven where he remained until his death. The stipends of the two parishes amounting to '80 bolls victual' were to be divided between Mr. Chrystison, the minister at Logiebride, and Alexander Anderson. The two ministers also contracted with each other to divide the stipends as modified at the union of the parishes. This contract was also delivered to the bishop.

In 1629, however, the bishop presented Mr. Chrystison to both benefices. As a result, a dispute arose between the two ministers concerning the stipend. Mr. Chrystison claimed the whole of it by virtue of his presentation. Alexander Anderson affirmed his right to half of the stipend under his translation by the bishop and Presbytery which he alleged to be equivalent to presentation and also under the terms of his contract with Mr. Chrystison. The subject came before the Court of Session and on 15 February 1631 the Lords delivered judgment on the case. They awarded the whole stipend to Mr. Chrystison, holding that a union of benefices appointed by parliament could be annulled only by parliament and not by the bishop. They also found that the contract did not bind the parties in that a presentation to the united parishes had been subsequently issued. Mr. Chrystison also alleged that Alexander Anderson continued to serve the parish of Dowally and to receive the stipend. The Lords found it unreasonable that Alexander Anderson should enjoy the whole stipend of Dowally and at the same time endeavour to obtain the half of another benefice. They, however, did not enforce their judgment. The Register of Acts and Discreets dated 31 March 1631 shows that they adjourned the case and recommended it to the bishop and Synod for settlement. Alexander Anderson, however, continued as minister at Auchtergaven.[3]

In 1647 the heritors and parishioners petitioned for the reunion of Auchtergaven and Logiebride. They drew their chief pleas from the hardship suffered by their minister, Alexander Anderson, who they said had been 'forced to live these sixteen years in great distress, being burdened with wife, children and family'. It may be that the stipend from Dowally had passed to another minister or that it was not sufficient on its own to support the minister and his family. Whatever the precise circumstances, by 1650 the parishes of Auchtergaven and Logiebride were combined. Before 7 March 1650, Alexander Anderson became minister of the united parishes, Prebendary of Fordischaw and Master of the Hospital of St George at Dunkeld.

Even during the period before the parishes were reunited, it is clear that Alexander was greatly involved in the wider affairs of the church. He was appointed moderator of the Presbytery of Dunkeld after the meeting of the Synod in October 1641. In 1643 the General Assembly met and Alexander was a member. At this Assembly the bond of mutual defence and common action known as the 'Solemn League and Covenant' was drawn up as discussed in the introduction. Despite the oppressive actions of King Charles I, the influence of the Scottish clergy at the time of the king's death was still very great and they were much involved in the political events taking place. In 1650 there was, for example, what became known as the Ministers Regiment and on 24 July 1650 at Dunkeld, Alexander Anderson with others signed an obligation (witnessed by his son, John Anderson) to pay £1,000 imposed on the churches of the Presbytery for 'advancing and reaching forth ane regement to this presentt leavie and expedition'.

For a period under the rule of Cromwell, relative stability prevailed in the affairs of the church. Alexander Anderson as minister at Auchtergaven had the company of his son. John Anderson was admitted as colleague and successor to his father before 13 October 1657. Cromwell died in September 1658 and the commonwealth continued until 1659. In 1660 King Charles II was restored, not only to the Scottish but also to the English throne. By 1662 King Charles II had re-admitted bishops and changed the situation whereby many ministers held their charges direct from their congregations and presbyteries. It was this situation which had been argued by Alexander Anderson in his dispute with Mr. Chrystison and the bishop concerning the stipend at Auchtergaven as far back as 1631. Alexander Anderson conformed to Episcopacy for part of his ministry although, as explained in the next chapter, his son did not. He died on 30 January 1665. He had married Grisell Ballendene who must have been born in about 1597 as she died on 11 July 1665 aged 68. An interesting tombstone in memory of Alexander Anderson and his wife was erected in Auchtergaven churchyard, presumably by John Anderson and the parishioners. It bears the coat of arms which was eventually matriculated at the Lyon Office in 1780, together with a range of other symbols. The tombstone bears the following inscription:[4]

> Here lyes Alexander Anderson, Minister of the Gospel at this charge of Ochtergaven, who departed this lyfe 30 of Januarie 1665, and of his age 72, and of his ministerie here 38 years.

> Here lies the corps of Grissal Ballendene, his spouse, who departed the 11th of July 1665, and of her age 68.

> Thy dead men shall live, together with my dead body shall they arise. Awake and sing ye that dwell in the dust.

> Isaiah 26, 19.

> *Hodie — Nobis — Vobis*[5]

The tombstone can still be seen although it is deteriorating and part of the cement ornamentation is breaking away. It appears to have been moved several times. Originally it must have been a flat stone as the inscription goes all round it. Later it was set in the outer wall on the east side of the graveyard but it now stands upright, set in the ground, on the top of the slope beside the church.[6] It would be good if something more could be done to preserve this memorial.

The only known issue from the marriage between Alexander Anderson and Grisell Ballendene was John Anderson who was born in about 1627. His life is discussed in the next chapter. It would be interesting to know what happened to the other children indicated in the petition of 1647 which asked for the reunion of Auchtergaven and Logiebride.

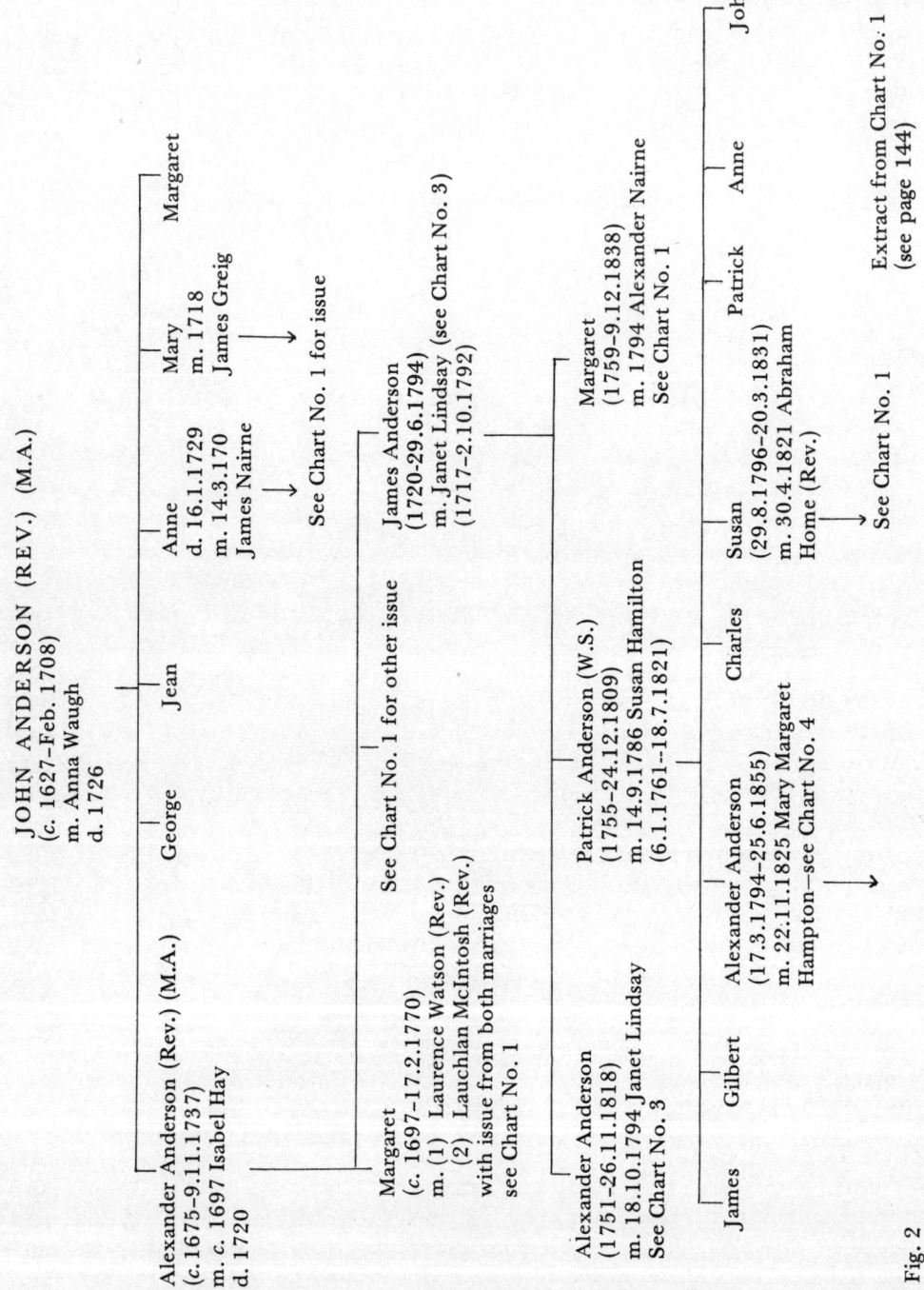

Fig. 2

CHAPTER THREE

John Anderson (*c.* 1627–1708)

BORN IN APPROXIMATELY 1627, John Anderson was a student at Edinburgh University and graduated as a Master of Arts on 26 July 1649.[1] In October 1650 he was bursar of the Presbytery of Dunkeld at the New College, St Andrews, and continued to hold the bursary in June 1653. He was licensed before 26 March 1654 when he preached at Logierait. On 6 January 1656 he was admitted assistant minister, working with his father at Auchtergaven. In 1657 he was admitted colleague to his father as minister at Auchtergaven. As already explained, following his restoration, King Charles II in 1662 moved to reverse the Presbyterian form of the church in favour of Episcopacy. On 11 June 1662 it was enacted under the Act of Glasgow that all ministers should, before 20 September, 'receive presentation from their lawful patrons and collation from their Bishops, or demit their cures'. This period was in due course extended to 1663. From this time the troubles of the Presbyterian Church of Scotland continued throughout the reign of Charles II and indeed until the Revolution of 1688.

John Anderson refused to conform to Episcopacy despite the enactment. As a result he was deprived of his living but continued to discharge ministerial functions at Auchtergaven, no doubt because his father was still alive at that time. In consequence of his refusal to accept presentation he was reported to the Privy Council as one of the ministers in the Diocese of Dunkeld who with others

'doe continow at their former residences and churches and doe persist in their wicked practices, still labouring to keep the hearts of the people from the present government of church and state by their pernicious doctrin'.

They were ordered to 'remove themselves, their wyves, bairnes, families, servants, goods and geir furth and frae their respective dwelling places and manses and outwith the bounds of the presbyteries where they now live, and that they doe not take upon them to exerce any part of the ministerial function either privately or publictly — and also command and charge them and

everyone of them to compear before the saids Lords the   day of
to ansuer for their former disobedience with certification'.[2] The dates do not
appear to have been entered. There is apparently no evidence that the letters
issued by the Privy Council were ever served on John Anderson. That he
remained at Auchtergaven, discharging the duties of his ministry, appears from
a reference to him in the M.S. Register of the Presbytery of Meigle on 11
August 1663, when the minister of Coupar-Angus was appointed to write to
him in connection with a case of discipline. He was however one of the ministers suspended by the bishop at the Synod, in October 1663 and deposed at
the Synod in October 1664.[3]

In 1669, under what was called the First Letter of Indulgence, ejected
ministers were allowed to re-occupy their churches and manses provided they
accepted Episcopacy.[4] In fact, only 42 ministers accepted these conditions and
John Anderson was not one of them. Further indulgencies were offered — there
were three by 1680 — and a further number of ministers accepted the conditions. John Anderson still was not one of them and, as a result, for a time he
had to move to Ireland. In 1671 he was the minister at Glenarm in Ireland. It
appears, however, that he also became one of the ministers to preach at the
secret meetings in the hills and countryside called conventicles. It was reported
that 'A Mr. John Anderson, an outed, unlicensed minister is stated to have been
one of the preachers at conventicles held at Inverkeithing from September
1679 till May 1680'.[5] Many of all ranks who supported the Presbyterian principles had to flee the country, John Anderson among them. He again went to
Ireland and in 1685 became the minister at Antrim. King Charles II died on
2 February 1685 and was succeeded by King James II. The Presbyterians were
then faced with even graver difficulties which were only resolved by the
Revolution of 1688. In late 1688 a deputation of loyal parishioners from
Auchtergaven crossed to Antrim to invite John Anderson back to resume his
ministry and this he agreed to do. In 1689 it was possible for the exiled Presbyterian ministers to return home, although there were only a small number
still left.

After all the tempestuous years, the affairs of the church took a long time to
settle down. William III appointed the Presbyterian Earl of Crawford as the
President of the Parliament. The Earl cautioned that William would not be
secure until the Presbytery system was the established religion of the country.
There were those who still sought to support the exiled King James and others
who were not happy with the apparent re-establishment of the Presbyterian
form of church affairs, preferring instead the Episcopalian system of bishops.
In September 1689 certain ministers in Perth were deprived of their ministries
because they would not accept the post-revolution new conditions, which
included offering prayers for King William and Queen Mary. The Earl of
Argyle, who was in command of the troops in Perth, was authorised to appoint
a suitable Presbyterian minister to fill the vacancy. To the regret of the

parishioners of Auchtergaven, John Anderson was called by the Earl of Argyle to become minister at the East Church (part of St John's Kirk), Perth. This move was also to the regret of the parishioners and the town council of Perth because they were, at that time, in favour of Episcopacy. It is said that the services of the military were required for the protection of John Anderson, even in the celebration of public worship.

In 1690 the Perth town council tried to have John Anderson moved. It appears that attempts were also made to stop him being paid the stipend due to him. As a result, he had to take out a petition to obtain the payment of the stipend. The town council opposed the petition in a long document which is now in the archives of the City of Perth. Hunter reproduces the full text of this document containing the council's objections to the petition. The Lords of the Privy Council, however, found in favour of John Anderson and agreed that the stipend should be paid. The town council still tried to oppose making the payment. After they had made approaches to John Anderson to reduce the stipend, it was reported 'that he will not condescend to quit one farthing thereof'. The council accordingly arranged to obey the order of the Privy Council and paid the stipend legally due for 1689 and 1690.

In 1690 an Act was passed restoring the Presbyterian church. It was voted that all the Presbyterian ministers who had been ejected since 1 January 1661 should at once be restored to their respective parishes. Only 60 such ministers remained and John Anderson was one of them, although as has been seen, he had already been restored to Auchtergaven and moved from there to Perth. On this group fell the duty of restoring the church to the form in which they remembered it.

Since 1653 no General Assembly had been held and the first one since then met in October 1690 for the express purpose of setting the re-established church in order. John Anderson was appointed a commissioner from the Presbytery of Perth to this first post-Revolution Assembly. He also opened the first meeting of the Synod of Perth and Stirling after the Revolution on 4 March 1691 with prayer and was elected moderator for the Synod. On 7 April 1691 he opened the meeting of the Synod with a sermon on Isaiah 62:6.[6] John Anderson was translated to Leslie in Fife on 30 June 1691 and he was Moderator of the Presbytery of Kirkcaldy. Then on 1 September 1697 he was translated to St Andrews. He was appointed to the University of St Andrews as Principal of St Leonard's College which was one of the colleges concerned with the teaching of theology. It was perhaps fitting that one so involved in the principles of the Presbyterian Church should help in the instruction of the new generation of ministers. John Anderson remained the Principal of St Leonard's College until his death in February 1708. He was buried in the cathedral burial ground at St Andrews together in due course with his wife, son and grandson and their wives. Details of the memorial to them are given in Chapter Five.

John Anderson had married Anna Waugh of Schaws in Cumbria and she died in 1726. One wonders whether they met during the time of one of his periods in exile. In this connection, it is noted that the theory receives some further support since Scaw in the area of Harrington, near Workington in Cumbria, was called Skaw in 1652.[7] Skaw may have been the Schaws in Cumbria, understood to have been the home of Anna Waugh. That part of the Cumbrian coast could have been a point from which crossings were made to northern parts of Ireland.

Despite all the difficulties in the church which prevented them from having a settled home life in the early years of their marriage, John Anderson and Anna had several children.[8] They were:

1. Alexander Anderson who was born in about 1675. His life is discussed in the next chapter.

2. George Anderson. He died abroad before 27 August 1707 according to his testamentary document.

3. Jean Anderson. She was named in the testamentary document dealing with the affairs of her brother George, and so was living in 1707.

4. Anne Anderson was married in 1706 and so was probably born in approximately 1685 — see below for fuller information about her marriage and descendants.[9]

5. Mary Anderson married in October 1718 Rev. James Greig, M.A., who was minister of second charge at Cupar in Fife. They had a daughter named Ann who was born in 1720. Mary must have died shortly after this because James Greig married for a second time. He married Janet Hedderwick who died on 18 November 1748. James Greig however died on 14 May 1727 aged about forty-six. It would be interesting to know if Ann Greig survived to become an adult.

6. Margaret Anderson was also named in the testamentary document dealing with the affairs of her brother, George, and was therefore living in 1707.

Anne Anderson married the Rev. James Nairne of Claremont, the minister of Anstruther Easter. He was born in 1680, the son of James Nairne of Claremont, skipper of Elie, and his wife, Janet Small. Rev. James Nairne was educated at St Andrews. He received his M.A. on 23 July 1697, which was the same date as Alexander Anderson, Anne's elder brother. He was licensed by the Presbytery there on 17 June 1702 and ordained to Forgan on 2 February 1703. He was admitted to Anstruther on 7 August 1717 and he eventually died 'Father of the church' on 12 May 1771.

James Nairne and Anne Anderson married on 14 March 1706. They had at least four children but three of them died young. John Nairne, however, survived and entered the church like his father and became his successor at Anstruther. Anne Anderson died at a fairly young age on 16 January 1729. John Nairne of Claremont was born on 20 January 1711. He also went to St Andrews University and obtained his M.A. on 7 May 1729. He was ordained on 18 June 1741 and eventually he too became 'Father of the Synod' and died on 15 February 1795. John married Elizabeth, the daughter of Alexander Gordon, a writer in Edinburgh. They had seven children who are detailed below with information about subsequent generations also, where known.

1. James Nairne, born 30 August 1750. He attended St Andrews University and subsequently in 1809 became a Doctor of Divinity. Like his father and grandfather, be became 'Father of the Presbytery' and died on 15 July 1819. He was minister of Pittenweem. James Nairne married on 12 January 1778 Helen, the daughter of James Kyd of Craigie (she died in London on 3 February 1836 aged eighty-one). They had several children as follows:

   a. John Nairne who was born on 14 October 1778 and became captain of *The Favourite*, a sloop-of-war. He died on the coast of Africa on 23 July 1807.

   b. Hannah Nairne, who was born on 29 May 1780, married on 29 May 1805 John Forman, Writer to the Signet, and died on 19 October 1849. He was born on 26 September 1775 and died on 4 December 1841. They had a son:

      John Nairne Forman, W.S., who was born on 6 April 1806 and died on 30 January 1884. He married on 16 October 1835 Jane, the daughter of Robert Mitchell of Airth, Stirlingshire. She died on 10 November 1881. Their issue included:

      (1) John Forman, W.S., who was born on 4 January 1838 and died on 18 February 1882. He married on 23 April 1872 Catherine, the daughter of Bernard Gilpin Cooper of Hazel Grove, Cheshire. She died on 27 November 1910.

      (2) Alexander George Forman, W.S., who was born on 17 April 1845 and died on 25 January 1925, unmarried.

   c. James Nairne of Claremont, W.S., was born on 29 August 1782 and died on 20 October 1847. He married on 9 April 1807 Elizabeth, the eldest daughter of Dr. John Hill of Brownhills, Fife, Professor of Humanity in the University of Edinburgh. She died in 1869.

   d. Alexander Nairne was born on 20 February 1785. He joined the Naval Service of the Honourable East India Company and became captain of the *General Kyd*.

e. Elizabeth Nairne was born on 4 November 1787 but died as an infant on 16 December 1788.

f. Ann Elmsall Nairne was born on 11 January 1791. She married on 5 June 1817 William Scott, a stockbroker in London.

g. Charles Nairne, W.S., who was born on 23 December 1794, died on 20 January 1837. He married on 20 September 1820 Amelia Forbes, the daughter of Rev. Andrew Bell of Kildunean, minister of Crail. She died on 20 March 1874. Their eldest son was:

James Nairne, W.S., who was born on 8 August 1821 and died on 26 March 1866, unmarried. He became the Secretary of the North British Railway Company from 1852 to 1866.

2. Helen Nairne, who was born on 6 January 1752, married on 17 July 1780 George Hall, a merchant in Dundee.

3. Alexander Nairne, who was born on 27 August 1753, became an accountant in Edinburgh. He married Margaret Anderson, the daughter of James and Janet Anderson — see Chapters Five and Six for further references to her. She died on 9 December 1838 aged 79 and Alexander died before her.

4. Ann Nairne was born on 16 February 1755 and married Alexander Wood, a merchant from Elie, on 25 December 1780. Their children were:

a. James Wood who was born in 1781. He died in 1806 while travelling in Persia. He was unmarried.

b. John Wood, who was born in 1785, died unmarried in 1813.

c. Mary Wood was born on 18 February 1783 and married in 1811 her cousin, Dr. James Wood. James and Mary Wood had several children including Walter Wood who was born at Dundee on 31 October 1812. He became the Rev. Walter Wood who wrote the book called *The East Neuk of Fife* in which fuller details of this family can be found as well as many other genealogical references.

5. Mary Nairne of whom no details are known.

6. Jean Nairne, who was born on 22 January 1759, married on 27 January 1779 Rev. James Forrester, the minister of Anstruther Wester. However, she died nine months later on 30 October 1779.

7. Peter Nairne, who was born on 17 June 1761, died on 6 August 1786.

Having summarised information concerning the other members of the family of John and Anna Anderson and their known descendants, the next chapter turns to their eldest son, Alexander, and his family.

CHAPTER FOUR

Alexander Anderson (*c*. 1675–9 November 1737)

ALEXANDER ANDERSON was born in about 1675 during the time when his father, John, was in exile. In all probability he received his early education in Ireland, possibly at Antrim. After the Revolution and the restoration of the Presbyterian Church, he was able to proceed to St Andrews University. He graduated with a degree as Master of Arts on 23 July 1697, just before his father moved to St Andrews University to become minister of St Leonard's Church and Principal of St Leonard's College in September 1697. Alexander was licensed by the Presbytery at St Andrews on 22 February 1700. He was subsequently ordained to the parish of Kemback in Fife on 26 September 1700. It appears that Alexander very nearly followed his father and grand-father by becoming the minister at Auchtergaven. Hunter notes that Lord Nairn was 'very willing' to have John Anderson's son, Alexander, settled in the ministry at Auchtergaven, but he had already accepted a call to Kemback. Lord Nairn was presumably the patron for Auchtergaven at that time. Alexander remained at Kemback for nearly two years. Then, on 13 May 1702, he was transferred to Falkland where he remained until 1725.[1]

It seems likely that shortly after graduating from St Andrews University in 1697, Alexander married. He married Isabel (she is sometimes described as Isabella), the daughter of Francis Hay of Strowie. They had a number of children but it is thought that only two survived. These were the eldest and the youngest. The following are details of the known children but others may have been born at St Andrews or Kemback before the move to Falkland.

1. Margaret Anderson was born in about 1698. Details about her and her children are given near the end of this chapter.

2. Anne Anderson was baptised on 14 June 1706 at Falkland. The witnesses were Robert Hay of Strowie and Charles Arnot Bailie.

3. John Anderson, baptised at Falkland 12 May 1709.

4. Anne Anderson, baptised at Falkland 6 May 1711.

5. John Anderson, baptised at Falkland 11 October 1712.

6. Alexander Anderson, baptised at Falkland 28 April 1714.

7. George Anderson, baptised at Falkland 18 June 1716.

8. Robert Anderson, baptised at Falkland 31 October 1717.

9. James Anderson who was baptised at Falkland on 1 December 1720. Some records show him as having been born in 1719. His life is outlined in the next chapter.

Isabel died in 1720 but no information is available as to the cause or actual date of her death. The old parish records for Falkland covering births are available for this period but the record of deaths is missing. Isabel is remembered on the family memorial at St Andrews which is described in the next chapter.

Alexander Anderson came into prominence through an apparent antagonism with Ebenezer Erskine who later became the leader of the breakaway church. For some time the two were close friends but diverging views about church affairs led to a breakdown in their friendship.[2] The difference of opinion arose first out of their attitude towards the Oath of Abjuration. Some ministers thought the Oath did not recognise the independence of the church in Scotland. Alexander agreed to the Oath but Erskine did not. Apparently, on the Monday after a communion at Dysart in October 1714, the two ministers were engaged to preach. Erskine, when preaching in the morning from John vi. 66, spoke of defection from Christ and, referring to some who had subscribed to the Oath, charged them with 'a design to serve the Pretender's cause'. Alexander Anderson preached in the afternoon from Colossians ii. 6. He stated that 'walking in Christ implied walking in love towards each other. All divisions about lesser matters where it is hard to tell who is in the right and who is in the wrong, are to be avoided, and I entreat you to guard against all insinuations that have a tendency to alienate you from those ministers whom you reproach as guilty of defection'. These extracts from sermons show how intense feelings were at the time. (Although this may surprise the reader in view of the nature of the Oath, this incident is related precisely as in the original source.)

In correspondence in July 1715, it appears Erskine tried to reconcile the matter. He wrote on 20 July 1715 to Alexander Anderson and asked him to help him at his August communion, and expressed the hope that any misunderstanding between them might be for ever buried. He wrote:

> It is uneasy for me to think that there should be any misunderstanding betwixt me and a person whom I so much love and value; and therefore, dear brother, let all unhappy differences be buried for ever in silence, and let us in time coming construe favourably one another's words and actions as becomes brethren — which I hope we are in more respects than one. For my own part, whatever harsh thoughts you may have of me, I can freely declare with the utmost sincerity, that (though indeed of small value, yet such as they are), you have my cordial sympathy in your late affliction, and

prayers for the Lord's countenance on your labours, and particularly on the great work you have in hand, and I hope I shall on all occasions show myself, Rev. and Dear Sir your very affectionate Brother and Servant, Ebenezer Erskine.[3]

The two one-time friends were not reconciled and differences continued for many years. These are detailed in the Rev. John Warrick's book *The Moderators of the Church of Scotland*. Reference to Alexander Anderson's late affliction may well have been connected with the death of some or one of his children. The sixth known child, Alexander, had been born in 1714 and perhaps he died in infancy as may also have been the case with all of the earlier children except Margaret who was the eldest.

In 1715 Fife was the centre for much activity concerning the Jacobite uprising. Despite Erskine's words, it is very unlikely, in view of his father's experience, that Alexander Anderson could have supported that cause. Many of the Jacobite troops were in Falkland and other areas. They 'vented their malice against the Presbyterian ministers in those parts, plundering and spoiling the houses of some, taking others into custody and making them prisoners'. In such a state of affairs Alexander Anderson thought it would be wise to leave Falkland. He took refuge in Edinburgh but after a time returned to his manse, which he reached on 23 December. Alexander apparently had reason to believe that the Jacobites were plotting to sieze him. Having been alerted, he put on his clothes very quickly and made his escape. This was only just achieved as it appears the rebels came in at one door as he escaped from another. The house was searched in an attempt to find him. Not having been successful, the rebels threatened to plunder his house but, with the aid of a small bribe, his servant managed to persuade them not to do so. Instead, they took only a few things and the minister's horse, but this was later recovered.[4]

At about this time, in January 1716, Rob Roy, with 150 men, took possession of the Palace at Falkland for a garrison on behalf of the Jacobites. They robbed and plundered the countryside, destroying and eating no less than 3,000 sheep in Falkland and district. It was observed by Warrick that 'evidently Anderson's Parish was no place of safety during Rob Roy's stay in it. He showed no little courage in coming back to it from Edinburgh before the danger was over'. Warrick further observes that 'the vigour of his opposition to Erskine, though it is not possible to approve of the animus he showed towards him, reveals Anderson as a man of vast energy, and doubtless his pulpit ministrations where characterized by great zeal'.

Apparently in 1724 or 1725, a call came to Alexander Anderson from St Andrews. The Presbytery declined to translate Alexander from Falkland. An appeal was therefore taken against this decision. It came before the commission in March 1725. It was reported that 'Mr. Alexander Anderson's transportation from Falkland to St Andrews took up some time and was carried pretty unanimously. Mr. Anderson seemed not much against it, but left himself to the judgement of brethren'. The claims of the University town were regarded as

paramount and so Alexander Anderson was admitted to the first charge at
Holy Trinity Church, St Andrews, on 14 April 1725. He is described as taking
a considerable share in the business of the church where he remained until his
death. Warrick observes that 'Anderson's interest in the public business of the
Church, whether we agree with his opinions or not, marks him out as one of
the most capable leaders of the day. His brethren so believed in him that he was
called to occupy the chair of the Assembly in 1735'.

Although the Presbyterian Church had become the established church of
Scotland from 1690, it had many problems to overcome. One of these matters
concerned the old question of patronage or who had the right to appoint
ministers. This question was taken a stage further in 1730. Twelve cases were
brought before the General Assembly and much debate on this subject
followed during the next few years. In 1732 it was decided that the right of
calling a minister was to lie with the heritors and the elders if the patron failed
to exercise his right of presentation within six months. If the congregation dis-
approved of their choice, the decision was to be with the Presbytery. The
Assembly in 1734, taking note of the warnings on the policy of patronage,
tried to get the position corrected. The next General Assembly was held in May
1735 and, as has been mentioned, on 8 May 1735 Alexander Anderson was
elected moderator.

A deputation was appointed by the Assembly to go to London to press for
the repeal of the Patronage Act of Queen Anne. Alexander Anderson was a
member of the deputation together with James Gordon of Alford, the late
moderator, and John Erskine of Carnock, one of the most trusted elders in the
church. It is reported that the deputies were very successful in their efforts and
that leave was given in parliament to bring in a bill abolishing patronage. A bill
to this effect was drawn up but the legislature 'was apathetic and nothing came
of it'. The matter came before the next Assembly in 1736, when it was again
declared that it was contrary to the principles of the church that ministers
should be thrust on unwilling congregations. This unsatisfactory situation was
to continue to cause discontent right through to the next century. It led to
the break up of the Church of Scotland through the disruption of 1843. It was
not until 1874 that patronage was finally abolished although it then took until
1929 before the various branches of the Presbyterian church reunited.

A number of other matters were also dealt with by the Assembly of 1735.
For instance, the Assembly considered the complaints which had become
general regarding the style of preaching which was reported to be common
among the younger ministers. It was said that they put into their sermons
'little that might not have been found in Seneca and Plato'. The Assembly
asked Presbyteries to support the request that all ministers should give in their
sermons a full and clear declaration of the essential doctrines of the gospel of
the grace of God. Warrick observes that the very passing of such a resolution
was hopeful and showed that at the time the church was in some real degree

alive to the weakness within its borders. It is an indication, too, of the change which had come over the preaching of the church since the years that followed the Revolution.[5]

Alexander Anderson must have been responsible for bringing up James, his surviving son, following the early death of his wife. They moved to St Andrews in 1725. It appears that Alexander acquired the property just outside St Andrews, known as 'Kingask'. Certainly, he is described as Alexander Anderson of Kingask on the memorial in the cathedral burial ground at St Andrews. Kingask appears to have been retained by members of the family for the next 100 years. Alexander died on 9 November 1737 and it is noteworthy that he was the last of a series of ministers in the Church of Scotland drawn from this line of the Anderson family. They had spanned a period of nearly two hundred years which had seen such radical changes in the religious life of Scotland and in which they had played no small part.

Margaret, the only known surviving daughter of Alexander Anderson and his wife, Isabel, married twice. She married Laurence Watson, one of the ministers of St Andrews (minister of the second charge). He was the second son of Dean of the Guild, Watson, who was formerly precentor in the Town Church. Laurence was presented to the second charge by the town council on 14 August 1712. He had graduated with a Master's degree on 14 April 1704. Laurence Watson and Margaret had two children.

1. John Watson who was born in 1716.
2. Elizabeth Watson who was born in 1718.

It is assumed that Laurence Watson married Margaret Anderson in 1715 or early 1716. This suggests that Margaret must have been born in about 1698 so she was only about seventeen when she married. She married before her youngest brother, James, was born. Laurence Watson died on 25 August 1718 which was in the same year that his daughter Elizabeth was born. It is not known whether the two children lived to become adults and any information about them would be welcomed.

Following the death of her first husband, Margaret married Lauchlan McIntosh, the Minister of Errol. He was descended from the McIntoshes of Dalmunzie and Dalreoch in the county of Perth and as such it appears that he had considerable wealth. Lauchlan took his Master's degree at St Andrews in 1710. His career is outlined in Warrick's book on the moderators of the Church of Scotland where he makes an interesting point. It appears that Lauchlan also married twice, first to Margaret, the daughter of John Murray, Minister of Trinity Gask by whom he had two sons and five daughters. Secondly, he married Margaret, daughter of Alexander Anderson and the widow of Laurence Watson. As has been noted, Alexander Anderson was moderator of the General Assembly of the Church of Scotland in 1735. Lauchlan McIntosh was elected moderator of the General Assembly on 13 May 1736. Warrick comments that if McIntosh's second marriage took place before 1736, as is likely, the interesting fact appears that he was welcomed to the Chair of the Assembly by his father-in-law. Warrick observes that this is a unique episode in the annals of the church. One wonders whether it has happened since. Warrick was correct in his assumption that the marriage took place before 1736. Lauchlan McIntosh and Margaret, his second wife, had five children and the dates of birth of these indicate that the marriage took place in the early 1720s. Some information is available about their issue as follows:

1. Jean McIntosh married Rev. John Ballingal on 1 November 1739. This date suggests she would have been born not later than 1722. Jean died on 8 March 1759 and John Ballingal died on 25 April 1758, aged about fifty-eight. In the 20 years of their marriage, they had nine children as follows:

    a. Margaret Ballingal, born 12 July 1742 and died 31 March 1808.

    b. Eupham Ballingal, born 1 July 1744 and died in April 1753.

    c. Jean Ballingal, born 20 November 1745 and died in July 1746.

    d. James Ballingal, born 28 August 1747 and died 16 April 1753.

    e. Lachlan Ballingal, born 14 January 1749.

    f. Elizabeth Ballingal, born 26 July 1750 and died 10 May 1752.

    g. Jean Ballingal, born 14 October 1752.

    h. Eupham Ballingal, born 26 November 1755.

    i. Elizabeth Ballingal, born 31 October 1757.

2. John McIntosh of Dalmunzie was baptised on 17 July 1726. He was apprenticed to James Mansfield, a merchant in Edinburgh. He became a merchant in London and died in 1790.

3. Robert McIntosh of Ashintully was baptised on 6 August 1727. He became an advocate and died on 15 April 1805.

4. Bethia McIntosh who was baptised on 20 October 1728.

5. Lauchlan McIntosh was baptised on 23 October 1730.

At this stage, it is not known how many other descendants can be traced from Margaret Anderson.

Lauchlan McIntosh was moderator in 1736 and was nominated to become moderator a second time in 1743. However, he declined to accept the nomination. While he was attending the General Assembly in 1743 he was taken ill as a result of an epidemic which was raging in Edinburgh at that time. As a result of this illness he died on 13 May 1744, aged about fifty-four. Margaret lived on in St Andrews for many years. She died there on 17 February 1770 leaving her estate to her brother, James. No doubt her surviving children had been provided for under the will of Lauchlan McIntosh. One of the items which was probably included in the estate left by Margaret to her brother was a painting which has recently been identified by the Scottish National Portrait Gallery. It appears to be one of several versions of a portrait of Andrew Macpherson of Cluny (1640-66) by Richard Wait. A copy is also in the collection of the National Portrait Gallery in Edinburgh. Another version is reproduced in·a book by John Telfer Dunbar called *The Costume of Scotland* (1981). The portrait was probably painted in about 1720. The notes from the Gallery about Andrew Macpherson describe him as being the 15th Chief and apparently 'Andrew was the Chief who got Macintosh to give the famous declaration of 12th September 1665 that the Macphersons would support Macintosh against the Camerons out of their "meir guidwill and pleasure"'.

A fuller explanation about the declaration can be found in *The Loyall Dissuasive*. The main subject of this book is a history of the relationship between the Macphersons and the Macintosh clan. The author is arguing against the Macphersons recognising themselves as being joined into and becoming a part of the Clan Macintosh. This case was being presented by the author, Sir Aeneas Macpherson, many years after the time of Andrew Macpherson of Cluny, the 15th Chief. However, in the course of his narrative, Sir Aeneas supports his contention by explaining how Andrew Macpherson obtained the declaration from the Macintoshes. The background is that after many years during which the Macintoshes had regarded the Macphersons as a branch of their family, the Macintosh family were engaged in a dispute with the Camerons over lands. They called on the Macphersons to help and knew they could not succeed without them. Andrew Macpherson, the 15th Chief, stopped on his march and sent a message to Macintosh to tell him

> that he did not grudge to serve his friend but least Macintosh might be ready to misconstrue his kindness, and place it to the store of duty as a supposed kinsman; he told Macintosh that he must renounce this claim and agree that it was on no such basis that the Macphersons went along with him, but as a kind friend and neighbour, for the like service from Macintosh if the Macphersons needed their services.

The outcome was that the Macintoshes did acknowledge the Macpherson claim to independence from them. In brief the reply read

> I Lauchlan McIntosche of Torcastle do declare that Andrew Mcpherson of Cluny and others have out of their meir guidwill and pleasure joined me at this time for recovering my lands.

The full statement and a reproduction of it are given in the book. The book also contains a photograph of one of the paintings of Andrew Macpherson of Cluny, 1661. Alexander Brodie described Andrew Macpherson of Cluny in the following fulsome terms

'as an Absolom for beauty
a Joseph for contenance
a Tully for Eloquence, and
a Jonathan for friendship'.

Having made such a mark on his contemporaries by his actions and his character, unfortunately Andrew Macpherson died while still a young man and just before he was due to be married. His family descent in the clan came from his brother, Duncan, who became the 16th Chief.

A copy of the painting of Andrew Macpherson of Cluny, 15th Chief, is also reproduced in the book called *The Chiefs of Clan Macpherson* by Macpherson of Dalchully. This book also details the genealogy of the Macpherson clan through to 1947 when the book was published. It may be noted that the Chief of the clan at the time supported the Jacobite cause in the 1745 uprising and suffered severe penalties as a result. Further aspects of the Macpherson clan are detailed in the book *Glimpses of Church and Social Life in the Highlands in Olden Times* by Alexander Macpherson, 1893.

It appears likely that Rev. Lauchlan McIntosh had a version of the painting of Andrew Macpherson because of his probable connection with the Macintosh family concerned with the events mentioned above. The portrait, after passing to the Anderson family, remained with them until it was sold with other portraits in the early years of the 20th century. Although the location of this painting is not now known, fortunately a photograph was taken of the portrait and this is still available.

Having discussed what is know about Margaret Anderson, her marriage and descendants, the life of her brother James, the only known surviving son of Alexander Anderson, is discussed in the next chapter.

CHAPTER FIVE

James Anderson, baptised 1 December 1720, died 29 June 1794

JAMES ANDERSON was the only surviving son of Alexander Anderson and his wife, Isabel. According to the parish register, he was baptised at Falkland on 1 December 1720. Some records show him as having been born in 1719. Since the normal Scottish practice was for infants to be baptised very shortly after birth, it is more likely that he was born in November 1720. Isabel, his mother, died in 1720 and if he was born in 1719, her illness may have been the reason for the long delay before baptism took place.

It appears that from all the children born to his parents, only the eldest, Margaret, survived before the birth of James. Margaret must have been about twenty-two years of age and already married when James was born. The first five years of his life would have been at Falkland until presumably he was taken by his father to St Andrews. The main part of his life was then centred on St Andrews and Edinburgh. It may be that Anna Waugh, the widow of John Anderson and the mother of Alexander Anderson, was of considerable help in the first few years of James's life following the death of his mother. Anna lived until 1726, by which time the family had moved to St Andrews. It is also likely that his aunts and his sister helped in bringing up James as his father was greatly involved in church affairs.

Little is known at this time about the early career of James Anderson. He was only 17 when his father died. Unlike his father and grandfather he did not enter the church as might have been expected. Instead he trained in law and in due course became an advocate. It is not known what influences led him to this decision about his career. However, he may have influenced his nephew, Robert McIntosh, who also became an advocate. James was admitted as an advocate on 31 July 1742. The record in the Register of Advocates reads:

> James Anderson of Newbigging 31st July 1742 son of Rev. Alexander Anderson of St Andrews born 1719 died 29th June 1794 married Janet (died 2nd October 1792) daughter of Patrick Lindesay, Lord Provost and M.P. Edinburgh.

After being admitted as an advocate in 1742 at the age of 22 or 23, about five years after the death of his father, James Anderson presumably spent most of his time on legal affairs in Edinburgh. In approximately 1750, when he was about thirty, he married Janet Lindsay. They had two sons and a daughter. It is likely that, in view of their family associations with St Andrews, the Lindsay and Anderson families were well known to each other and, as shown in subsequent chapters, the family friendship continued for many years. Janet Lindsay was the second child of Patrick Lindsay who had been Lord Provost of Edinburgh and an M.P. Patrick Lindsay had been admitted to the freedom of the city of St Andrews on 10 September 1722. His father had been the headmaster or rector of the grammar school in St Andrews. His name was also Patrick Lindsay and the family was descended from a younger branch of the eldest son of Patrick, 4th Lord Lindsay of the Byres. More information about Patrick and the Lindsay family is given in Chapter Fourteen which also shows the subsequent family connection.

In addition to Kingask, which he inherited from his father, James Anderson established a house farther along the Fife coast at Burntisland. The property was called Newbigging (or new building, based on the Anglo-Saxon Niwe byggan).[1] The list of landowners in Scotland lists him as James Anderson of Newbigging with lands both at St Andrews and Burntisland. In the entry about his father-in-law in the *Dictionary of National Biography*, James Anderson is described as being of Monthrieve, Fifeshire. This is the property now known as Montrave, near Leven in Fife, which is dealt with in more detail in Chapter Seven.

On 24 August 1763, James Anderson was admitted a burgess of Edinburgh. The record reads:

> Anderson of Newbigging Esq. advocate, burgess of Edinburgh and gild brother by right of wife Janet daughter of deceased Patrick Lindesay Esq., late Lord Provost, gratis by Act of Council for good services 24th August 1763.

James Anderson must have had various records of his family available as he matriculated the existing coat of arms in the Public Register of All Arms and Bearings in Scotland. This Register is maintained by the Lord Lyon, King of Arms. The entry in the Lyon Register reads:

> James Anderson of Newbigging Esquire Advocate only son and heir of the Reverend Mr. Alexander Anderson of Newbigging Minister of the Gospel at St Andrews and Isabel daughter of Robert Hay of Strowie Esquire which Alexander was only son and heir of the Reverend Mr. John Anderson Principal of St Leonards College in the University of St Andrews and Ann daughter of ... Waugh of Shaws Esquire which John was eldest son and heir of the Reverend Mr. Alexander Anderson Minister of the Gospel at Auchtergaven and Grizel daughter of ... Ballantyne of Spolt Esquire which last Alexander was eldest son and heir of the Reverend Mr. James Anderson Minister of the Gospel and one of the Reformers of religion in this Kingdom which last James was grandson by a younger son of the family of Anderson of Westertown in the county of Banff. Bears – Argent – a Cheveron Gules between three stars in chief and a crescent in base all azure. Crest a star azure. Motto Nil Conscire Sibi. Matriculated 5th October 1780.

This entry is recorded in the Public Register of All Arms and Bearings in Scotland in Volume I, Folio 243 and dated 5 October 1780.

For the continuation of the record shown in the matriculation of 1780 to cover the next 200 years, see the cadet matriculation of 1980 detailed in Chapter Eleven. It will be noted that James Anderson appears not to have had a record of Henry Anderson, the son of the first James Anderson referred to in Chapter One. This is not surprising in view of the limited information available even now with all the additional records and sources which have been published in the last 100 years.

The motto used is of some interest. *Fairbairn's Book of Crests* translates 'Nil conscire sibi' as 'Conscious of no wrong'. Elvin's *Mottoes Revised* suggests a development on this interpretation 'To have a conscience free from guilt'.[2] The motto clearly sets a high standard of conduct for members of the family. From what has been said earlier (see Chapter Two), it appears that the arms had been used in the family for well over a hundred years previously. It is slightly surprising that the arms were not entered on the Register in the period when existing arms could be entered under the statute of 1592 and the later statute of 1672 which regulates the use of arms. It was this second statute which established the single 'Public Register of All Arms and Bearings'. At first there was free registration of arms after they had been suitably verified and if necessary corrected for differences due to the position in the family. The explanation for this omission no doubt lies in the troubled times which affected the lives of ministers in the church during the 17th century. However, the correct action in the matriculation of the family arms was eventually taken in 1780 with the above matriculation dated 5 October 1780.

In 1792 James Anderson made a bequest to his daughter, Margaret. This document, which was recorded in the Register of Deeds, Durie, 8 July 1794, after his death, also refers to a bequest to Margaret from her uncle, Captain James Lindesay. He had been a captain of a ship in the service of the East India Company (see Chapter Fourteen). In 1794 Margaret Anderson married Alexander Nairne, an accountant in Edinburgh. He was descended from Anne Anderson, the daughter of Rev. John Anderson (see Chapter Three) who married James Nairne, the minister of Anstruther Easter.[3] Margaret died on 9 December 1838 and is buried at Greyfriars in Edinburgh (see Chapter Six).

Janet Lindsay or Anderson died on 2 October 1792 aged 75 years. James Anderson died at the age of 75 on 29 June 1794. He and his wife are both buried at the Cathedral burial ground in St Andrews. On a wall nearby is a large memorial to John, Alexander and James and their wives. Presumably erected by the sons of James, it incorporates the newly matriculated coat of arms complete with motto and crest.

The memorial in Latin reads—

IN TERRA SACRATA
JUXTA HOX MONUMENTUM
CONDUNTUR RELIQUIAE
REVERENDISSIMI VIRI
JOANNIS ANDERSON
IN ACADEMIA ANDREANA
COLLEGII LEONARDINI
PERFECTI
OUI OBIIT AD MDCCVIII
ET EJUS CONJUGIS ANNAE WAUGH
DI SCHAWS IN CUMBRIA
QUAE OBIIT AD MDCCXXVI
NECNON EORUM FILII
ALLEXANDRI ANDERSON DE KINGASK
ECCLESIAE ANDREAPOLITANAE MINISTRI
OUI OBIIT V ID NOV AD MDCCXXXVII
ET ISABELLAE HAY DE STRUIE
EJUS CONJUGIS
QUAE OBIIT AD MDCCXX
NECNON ET JACOBI ANDERSON DE KINGASK
INCLYTAE FACULTATIS JURIDICAE SOCII
OUI OBIIT III CAL JUN MDCCXCIV
AETATIS SUAE LXXV
ET EJUS CONJUGIS JANETTAE LINDESAY
FILIAE PATRICII LINDESAY MP
QUAE OBIIT V CAL OCTOB AD MDCCXCII
AETATS SUAE LXXV

James and Janet Anderson had two sons in addition to their daughter, Margaret, born *c.* 1759:

1. Alexander Anderson, born in 1751.
2. Patrick Anderson, born in 1755.

An outline of their lives is given in the next chapter. A fuller outline of the Lindsay family and, in particular some of the life of Patrick Lindsay, the father of Janet Lindsay, will be found in Chapter Fourteen.

CHAPTER SIX

Alexander Anderson (1751–26 November 1818)
Patrick Anderson (1755–24 December 1809)

ALEXANDER ANDERSON was born in about 1751, the elder son of James and Janet Anderson. Little is known about his career, although he was clearly a man of substantial means and became the owner of several properties. It seems that Alexander Anderson's life was mainly centred on St Andrews in Fife and the Edinburgh region. He was known as Alexander Anderson of Kingask which was the property originally acquired by his grandfather, Rev. Alexander Anderson of St Andrews. The estates he owned included Kingask, Newbigging and Monthrive, all in the county of Fife. It is possible that he farmed part of the various estates, in addition to drawing rental income from the properties which were let. He must also have been in business as he became a merchant burgess of Edinburgh. The Roll of Edinburgh burgesses records:

> 'Anderson, Alexander, Merchant burgess of Edinburgh and gild brother in or by right of father James Anderson of Newbigging Esq. advocate burgess of Edinburgh and gild brother' dated 10th June 1772.

This means that Alexander Anderson was admitted as a merchant burgess at the age of about twenty-one. No evidence has been found that he trained in the law as was the case with his father and his brother. He remained a bachelor for many years but clearly retained a close relationship with his brother. On 19 March 1794 he was present at the baptism of his brother's third son (also Alexander) who became his heir and later that year he himself married. On 18 October 1794 he married his cousin, Janet, the second daughter of one of his mother's brothers, Patrick Lindsay of Eaglescairnie (see Chapter Fourteen). Alexander Anderson was about forty-three years of age when he married his cousin who was about thirty-seven years of age. They did not have any children.

Alexander Anderson died on 26 November 1818. His younger brother had died in 1809. Janet Lindsay, his wife, died on 17 December 1825. They are both buried in Greyfriars churchyard, Edinburgh. A monumental inscription reads:

Alexander Anderson Esq. of Kingask

The Burial-ground of Alexander Anderson Esq. of Kingask whose remains are here
deposited. He died 26th November 1818 aged 67 years. Also the remains of Janet,
his wife, daughter of Patrick Lindsay Esq. of Eaglescairnie who died 17th December
1825 aged 68 years.[1]

Other entries follow which are detailed below.

The second son of James and Janet Anderson was Patrick Anderson who was
born in 1755 and clearly named Patrick after the long line of Patrick Lindsay's
from his mother's family as explained in Chapter Fourteen.

Patrick Anderson entered the legal profession like his father. However, he
trained in different aspects of the profession, first becoming a Clerk to the
Signet and later a Writer to the Signet. It is interesting to note that in 1792 he
personally handwrote his father's will in which James Anderson made a bequest
to his daughter, Margaret, as a supplement to his marriage contract with Janet
Lindsay. James Anderson wrote the final section of the document himself.
Patrick Anderson also wrote his own will which was dated 1797. It is a valuable
feature of the Scottish record system that copies of these old documents are
still available. The more normal course would have been for these documents
to be handwritten by a clerk in the office of a firm of Writers to the Signet.

The list of Writers to the Signet records—

Anderson Patrick   2nd December 1779

Apprentice to Walter Scott — second son of James Anderson of Kingask and New-
bigging. Advocate. Died 24th December 1809 aged 54. Married 14th September 1786,
Susan (died 18th July 1821) daughter of Rev. Gilbert Hamilton D.D. Minister of
Cramond.

The Walter Scott to whom Patrick Anderson was apprenticed was the father
of Sir Walter Scott, the well-known author who was himself apprenticed to his
father a few years after Patrick Anderson.

Patrick Anderson would have been about thirty-one years of age when he
married Susan, the daughter of Rev. Gilbert Hamilton, D.D., on 14 September
1786. She was born in 1761 and so was about twenty-five years of age when
she married. The Hamilton family is very extensive and has well-documented
records. For example, A History of The House of Hamilton by Lt.-Col. George
Hamilton was published in 1933. Here, however, a short outline is given from
various sources showing the lineage of Susan Hamilton.

Gavin Hamilton, born 27 October 1614, a relative of Sir Robert Hamilton,
was a staunch covenanter who accompanied Charles II on his 1651 expedition
into England. He was a member of the General Assembly in 1650. Gavin
married a kinswoman, Jane, the daughter of Robert Montgomery of Hazlehead.
Their eldest son was Robert, born in 1650, who succeeded to the estates. The
second son, William, was born in 1669. William's father, Gavin, died before 11
January 1675 so that his brother, nearly twenty years older, had a significant

influence on William's life. Owing to the times in which they lived (see Chapter Three), William was not baptised until he was six and then at a conventicle held in 1675. William Hamilton in due course took a leading part in church affairs. He became minister of Cramond from 1694 until 1709 and was the moderator of the General Assembly no less than five times in 1712, 1716, 1720, 1727 and 1730. He also became Professor of Divinity in the University of Edinburgh. His career is discussed in some detail in Warrick's book *The Moderators of the Church of Scotland 1690 to 1740* and this book also contains a photograph of him taken from a painting.

In 1696, William Hamilton married Mary, the daughter of John Robertson. She died on 22 January 1760 aged 85. It is reported that they had 16 children and a little is known about nine of them:

1. William — second son.

2. Gavin — third or fourth son, born 1704, became a bookseller who during an illness made a model with improvements of the new town of Edinburgh. As the youngest bailie at the time, he took part in dealing with the Porteous mob and had to superintend the taking down of Captain Porteous' body from the dyer's pole on which he was hanged (see also Chapter Fourteen).

3. Alexander — died 1778.

4. Robert — born 1707, became a Doctor of Divinity. He was minister of Cramond from 1731 to 1736 and was moderator of the General Assembly in 1754 and in 1760.

5. Gilbert — born 1715 (see below).

6. Ann — born 1703, married John Horsley, rector of Newington in Surrey. She was the mother of Samuel Horsley who became Bishop of St Asaph.

7. Jean — married 1718 Hugh Cleghorn.

8. Margaret — married 1731 William Tod.

9. Janet — married 1731 James Smith.

The father of Susan Hamilton was Gilbert Hamilton who was born on 16 May 1715. He was educated at the University of Edinburgh where his father was a professor. He was ordained on 28 March 1737 and presented by John, Earl of Duglen, 21 September 1739. He became a Doctor of Divinity from King's College, Aberdeen, in 1760. Following his father and brother he was minister of Cramond from 1737 to 1772 and became moderator of the General Assembly of the Church of Scotland on 19 May 1768. He died on 17 May 1772.

On 9 January 1742 Gilbert Hamilton married Isabel, daughter of James Smith of Nether Alderston, and on 4 March 1754 he married Margaret, daughter of John Craigie of Dunbarne, and had issue:

1. Anne Cockburn Hamilton, born 27 June 1756, who married William Dinwiddie of Manchester (see below and also Chapter Seven).

2. Mary Hamilton, born 24 February 1758, who remained unmarried and died 13 February 1838 and was buried near her younger sister.

3. Susan Hamilton, born 6 January 1761 and who married Patrick Anderson, W.S.

A number of references incorrectly state that it was Mary Hamilton who married William Dinwiddie.[2] That this was not the position is clearly shown by two pieces of evidence. The tombstone memorial for Mary Hamilton shows she did not change her name — see later in the chapter for the entry. Patrick Anderson's wills, one for Scottish property and one for property not in Scotland, refer to his wife's sisters, Mrs. Ann Hamilton, wife of William Dinwiddie, merchant in Manchester and to Miss Mary Hamilton.

Patrick and Susan Anderson lived on the north side of Princes Street according to his will where he describes and identifies the property.[3] They had eight children as follows:

1. James Anderson born 6 October 1789.

2. Gilbert Hamilton Anderson born 24 March 1793.

3. Alexander Anderson born 17 March 1794, of whom more detail is given in Chapter Seven.

4. Charles Inglis Anderson born 14 August 1795 (see below).

5. Susannah (Susan) Anderson born 29 August 1796 (see below).

6. Patrick Anderson born 11 April 1798.

7. Anne Anderson born 20 March 1800 (see below).

8. John Anderson born 21 August 1802 (see below).

An interesting feature may be noted in the case of two of the sons in that they had two forenames. Having more than one Christian name was a rare event in Scotland until the end of the 18th century. It has been estimated that in Edinburgh in 1760 only 1 per cent. of the people had two names. By 1790 this had risen to 7 per cent. which is the time of the two named above. By 1820 the figure had risen to 25 per cent.[4] In the case of Patrick and Susan Anderson they clearly gave the additional Christian names to their children as a compliment or mark of respect to people they knew with the same names, but they included the surname. Thus Gilbert Hamilton Anderson is clearly incorporating the name of Susan's father who was Gilbert Hamilton. The first son's name, James, would appear to be after Patrick Anderson's father. The third son, Alexander, would have been so named to follow the name given to several members of the family and more recently to Patrick's grandfather and to his elder brother who up to this time had not married although he did so in the year following Alexander's birth. The two Christian names given to the fourth son are explained by reference to the old parish registers.

Each of the baptisms of the children is fully recorded. All took place at St Andrew's church which lies just behind Princes Street in Edinburgh where Patrick and Susan lived. The entry for the eldest son, James, records that the witnesses included the Rev. William Simpson (present for the first three children's baptism and presumably the minister at the time) and Charles Inglis Esq., Captain in the Royal Navy. Reference to the Navy biographies of the time show that a Charles Inglis eventually became an Admiral and a painting of him can be seen in the Scottish Portrait Gallery in Edinburgh. He had two sons who were also in the Navy: Charles, who entered the Navy in 1807 and Patrick who entered the Navy in 1812. It may be concluded that the Inglis family were friends of the Anderson family at that time, sufficiently so for one of their sons to be named Charles Inglis Anderson. This family friendship may be further evidenced by the fact that at the baptism of the sixth child named Patrick, one of the witnesses was Patrick Inglis of Sunnyside who may have been the son of Charles Inglis referred to above.

Other family or connected names were present at other baptisms. Patrick's brother, Alexander, was present at the baptism of Gilbert Hamilton, Alexander, Susannah (Susan), Anne and John. His designation changed in this time. In 1793 and 1794 he was described as Alexander Anderson, younger, of Newbigging Esq. From 1796 he is described as Alexander Anderson of Kingask Esq. Witnesses to the baptism of Charles Inglis Anderson were the Rev. James Nairne, minister of Pittenweem (see Chapter Three) and Mr. Alexander Nairne, accountant, Edinburgh. The latter was of course married to Margaret, the sister of Patrick Anderson. Alexander Nairne was also present at the baptism of Susannah. The other witness at the baptism of the eighth child, John, was Patrick Lindsay, 39th Regiment of Foot. This will almost certainly have been Patrick Anderson's cousin, Patrick Lindsay, son of John Lindsay and cousin also to Janet Lindsay, the wife of Alexander Anderson of Kingask, who was later to become Sir Patrick Lindsay and in due course to be recognised as the 8th Earl of Lindsay and 17th Lord Lindsay of the Byres (see Chapter Fourteen).

Little is known about the lives of several of the children and it may be that James and Gilbert Hamilton both died in infancy. The life of Alexander is fully discussed in the next chapter. Charles Inglis Anderson, who it has been noted was born on 14 August 1795, appears not to have married and died on 1 March 1853 at the age of fifty-seven. He was buried in the Greyfriars burial area designated by his uncle, Alexander Anderson of Kingask. Charles appears to have owned various properties in Edinburgh but at this time it is not clear whether he pursued a particular career. In his will he left most of his property to his brother, Alexander Anderson of Montrave, with bequests to various of his nephews and nieces and also £500 each to his cousins, Elizabeth Dinwiddie, Jane Dinwiddie and Gilbert Hamilton Dinwiddie who was the Assistant Commissary General in H.M. Service at Gibraltar.

Susan Anderson, as she was known, was born on 29 August 1796. A needlework sampler made by her in 1804 when she was eight still exists.[5] She married Rev. Abraham Home of Windshield and Gunsgreen on 30 April 1821. He was born on 25 December 1775 and was therefore about twenty-one years older than Susan. Abraham Home was the son of George Home, the minister of Ayton and he was educated at the University of Edinburgh.[6] Susan and Abraham are known to have had six children as follows:

1. Susan Hamilton Home who was born on 22 January 1822 and died in January 1831.

2. George Home who was born on 12 February 1823 and died in March 1858.

3. Patrick Anderson Home, born on 27 April 1824, may have become a Doctor of Medicine. He died in June 1874.

4. Margaret Home who was born on 18 September 1825 and died on 11 September 1907.

5. Ann Mary Home who was born on 5 February 1827 and died in June 1866.

6. Elizabeth Hay Home, who was born on 15 April 1830 but died on 20 March 1831 on the same day as her mother died.

It is interesting to note that following the example of her parents, Susan gave the names of her mother and her father to two of the children, Susan Hamilton and Patrick Anderson.

In the will of Charles Inglis Anderson written on 10 March 1844 he left £3,000 to be divided equally between George, Patrick, Ann(e) and Margaret, because the other two girls, Susan and Elizabeth, had died before that time. It would be interesting to learn something more about the lives of the members of the Home family descended from Susan Anderson. It is believed that Margaret Home did not marry. As noted later, when she died she left certain bequests to her cousins, the descendants of Susan's brother, Alexander Anderson of Montrave (see Chapter Nine).

Susan Home died after only ten years of marriage on 20 March 1831. Her husband, Abraham, died at Gunsgreen, Eyemouth, on 3 March 1856. Included as an appendix at the end of this book are some notes dealing with the Home family of Wedderburn and Paxton. These notes raise some interesting questions concerning Abraham Home and other members of the family.

The sixth child was Patrick Anderson (younger) and apart from the fact that he was born on 11 April 1798, nothing further is known. In the case of

Anne Anderson, nothing is known about her life. She was born on 20 March 1800 and she lived until she was 75, her death being on 25 July 1875. She is the last known member of the family buried in the area reserved for Alexander Anderson of Kingask and members of the family at Greyfriars in Edinburgh.

The eighth and final child born to Patrick and Susan Anderson was John, born on 21 August 1802. Whilst no further specific information is known at this stage it is possible that like his father he may have been trained in the law. In 1825 Alexander Anderson, the third but the eldest surviving son of Patrick and Susan, entered into a marriage contract. This document was written by 'John Anderson clerk to Alexander Moneypenny Writer to the Signet'. The document was dated 21 November 1825. It is not unreasonable to believe that John Anderson could be providing this service to his eldest brother. In due course it is hoped to obtain more information concerning the lives of these other members of the family of Patrick and Susan Anderson.

A significant feature of the early 19th century is the martial spirit which prevailed because of the wars with France and knowledge of international expansion through a growing Empire. As a marked departure from his own, his father's profession or his Anderson forebears, in 1809 Patrick Anderson entered his eldest surviving son into the service of the Honourable East India Company. The influence of the East India Army was to dominate the lives and affairs of the family for the next fifty years and more.

Patrick Anderson died at the young age of fifty-four. He and Susan, his wife, were buried in the burial ground at Greyfriars churchyard, set aside by his brother Alexander. The inscription referred to before continues:

> Here lie interred the bodies of Patrick Anderson, Esq. Writer to the Signet, who died on 24th December 1809 aged 54 years.
> And Mrs. Susan Anderson, daughter of the deceased Rev. Dr. Gilbert Hamilton, Minister of the Gospel at Cramond, his wife, who died on the 18th of July 1821 aged 60 years.
> And Miss Mary Hamilton, daughter of the said Dr. Gilbert Hamilton who died on the 13th day of February 1838 aged 79 years.

Other references are to John Hampton Anderson — see Chapter Seven — and:

> Also the body of Mrs. Margaret Anderson, relict of Alexander Nairne Esq. Accountant in Edinburgh who died on the 9th day of December 1838 aged 79 years.
> Charles Inglis Esq. 2nd son of P. Anderson Esq. who died 1st March 1853 aged 57.

The final entry records the death of Anne Anderson on 25th July 1875.

The next chapter discusses the life and family of Alexander Anderson, the son of Patrick and Susan Anderson.

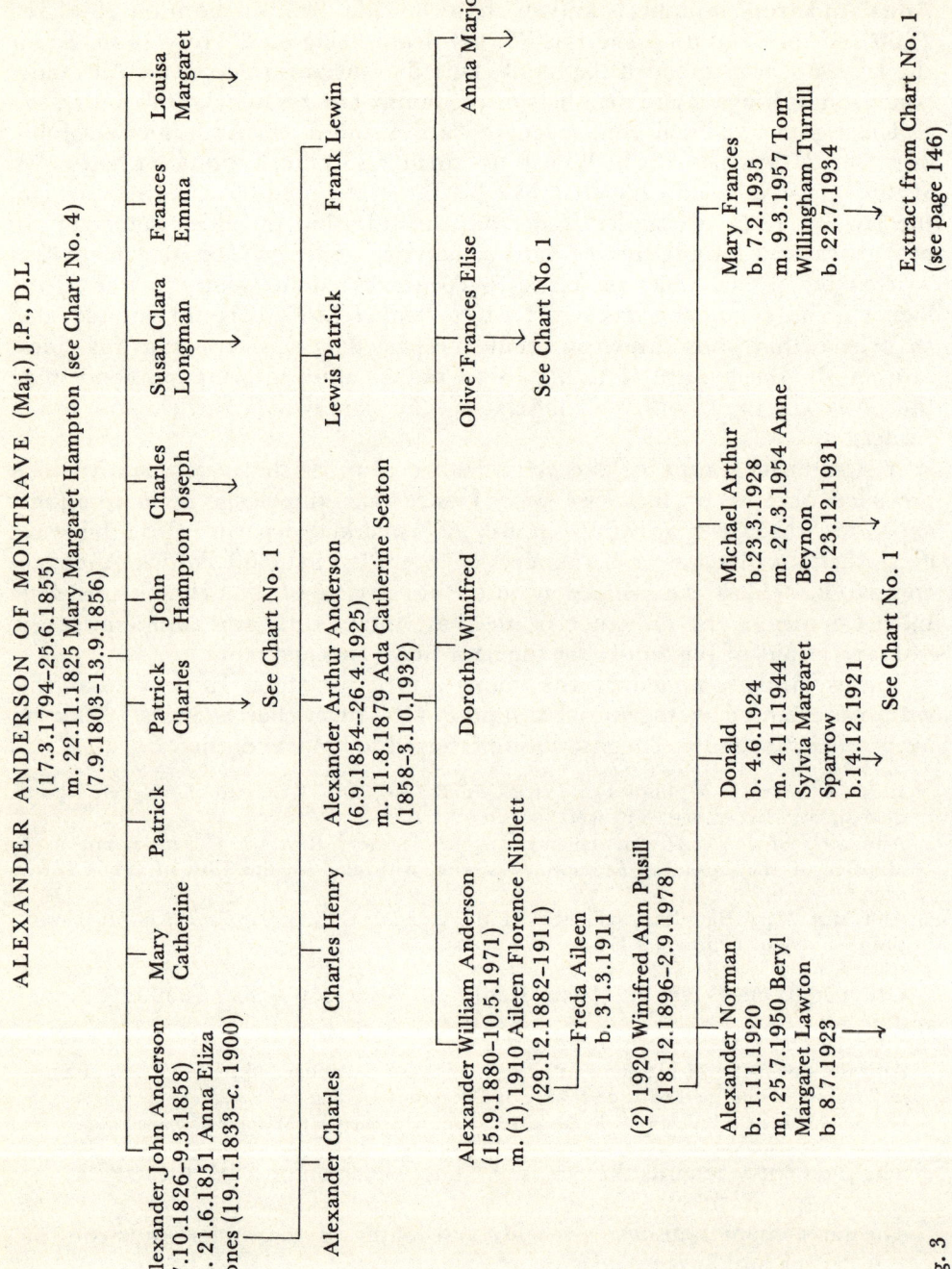

ALEXANDER ANDERSON OF MONTRAVE (Maj.) J.P., D.L.
(17.3.1794–25.6.1855)
m. 22.11.1825 Mary Margaret Hampton (see Chart No. 4)
(7.9.1803–13.9.1856)

Alexander John Anderson
(7.10.1826–9.3.1858)
m. 21.6.1851 Anna Eliza
Jones (19.1.1833–c. 1900)

Mary
Catherine

Patrick
Charles

John
Hampton
Joseph
→
See Chart No. 1

Patrick
Charles

Susan Clara
Longman
→

Frances
Emma

Louisa
Margaret
→

Alexander Charles

Charles Henry

Alexander Arthur Anderson
(6.9.1854–26.4.1925)
m. 11.8.1879 Ada Catherine Seaton
(1858–3.10.1932)

Lewis Patrick

Frank Lewin

Dorothy Winifred

Olive Frances Elise
→
See Chart No. 1

Anna Marjorie
→

Alexander William Anderson
(15.9.1880–10.5.1971)
m. (1) 1910 Aileen Florence Niblett
(29.12.1882–1911)

Freda Aileen
b. 31.3.1911

(2) 1920 Winifred Ann Pusill
(18.12.1896–2.9.1978)

Alexander Norman
b. 1.11.1920
m. 25.7.1950 Beryl
Margaret Lawton
b. 8.7.1923
→

Donald
b. 4.6.1924
m. 4.11.1944
Sylvia Margaret
Sparrow
b.14.12.1921
→
See Chart No. 1

Michael Arthur
b.23.3.1928
m. 27.3.1954 Anne
Beynon
b. 23.12.1931
→

Mary Frances
b. 7.2.1935
m. 9.3.1957 Tom
Willingham Turnill
b. 22.7.1934
→

Extract from Chart No. 1
(see page 146)

Fig. 3

CHAPTER SEVEN

Alexander Anderson of Montrave (17 March 1794–25 June 1855)

THE EARLIEST INFORMATION about this Alexander Anderson, who was the eldest surviving son of Patrick and Susan Anderson, is that he was baptised on 19 March 1794 only two days after he was born. Early baptism was the normal custom in Scotland at that time. The ceremony was performed in St Andrews church, Edinburgh, and one of the witnesses was his uncle, Alexander Anderson of Kingask.

It is interesting to speculate on the influences which led to Alexander Anderson joining the military service of the Honourable East India Company at the early age of 15. His grandmother was Janet Anderson or Lindsay and her father had been in the army in his younger days in the 18th century. Her three brothers were all involved with military matters. The eldest, Patrick Lindsay, of Eaglescairnie, had been Deputy Secretary of War but had died in 1801. The second brother was John Lindsay who became a Lieutenant Colonel and died in 1780. His son, Patrick Lindsay, born 24 February 1778, became Sir Patrick Lindsay, K.C.B. in recognition of his outstanding military services in India. Sir Patrick did not complete his claim to the titles of 8th Earl of Lindsay, 7th Viscount Garnock and 17th Lord Lindsay of the Byres, in his lifetime. However, as explained in Chapter Fourteen, he was subsequently recognised as the holder of these titles. As noted in the previous chapter, this Patrick Lindsay was present at the baptism of Alexander's youngest brother, John, in 1802. It is concluded that it may have been his example, though he was with the British Army (rather than H.E.I.C.S.), which influenced Alexander Anderson and his parents into thinking of a military career, coupled with the martial spirit which existed at that period.

In 1809, the East India Company founded a new seminary for the training of their military cadets. It was called Addiscombe and was situated near Croydon in London. Alexander Anderson was one of the first cadets to enter.[1] He passed his public examinations with 13 other cadets on 22 December 1809, two days before the death of his father, Patrick Anderson. Subsequently, he was admitted on Establishment 24 August 1810, having been directed to join an expedition preparing for foreign service. During the time following the death of his father and his embarkation for India, he obtained a range of interesting entries in his autograph book which still exists.[2] These include contributions from members of the Lindsay family at Eaglescairnie, and his uncle, Alexander Anderson.

It appears likely that the autograph book was given to Alexander by his cousin, Gilbert Hamilton Dinwiddie, or Gilbert's parents, his mother's sister and her husband. Entries by members of the Dinwiddie family are the earliest recorded in the autograph book. The front page has been beautifully illustrated and, although unsigned, appears to be in the same style as a subsequent entry dated 22 January 1810 in London and signed by Gilbert. The members of the Dinwiddie family appear to have had an artistic talent as on the same date there is a delightful water colour painting of Edinburgh Castle with a note signed E.D. and almost certainly Elizabeth Dinwiddie. Entries on 18 January 1810 appear to be by Anne Dinwiddie (A.D.) and her husband, William Dinwiddie (W.D.). Other entries obtained by Alexander are by his mother, Susan, his sister, Susan, and his brother, Charles Inglis Anderson. Additional entries are by Lady Catherine Blantyre, his aunt, married to Alexander 10th Lord Blantyre, Mrs. Craigie, the mother of Margaret Lindsay (widow of John Lindsay and mother of Patrick Lindsay — see Chapter Fourteen) who also recorded an entry in the autograph book on 2 March 1810. Further entries were by the Hon. Mrs. Stewart of Bolton, Miss Lindsay of Eaglescairnie, Mrs. Blair, Miss Isabella Blair and William Blair, M. Erskine, Miss C. Halkett, Susan Findlay, Ann Wanahope and John Wanahope, Mrs. Adam, formerly Kenny, Mrs. R. Adam. Dr. Cochrane, Jane Cochrane and M. C. Cochrane.

Four entries of particular interest were made by members of the Scrymgeour family. H. Scrymgeour, subsequently H. Scrymgeour-Wedderburn (later to be recognised as *de jure* 7th Earl of Dundee) wrote a message which must have been particularly meaningful for the young Alexander. It reads:

'To be prosperous and truly happy, you have only to copy the example of your late worthy Father' Edin. 24th March 1810.

His wife, Mrs. Scrymgeour, also made an entry as did two of their daughters, Eliza and Catherine, who later became Mrs. Cathcart.

Another entry in the autograph book was made by Miss Elizabeth Brodie. This is an attractive pencil sketch of an old castle. She was born on 20 June 1794 and was therefore some three months younger than Alexander. A little later, on 11 December 1813, Elizabeth married the Marquis of Huntly who was the eldest son of the 4th Duke of Gordon. He was some twenty-five years older than his wife and they unfortunately had no children. The 4th Duke died in 1827 and the 5th Duke in 1836 when the Dukedom of Gordon became extinct. The Duchess lived until 1864 when she died on 31 January. It would be fascinating to know if other examples of her sketches are still in existence.

The book also contains an entry by Alexander's cousin, Grizell Bell. Grizell was the daughter of Robert Hamilton, the brother of Gilbert Hamilton. She married Benjamin Bell, the eminent surgeon.[3] The entry may perhaps have been by her daughter if she had the same name.

The autograph book makes a most valuable record because of the high standard of its numerous entries and the interest in the people who made them. All the entries were made in the period of January to March 1810, being the three months following the death of Patrick Anderson.

Having spent his leave after passing out from Addiscombe in visiting friends and relations, as evidenced by the autograph book, Alexander proceeded to India. At the age of 16 he was appointed as a cadet in the Madras Engineers of the Honourable East India Company. On his way to India, he received his first involvement in action. He was aboard the East Indiaman ship named *Astell* in company with two other Indiamen when they were involved in a campaign at sea with two French frigates and a corvette off the coast of Mauritius. The battle lasted for six hours. The other two Indiamen were captured but the *Astell* managed to escape, with however, heavy losses in killed and wounded.[4]

Records of the East India Company show that as an ensign in the Engineers, Alexander Anderson was employed in the successful campaign for the capture of Java.[5] Resulting from this campaign, he received a share of the prize money. In 1817 he was engaged in the Matratta war in the Hyderabad Subsidiary Force. His services in the attack upon Talneir were extolled. He received official regrets for the wound he received there. He was wounded in the right wrist in the action at Talneir on 27 February 1818.[6] As a result, he was incapacitated from using his sword and was granted a wound pension. He was extolled for his services at the reduction of the fortress of Chanda and Mundela. He also received approbation of his conduct by the Governor General on 18 June 1818 at the close of the operations within the Nagpore territory. He shared in the prize money for the capture of Malidpore in 1817.

After 14 years' service, Alexander Anderson was given leave in Europe from 1824. Later he apparently submitted to the Court of the East India Company a memorandum for their favourable consideration. In this he outlined the disadvantages under which the Engineer Corps laboured as compared with other branches of the Company's army in respect of the number of field officers. In 1832 he requested permission to retire. At the same time he transmitted a certificate on the state of his health. He was permitted to retire on a pension of 9s. 6d. per day. Official retirement to England was from 3 March 1832. However, it appears that Alexander may not have been required to return to India from his leave in 1824.

In 1824 Alexander Anderson presumably returned to Scotland. His mother had died in 1821 and his uncle, Alexander Anderson of Kingask, had died in 1818. However, his aunt, Janet Lindsay, widow of Alexander, did not die until

17 December 1825. From the combination of deaths, Alexander, now a captain, was the main beneficiary of the various estates in Scotland. That this was so can be seen from the references in his marriage contract dated 21 November 1825. Alexander was married on Anglesey in North Wales. Whilst one can only speculate on the circumstances which took him to Anglesey, the source of the introduction seems fairly clear. Joseph Hampton Hampton, who was born on 2 February 1800, was in the East India Company military service also. He arrived in India on 5 September 1823, the year before Alexander went on leave. His elder brother, John Lewis Hampton, was also in the army, but in the Fifth Regiment of Dragoon Guards and may have seen service in India. Other members of the family may have visited India or alternatively Alexander Anderson may have been invited to visit Henllys at Beaumaris, Anglesey. He met Mary Margaret Hampton, the eldest surviving sister of the two brothers just mentioned and the daughter of John Hampton Hampton. As a result of this introduction, in due course a detailed marriage contract was entered into on 21 November 1825 and they married the next day. The ceremony took place on 22 November 1825 at Llanfaes church near Henllys, Beaumaris.[7] For additional information on the Hampton and associated Lewis families, see Chapter Fifteen which outlines the fascinating history of this family.

After their marriage, Alexander Anderson and his wife must have travelled for some time. They were staying in Italy the next year as their eldest son, Alexander John Anderson, was born at Leghorn (Livorno) in Italy on 7 October 1826. A little over a year later, Mary Catherine was born on 7 November 1827. A son, Patrick, was born in 1829 but died after 14 days. Patrick Charles was born on 29 June 1831. In 1832, as mentioned above, Alexander Anderson retired from the East India Company Service. In 1833, a further son named John Hampton Anderson was born but he died when he was five and a half months old and is buried at the family burial area in Greyfriars churchyard in Edinburgh. In 1835 Charles Joseph Anderson was born, also in Edinburgh, on 21 February and he was baptised on 25 March. The baptism certificate described his father as Major Alexander Anderson, Kingask, County of Fife. The next three children, Susan Clara Longman Anderson, born 10 November 1836, Frances Emma Anderson, born 2 February 1839 and Louisa Margaret Anderson, born 4 April 1840 (baptised 16 May 1840) are all recorded at the same time in the old parish register for Scoonie, near Leven in Fife, not far from Montrave.[8] The influence of Mary Margaret in the naming of the children can be seen in the use of Hampton family names in several cases — see Chapter Fifteen and Chart 4.

After his retirement from the East India Company, Alexander Anderson must have decided to settle at Monthrive, the estate in Fife originally acquired by his grandfather, James Anderson, in the previous century. Presumably at around this time the properties near St Andrews (Kingask and Newbigging) were sold. A house was built on the Monthrive estate and the name of the

1. Assumed to be Anna Waugh (d. 1726), the widow of Rev. John Anderson

2. Thought to be Isabel Hay (d. 1720), the wife of Rev. Alexander Anderson

3. Thought to be Rev. Alexander Anderson (1675-1737)

4. Thought to be Margaret Anderson (1698-1770), the daughter of Rev. Alexander Anderson and his wife Isabel

5. Andrew MacPherson of Cluny (1640-1666), by Richard Wait

6. Thought to be James Anderson
(1720-1794)

7. Alexander Anderson of Montrave
(1794-1855)

8. (*Left*) Mary Margaret Hampton (1803-1856), the wife of Alexander Anderson of Montrave

9. (*Below*) Montrave House *c.*1850. A sketch by John Coombs

10. (*Opposite*) Alexander John Anderson of Montrave (1826-1858)

11. Anna Eliza Jones (1833-1900), the wife of Alexander John Anderson of Montrave

12. Alexander Arthur Anderson (1854-1925)

13. (*Left*) Ada Catherine Seaton (1858-1932), the wife of Alexander Arthur Anderson

14. (*Below*) Alexander William Anderson (1880-1971) and his second wife, Winifred Ann Pusill (1896-1978)

15. (*opposite*) Extract of the Matriculation of the Arms of Michael Arthur Anderson.

EXTRACT of MATRICULATION of the Arms of MICHAEL ARTHUR ANDERSON

MICHAEL ARTHUR ANDERSON, Holder of the Degree of Bachelor of Science (Economics) of the University of London, Fellow of the Institute of Chartered Accountants of England and Wales, Fellow of the Institute of Cost and Management Accountants, Company Director, residing at Rhettave, Meadow Court, Mollington, Chester, having by Petition unto the Lord Lyon King of Arms of date 20th June 1979 Shewn, THAT he, the Petitioner, born Wellington in the County of Oxford, 23rd March 1928 (who married 27th March 195., Anne, daughter of Joseph Byrion and his wife Winifred Mason) is the third son of the late apparent Michael Grame Anderson, born 5th January 1950, and his wife Winifred Annie daughter of the late apparent William Anderson, civil engineer formerly in the Colonial Service, and his wife Winifred Annie daughter of John Charles Busill; THAT the Petitioner's said father (born Camberwell in the County of Surrey, 15th September 1880 and died 10th May 1971) was the only son of Alexander Arthur Anderson, architect, and his wife Ada Catharine Sexton; THAT the Petitioner's said grandfather (born on September 1854 and died 20th April 1925) was the third son, but eldest son with issue of Alexander John Anderson, Captain in the late 38th Native Infantry Honourable East India Company Service, and his wife Anna Eliza daughter of John Lawton Jones; THAT the Petitioner's said great-grandfather (born 7th October 1826 and died 9th March 1859) was the eldest son of Alexander Anderson of Mountarue, in the County of Fife, sometime Major in the Madras Engineers of the Honourable East India Company Service, and his wife (married 22nd November 1825) May Margaret, eldest daughter of John Hampton Hampton of Henllys, Anglesey, North Wales; THAT the Petitioner's said great-great-grandfather (born 17th March 1794, and died 25th June 1855) was the eldest son of Patrick Anderson, Writer to His Majesty's Signet, and his wife (married 14th September 1786) Susan, daughter of the Reverend Gilbert Hamilton, Doctor of Divinity, Minister of Cramond; THAT the Petitioner's said great-great-great-grandfather (born 1741 and died 24th December 1809) was the second son of James Anderson of Newbigging and Hugrass (who married at Edinburgh 18th October 1794) Janet daughter of Patrick Lindsay of Eaglescairnie and died without issue 20th November 1816) succeeded his uncle Alexander Anderson of Newbigging and Hugrass, daughter of Patrick Lindsay, Lord Provost of Edinburgh and a Mountarue, Advocate, and his wife Janet, daughter of Patrick Lindsay, Lord Provost of Edinburgh and a descendant of Patrick, 4th Lord Lindsay of the Byres; THAT Alexander Anderson of Mountarue aforesaid eldest son of the said James Anderson of Newbigging, Hugrass and Mountarue aforesaid; THAT certain Ensigns Armorial were recorded in the Public Register of All Arms and Bearings in Scotland (Volume 1, Folio 2.3) of date 5th October 1780 in name of the said James Anderson of Newbigging; AND the Petitioner having prayed that the foresaid Ensigns Armorial might be rematriculated of new in his own name with a suitable difference The Lord Lyon King of Arms by Interlocutor of date 5th February 1980 Granted Warrant to the Lyon Clerk to rematriculate in the Public Register of All Arms and Bearings in Scotland in name of the Petitioner the following Ensigns Armorial, videlicet:—

Azure, on a chevron Gules between three stars in chief, and a crescent in base Azure, a mullet Or

Above the Shield is placed an Helm befitting his degree with a Mantling Gules doubled Argent, and on a Wreath of the Liveries is set for Crest a Star Azure, and in an Escrol over the same this Motto "NIL CONSCIRE SIBI".

Matriculated the 30th day of April 1980.

Extracted forth of the 57th page of the 61th Volume of the Public Register of All Arms and Bearings in Scotland this 20th day of April 1980.

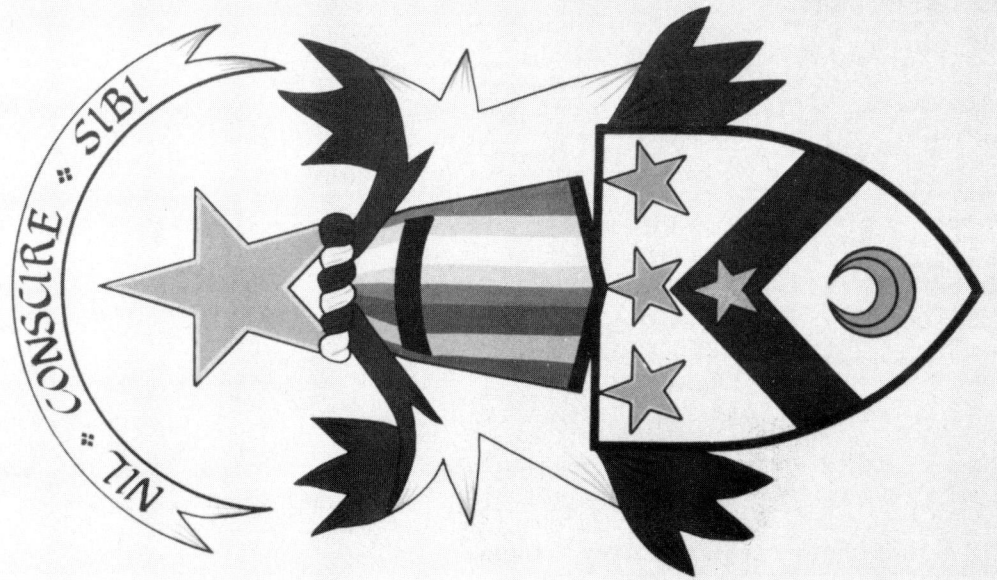

NIL :: CONSCIRE :: SIBI

Malcolm R. Innes of Edingight
Lyon Clerk and Keeper of the Records.

16. 'Grace Dieu', County Waterford

17. Henllys Hall and Llanfaes church, Beaumaris, Anglesey

property was modernised to the present Montrave. The original Montrave House appears to have been built around 1835.[9]

Apparently, much work over the subsequent years went into developing the Montrave Estate, including extensive tree planting. It is interesting to note that around this same period in Anglesey, at Beaumaris, the older established house of the Hampton family, called Henllys Hall, was extensively rebuilt. In the early 1850s John Coombs, who was in the East India Army and had married a sister (Sarah Louisa Jones) of Anna Eliza Jones, the wife of Alexander John Anderson, made a sketch of Montrave House. This shows the house before it was extended in the last quarter of the century by Sir John Gilmour, Bt.[10] The Gilmour family bought the property in the 1870s and have lived there ever since. Reference is made to the property in a number of books about Fife.[11] The house was considerably enlarged with a third floor being added. This lasted until the 1970s when the present Sir John Gilmour, Bt., formerly M.P. for East Fife, decided to have the house demolished. The present Montrave House is a most attractive conversion of another property on the Montrave Estate, a short distance from where the earlier house had been built.

It appears that from the time Alexander Anderson took up residence at Montrave, he devoted a considerable amount of his time to affairs in the county of Fife. He was engaged extensively in local authority matters as well as being a magistrate. Apparently, he was for some time chairman of the Finance Committee of the county. He also presided over the County Prison Board and over the Board for County Buildings. Shortly before his death his name was included in the list of Deputy Lieutenants for Fife. M. F. Connolly records:

> On the bench at Quarter Sessions and in the District Justices' Courts, we admired the deceased's uprightness and sagacity.[12] He dealt to all what he thought impartial justice, and without fear or favour. He never entered the courtroom in connection with any party or pledged to any particular course. He quickly saw where the truth lay, and gave his judgement accordingly. He was probably one of the best magistrates that ever sat on a bench — making the delinquent feel and smart for his offence, but without any approach to undue severity.

Connolly also records that the question of road reform was first started in Fife. At the May county road meeting before his death, Alexander Anderson obtained a committee to consider whether road money might not be raised by a better and more equitable system than collecting at toll-bars.

Although Alexander Anderson retired from the service of the Honourable East India Company in 1832, he must have continued to have a keen interest in affairs in India. All three of his sons were entered for the military training seminary of Addiscombe.[13] They were cadets there as follows:

Alexander John Anderson	cadet	1843–45
Patrick Charles Anderson	cadet	1849–50
Charles Joseph Anderson	cadet	1853–54

The relationship with the East India Military Service went even further than this. It is known that at least three of the four daughters married officers from the same service: Louisa Margaret Anderson married William Landon Jones who was a cadet 1840-2. Susan Clara Longman Anderson married Henry Leeuwin Dempster who was a cadet 1850-1. They had a son, F. E. Dempster.[14] Frances Emma Anderson married Frederick Edward Hadow, who was a cadet 1852-4.

Of these three it is interesting to note that William Landon Jones was the brother of Anna Eliza Jones who became the wife of Alexander John Anderson. William Jones and Louisa had three children, Margaret Julia Jones, born 1860, Edward Palmer Jones, born 1865 and James Alexander Landon Jones, born 1866. See also Appendix Two for fuller information about the Jones family.

There is reason to believe that one of these two sons may have married Anna Mary Vivienne, the daughter of William Dickinson who had been Deputy Finance Minister of Canada.[15] She married Roger Gordon, the fourth son of the 3rd Earl of Sefton on 4 October 1890. However, he died on 9 September 1893 and Anna Mary Vivienne lived until 3 January 1941 so she could well have married again. It is hoped in due course to obtain confirmation on this point.

Henry Leeuwin Dempster was born at DumDum in India and baptised 11 November 1834 at St Andrews church, Calcutta. His father was Thomas Erskine Dempster, a surgeon in the Honourable East India Company Service. His mother was Maria Christiana Innes, daughter of Major-General William Innes of No. 7 Grosvenor Place, Bath.[16]

Frederick Edward Hadow was born 28 October 1836, the son of Charles Scott Hadow, a merchant, and Marianne Sarah Hadow.[17] F. E. Hadow later became a Major-General in the Royal Artillery and retired 1 February 1892. He and Frances Emma had no children and she must have died before 1888 because F. E. Hadow married a second time. He died on 15 May 1915.[18]

To revert to Major Alexander Anderson, he died on 25 June 1855. According to a letter from his great-grandson, Alexander William Anderson, when he was very young he had heard about the circumstances of Alexander Anderson's death from one of his staff whom he had met.[19] Apparently Alexander Anderson was very particular that the whole household should gather for prayers at eight o'clock each morning. One morning in June 1855 everyone was assembled in good time, but eight o'clock passed and he had not come down. After waiting for him for some time, it was decided that someone should go to see where he was. Apparently, only one of his daughters, believed to have been the eldest, Mary, 'had the courage to intrude on his privacy'. When she got to his bedroom she found that he had started to dress and had suffered a stroke in the process. He lived on for a few days but died on 25 June 1855.[20]

Mary Margaret Hampton, now the widow of Alexander Anderson, continued to live at Montrave until her death at an early age in 1856. She was only 53 when she died on 13 September 1856. Alexander Anderson and Mary Margaret were both buried in Scoonie cemetery on the outskirts of Leven in Fife. A marble memorial tablet set in the wall next to the road reads:

TO THE MEMORY
OF
MAJOR ALEXR ANDERSON
OF MONTRAVE
MADRAS ENGINEERS
DIED 25TH JUNE 1855
AGED 61
ALSO OF
MARY MARGARET HAMPTON
HIS WIFE
DIED 13TH SEPT 1856
AGED 53

In his marriage settlement and in his will, Alexander Anderson had provided for his wife after his death. He also made substantial provision for payments to be made to the younger members of his family. His first son was to inherit the estate of Montrave and the residue, after specific provision had been made for his wife and other children. In addition to a capital sum to be divided amongst his children, he made a further provision for his daughters. In a codicil to his will, he explained that following the death of his brother (Charles Inglis Anderson) his means were substantially increased. In view of this he provided for a further capital sum to be divided between his daughters after his death. As trustees in his original will he named his brother, Charles Inglis, and his wife's eldest brother, John Lewis Hampton-Lewis, plus a Mr. Thomas Playfair Williams, in addition to Mr. Cook, the family solicitor (Writer to the Signet). He did not specify who Mr. Thomas Playfair Williams was, but presumably he was a friend. In a later codicil, he appointed his three sons as trustees as his brother had died and Thomas Playfair Williams no longer resided in Scotland.

Earlier in this chapter, an outline has been given concerning the marriages of three of Alexander Anderson's daughters. It is known that two of the three had children and in due course it is hoped additional information concerning their descendants can be obtained. Help from any reader concerning these members of the family and their lives would be appreciated. The eldest daughter was Mary Catherine Anderson. It is not known whether she married. One possibility is that she may have accompanied her younger brother,

Charles Joseph Anderson, when he went to Canada. No confirmation of this is available at present and any information concerning Mary Catherine would be welcomed.

The next chapter provides fuller information concerning the lives of Alexander John Anderson and his two brothers.

CHAPTER EIGHT

Alexander John Anderson (7 October 1826–9 March 1858)
Patrick Charles Anderson (29 June 1831–15 February 1882)
Charles Joseph Anderson (21 February 1835–18 December 1910)

ALEXANDER JOHN ANDERSON, the eldest son of Alexander Anderson and Mary Margaret Hampton, was born at Leghorn (Livorno) in Italy on 7 October 1826.[1] He is likely to have been brought up in Edinburgh until his parents moved to Montrave in Fife in 1835. For some time he attended school at Wimbledon, undertaking classical and mathematical studies. He was admitted to Addiscombe in 1843 as a cadet with the Honourable East India Company.[2] In 1845 he passed out from Addiscombe and proceeded to India. There he met and married Anna Eliza, the daughter of a former East India Army Officer, John Landon Jones, and his wife, Sarah Jacques. An outline of her father's family history, both on the Jones and Landon sides, is given in Appendix Two at the back of this book. The Appendix also shows the relationship with a number of other families.[3]

When she was 16, Anna Eliza accompanied her elder sister, Sarah Louisa Jones, on a visit to India. They sailed on the ship *Southampton* which was under the command of a Captain Bowen, leaving England on 27 July 1849. Their brother, William Landon Jones, had returned to India in 1842, having been a cadet at Addiscombe from 1840. As explained in Appendix Two, Sarah Louisa met Lt. J. R. Coombs and married him on 2 June 1851. Anna Eliza met Alexander John Anderson and married him in the same month, on 21 June 1851.

Their first son, Alexander Charles William Anderson, was born on 28 April 1852 but died a few months later on 7 December 1852. The second son, Charles Henry Anderson, was born in India on 21 September 1853. The third son, Alexander Arthur Anderson, was born on 6 September 1854 and baptised at Mussoorie, India, on 29 September 1854. At the time, Alexander John Anderson was a lieutenant in the 38th Regiment Bengal Light Infantry. A fourth son, Lewis Patrick Anderson, was born on 30 July 1856, the same year that Alexander John with his family returned to Scotland to live at Montrave.

55

Major Alexander Anderson had died in 1855 but Mary Margaret, his wife, was presumably still alive at the time the family returned from India. After the death of his mother, Alexander John Anderson prepared a will in Edinburgh which was signed on 19 November 1856. In his will he declared that he was living at Montrave and that he was entitled to the residue of the estate left by his father 'which will be of considerable amount'. He named his brothers, Patrick Charles Anderson and Charles Joseph Anderson, as trustees, together with Edward Jones, wine merchant in London (his wife's uncle). In the event of these three not being available, the will provided alternative names as trustees. Those were John Cook, Writer to the Signet, and Edward Kendall Jones, also wine merchant in London (the son of Edward Jones and cousin to Anna Eliza). In his will, provision was made for Anna Eliza and also for the children. It was specified that each child should receive a thoroughly good education.

In May 1857 the family left Montrave and took a furnished house in St Andrews. In that year, also at St Andrews, the marriage took place between Alexander John's sister, Susan Clara Longman, and H. L. Dempster. Montrave had been transferred to Alexander John and then let.

On 4 August 1857, a fifth son was born named Frank Lewin. At about this time Alexander John was called back to military duty because of the Indian Mutiny which had broken out earlier in the year. Before he left he signed, on 14 August 1857, a codicil to his will. The codicil provided for various items to be given to his wife and sons. Certain rings, guns and swords were to go to the boys. His mother's collection of coins and shells were for his wife and after her, his eldest son alive. His white crest ring given to him by his wife was to be kept by her. It was specified that 'the large pictures at Montrave of my father and mother to be preserved by my heir, also the family pictures in the hall at Montrave'.[4]

Alexander John started on his return to India in August 1857. His youngest son, Frank Lewin, died on 24 August 1857. Anna Eliza Anderson and the remaining three boys moved to Perth, having re-let the house in St Andrews.

Much has been written about the Indian Mutiny and a number of books are listed in the bibliography at the back of this book. A short outline of a part of the campaign may be of interest. The mutiny started in 1857. After preliminary troubles the full scale mutiny broke out in May 1857 with the massacre at Meerut. In July Lucknow was under siege and, although partly relieved by Havelock and Outram in September 1857, a new siege began. In November 1857 Lucknow was relieved and the garrison evacuated. The city was then abandoned to the rebels and it was not until the next year that preparations for the final recapture of the city were undertaken.

In January 1858 Sir Colin Campbell began a campaign for the recapture of Lucknow. Relief forces had now been brought in and more were on their way, including help from the Gurkha army. The assault on Lucknow took place in

March 1858. Alexander John Anderson was a member of the force engaged on this difficult operation. In the course of action he was killed on 9 March 1858. Lucknow was finally recaptured on 21 March. From April to December (1858), actions took place to recapture other northern Indian cities which had previously fallen to the rebels. The final stages of the campaign took place in the early months of 1859. In November 1859 there was a proclamation that brought the long rule over India of the East India Company to an end. The European members of the East India Company in India were not pleased with the way power was handed over to civil authorities without consultation. In due course, of the 15,000 men of the former company's army, over ten thousand left for England.

Returning to the news of the death of Alexander John Anderson, this event was clearly to have a marked effect on the well-being of the surviving members of his family. News of his death came in the form of a letter from his brother, Patrick Charles Anderson, addressed to the family solicitor, Mr. Cook, W.S. of Edinburgh. The letter reads as follows:

11th March
Campoonar

My Dear Mr. Cook,

It is my painful task to inform you of the death of my poor brother Alex.

He fell before Lucknow on the 9th shot thro the neck.

I enclose the letter which informed me of his death, and please send it and the enclosed to his poor wife.

I shall be thankful if you communicate with Mary and Charlie.

I remain

Yours sincerely

P. C. Anderson

The enclosed letter reads as follows:

My Dear Patrick,

I am deeply sorry to communicate the melancholy news of the death of your poor Brother. He fell yesterday morning at the 'Chukkur Khole' shot through the neck. I was unable to go to the place as the rest of my Regiment was ordered on to the pont to hold a garden, no officer was allowed to leave his post as we were engaged all day with the enemy. Excuse this short note as we are under a severe fire. I will write to you again by the first opportunity. We have got his watch, sword etc. but his Bi revolvers were taken by some European. I hope to be able to recover them. Let me condole with you in this severe loss and believe me

Yours affecty.

William Fischer

10th March.

Patrick Charles wrote a further letter to Mr. Cook, W.S., from Cawnpore dated 16 June 1858.[5] In this interesting letter he detailed how his brother's affairs in India were being dealt with. Alexander John had left comprehensive instructions for the disposal of his personal effects etc. In these instructions, he refers to 'my property at present in the hands of Mrs. J. R. Coombs, wife of Captn. Coombs 42 L I in Calcutta'. Sarah Louisa Jones, one of Anna Eliza Jones' sisters had married a John Coombs and would have been the Mrs. Coombs referred to. In a further reference in this letter, Patrick Charles reports:

> I fear I shall not be able to erect a tomb for his regiment has left Lucknow, shortly after his fall and the only person who knows where he is buried is the clergyman who performed the ceremony and he too I fear has left, at any rate I do not know his name, the present chaplain of Lucknow did not bury him.

Patrick Charles refers in the letter to the fact that he had been absent from home for seven years. This means he had been in India from the time following his training at Addiscombe which he left in 1850.

Concerning religious instruction, Patrick Charles understood that the children were to be educated according to the tenets of the Church of England. This statement is rather surprising in view of the role of the earlier members of the family in the Church of Scotland. Two factors must have contributed to this: one the state of disruption in the Church of Scotland itself and secondly the influence of being in the service of an English company, the East India Company, where presumably the main religious practice was in accordance with the Church of England.

Although a tomb could not be erected where Alexander John was killed for the reasons explained by his brother, he is remembered near Montrave. On a marble memorial set into the wall at Scoonie cemetery next to the memorial for his father and mother, is an inscription to the two children who died in infancy. To this has been added a memorial to Alexander John recording his death at the siege of Lucknow, 9 March 1858.

Under the circumstances of Alexander John's death, a number of legal matters had to be resolved concerning the provision for his wife and children. One of these concerned an entail taken out by a Mr. Robert Fairfall on 12 April 1796. This dealt with what are described as certain superiorities forming the barony of Struie Hay in the parish of Forteviot and county of Perth. The deed of entail provided for the lands to be disposed for himself and his heirs or, failing them, to Alexander Anderson of Kingask and his heirs or to Patrick Anderson and his heirs. The opinion of counsel (Alex. S. Cook) was that the entail was still good and the superiorities belonged to the surviving eldest son.[6] At that time, this was Charles Henry Anderson who was only five years old. It is not clear, however, what subsequently happened about this entail since presumably it should have continued to the surviving eldest male descendants from Alexander John. After the death of Charles Henry Anderson, this would have been Alexander Arthur Anderson but there is no known information that it did.

There is evidence that Anna Eliza continued to live in Perth for some time after the death of her husband. For instance, Frances Emma married Frederick Edward Hadow in Perth on 17 April 1860. Some sixteen years later the surviving eldest son, Charles Henry Anderson, died on 24 April 1876 in Edinburgh. He must have been about twenty-two years of age. Some time after the death of Charles, the family moved to England and lived for a time in Montrave House, St Marks Road, Notting Hill, London. No trace of a house with that name remains in the road which is now largely an immigrant area. Shortly after this, Anna Eliza remarried. She married Llewellyn Adolphus Pike and went to live in Reading, Berkshire. The youngest son, Lewis Patrick, emigrated to the United States of America. He went before 1880 because in that year Mr. Cook, W.S., wrote to Mrs. Anderson (probably Mrs. Pike by then) concerning her son's wish to borrow money to pay off the mortgage on his land at Kansas.[7] The nature of the proposed transaction makes interesting reading in these later years of inflation. The letter reads:

> You will observe that Mr. Lewis wishes £300 to be remitted to him to pay off a Mortgage over his land in Kansas — so as to effect a saving of interest.

There follows a note about the effect of sending this sum which would have reduced the annuity payable to Anna Eliza from the estate of her eldest son from £50 per annum to £38 per annum. It concludes with a summary:

> Mr. Lewis, as you will see, states that the interest on the mortgage is 9 per cent., so that the practical result of the proposed arrangement, if carried out, will be that Mr. Lewis will be saved the £27 of interest on the mortgage yearly and that you will lose £12 of income annually by the transaction.

The transaction was completed and Lewis Patrick entered a deed to ensure the repayment of the £300 to John Cook, W.S. By this time, August 1885, Lewis was residing at Acton, Polk County, Florida, in the United States of America. No further information is available concerning Lewis Patrick and the date of his death is not known at present. Thus, from five sons, only one is known to have married and had surviving children. That son was Alexander Arthur Anderson who is discussed in the next chapter.

Patrick Charles Anderson was the second surviving son of Alexander Anderson of Montrave. Only a limited amount of information is available at present concerning his life. He was born on 29 June 1831 and it is known that he was educated at the Edinburgh Academy where he was a pupil from 1844 to 1846.[8] He later went to the East India Military Training Seminary at Addiscombe where he was a cadet from 1849 to 1850.[9] Upon leaving Addiscombe he was appointed an ensign on 9 December 1850 in the Bengal Royal Artillery of the Honourable East India Company Service. He proceeded to the Indian sub-continent and subsequently served throughout the Burmese War of 1852–53. He was involved in the operations both before and during the capture of Rangoon. For his services he was awarded a medal with clasp. After this time he was engaged in the suppression of the Santhal insurrection in 1854. He served throughout the Indian Mutiny, including action at Khudjioa, for which he was awarded a medal. Earlier in this chapter, details have been given of some of the letters written by Patrick Charles in which he reported on the death of his brother, Alexander John.

Patrick Charles Anderson became a lieutenant on 8 June 1856 and a captain on 12 September 1859. At this stage he chose to remain in the Royal Artillery following the changes after the Indian Mutiny and the demise of the East India Company. He was appointed to the rank of major on 5 July 1872 and promoted to lieutenant-colonel on 4 October 1877. Finally he became a colonel on 4 October 1881. In the next year, Patrick was on passage between India and England on board the ship, *Amarapoora*, when on 15 February 1882, he died at sea.

Patrick Charles married Emma J. Bean in India in 1858. It is known that they had at least two children: a son named Ernest Chester and a daughter named Ruby. Ernest Chester Anderson was born 26 November 1863. In 1892 he entered the army in the Royal Army Medical Corps. In 1899 he married Aimee, the daughter of a Captain Harris. Ernest Chester was promoted captain in 1895 and major in 1904. After serving with No. 1 British General Hospital during the Trah Expedition 1897–8, he served in the South African War during 1900 and 1901. He was present at the relief of Kimberley and at the operation in the Orange Free State from February to May 1900, including the engagement at Paardeberg and the actions at Poplar Grove and Driefontein. He was mentioned in dispatches and was awarded the Distinguished Service Order and the Queen's Medal with four clasps and the King's Medal with two clasps. Ernest retired from the army in 1912. While he was on the retired list he served at Golden Hill Fort on the Isle of Wight. He is believed to have had two daughters and it would be of great interest to learn more about them. Ernest Chester Anderson died at Totland Bay on the Isle of Wight on 22 December 1913, aged only fifty-one.[10]

The third surviving son of Major Alexander Anderson of Montrave was Charles Joseph Anderson. He was born in Edinburgh on 21 February 1835, just before his parents moved to Montrave. His early education was obtained at St Andrews and Edinburgh before he entered Cheltenham College in August 1848.[11] He left Cheltenham in June 1852 and entered the East India Military Training Seminary at Addiscombe on 4 February 1853.[12] A letter from the headmaster of Cheltenham College dated 7 December 1852 is among his cadet application papers for entry to Addiscombe.[13] Charles Joseph remained at Addiscombe until 1854 when he became an ensign in the 8th Bengal Native

Infantry. He was also appointed an ensign in the Queen's Army in The East Indies 'as long as he holds a similar rank in the Honourable East India Company'. The commission was dated in Simla on 2 June 1855 and signed by Sir William Maynard Gomm with effect from 9 December 1854.

After serving in India for some time, Charles became ill. A medical certificate dated 5 November 1856 still exists in which details are given of his severe illness. It was recommended that he should be given leave to return to England for three years to recuperate. As a result of his ill health and his subsequent decision to emigrate to Canada, Charles finally resigned from the Honourable East India Company on 10 January 1860. Following his illness in 1856, Charles returned to Montrave and this must have been less than a year after his eldest brother, Alexander John, with his wife and children. His mother, Mary Margaret, had died in the September before he came home and so in the relatively short period he had been in India (1854–1856) both his parents died. This must have influenced his next major decision. Having spent some time recovering from his illness, Charles decided to emigrate to Canada in 1858. He entered the Civil Service of Canada on 16 November 1858. He was appointed a second-class clerk on 1 April 1860 and first-class clerk on 20 April 1861. In due course, on 1 July 1874, he was appointed chief clerk and head of the Savings Bank Branch. He was superannuated on 1 October 1898.

In October 1861 Charles joined the volunteer Militia Rifle Company at Quebec which was styled 'Civil Service Rifle Corps'. It is recorded that 'To be adjutant with the rank of Lieutenant, Charles Joseph Anderson, Gentleman, Late Lieutenant in The Honourable East India Company's service'. On 13 April 1865 he was commissioned captain in the Civil Service Rifle Company. Then on 21 September 1866, he was commissioned major. The Regiment was disbanded on 19 December 1868.

Charles Joseph married in about 1860 Ellen Augusta Barron, whose father was Professor Frederick William Barron, Principal of Upper Canada College, Toronto, and later Judge in the Supreme Court of Canada.[14] Charles died in Toronto on 18 December 1910 aged seventy-five. There were three children from the marriage: Frederic Charles, Ernest Stuart and Florence Maud.

1. Frederic (or Frederick) Charles Anderson was born on 23 June 1861. He attended Upper Canada College, Toronto, where his maternal grandfather, Professor Barron, was principal. On 5 September 1878 he entered the Royal Military College at Kingston, Ontario, and graduated 27 June 1882 with a first-class certificate and the rank of sergeant. He then joined the Post Office Department in Ottawa as an engineer. On 19 September 1889 Frederick Charles married Minerva Catherine Evangeline Kerr (born 15 July 1868). They had four children:

    a. Eric Anderson who was killed in World War I.

b. Stuart H. Anderson, born 1 September 1891. He married and had two children:

   i. Jacqueline Anderson, born 21 July 1921.

   ii. Frederick Stuart Anderson, now believed to be living in California.

c. Frederick Barron Anderson, born 23 September 1895, died 15 October 1963. He married Charlotte White of Milton, Ontario, who was born in 1895 and died without issue in September 1969. Frederick, known as Barry, and his wife obviously had some knowledge of their family history. They named their house in Picton, Ontario, 'Montrave'. Apparently, Barry was a musician and during World War I was a member of the Canadian Forces entertainment group known as the 'Dumbells'. Shortly before he died, he visited 'Montrave' in Fife. He had in his possession a copy of the sale particulars dealing with the sale of the Montrave estate by the executors of Alexander John Anderson in 1859. He gave this to Sir John Gilmour, the present owner. During a visit to Montrave, Sir John lent this document to me. It was found to have a note of Barry Anderson's address written on the back. As this discovery was not made until the summer of 1980, it was found that Barry Anderson had died some years before. However, through this information the necessary lead was obtained which enabled my brother, Donald Anderson, who lives in Canada (see Chapter Eleven) to obtain fuller information concerning the family and descendants of Charles Joseph Anderson. Prior to this they were completely unknown to the present generations of the family living in Great Britain.

d. Vaudrey P. Anderson, born c. 1897 and died in 1936. She married James Bryden Christie of Perth in Scotland. They had one son:

   Baron C. Christie who was born in 1920. He married Marion Harrison who was born in 1918 and they have three children:

   (1) James Frederick Christie, born in 1941, who is married and living in Melbourne, Australia, with two children, Laura Christie, born in 1973, and Blair Christie, born in 1976.

   (2) Eric Barron Christie, born in 1946 and married with two children, Jennifer Christie, born in 1974, and Jacqueline Christie, born in 1976.

   (3) Ann Christine Christie, born in 1950 whose married name is McLellen, and who has two daughters, Tracy McLellen, born in 1973, and Tara McLellen, born in 1980.

Reverting to the family of Charles Joseph Anderson:

2. Ernest Stuart Anderson, born *c.* 1862, was a manager with the Dominion Bank, St Thomas, Ontario. He married and had two children:

   a. Ernest Basil Anderson.

   b. Edith Vivian Anderson.

   It is hoped to obtain more information about these descendants.

3. Florence Maud Anderson, born in 1864, and died unmarried after 1929. She left a very comprehensive will dated 17 May 1929 which names and gives the relationship of 12 members of the family.

It is hoped in due course to be able to obtain fuller information concerning the various families outlined above. However, the next chapter returns to the descendants of Alexander John Anderson, the eldest of the three brothers whose lives have been outlined in this chapter.

CHAPTER NINE

Alexander Arthur Anderson (6 September 1854–26 May 1925)

ALEXANDER ARTHUR ANDERSON was born on 6 September 1854 in India. He was baptised on 29 September 1854 at Mussoorie. As explained in the previous chapter, he was taken to Scotland when his parents returned in 1856. Following the return of his father, Alexander John Anderson, to India in 1857 and his subsequent death at the relief of Lucknow on 9 March 1858, Alexander Arthur was brought up by his mother, Anna Eliza. He and his two brothers must have spent their childhood living in Perth. His elder brother, Charles, died in 1876 and his younger brother, Lewis, emigrated to the U.S.A., probably in 1878.

In 1879, Alexander Arthur was living at No. 10 Gloucester Place, Edinburgh, although other members of the family were living in London. At the age of 24, on 11 August 1879, he married Ada Catherine Seaton who was 21, the daughter of Henry Seaton, a Doctor of Medicine (deceased). Her mother was Frances Seaton, formerly Kanner, who resided at No. 1 Cambridge Street, Edinburgh. The marriage took place at that address by Declaration in the presence of William Reid, M.A., and Walter Thomas Prideaux Wolston, Doctor of Medicine.

By the following year, Alexander Arthur and his wife had moved to near London. Their first child, Alexander William Anderson, was born on 15 September 1880 when his parents were living at Dunstan Road, Peckham Rye, in Surrey. An outline of his life is given in Chapter Ten. It is understood that two others boys were born but both died in infancy. However, later three daughters were born as follows:

Dorothy Winifred Anderson, born 2 August 1887.

Olive Frances Elise Anderson, born 24 February 1891.

Anna Marjorie Anderson, born 30 December 1894.

A brief outline of their lives is given later in this chapter.

Very little is known about the life of Alexander Arthur Anderson but it is known that he trained as an architect and in engineering. He designed a very successful bakers' oven and was awarded a design prize for which he received a medallion.[1] For some time he lived at Doncaster in Yorkshire and had a prosperous business. However, it appears that Alexander did not enjoy very good health. While living in Doncaster, he was advised to go to Switzerland for treatment. The three girls accompanied their parents to Vevey and Alexander William was left in Doncaster to help in the business which was run by a manager. The family remained in Switzerland for two years. Apparently, however, the manager defrauded the business and left it in a critical financial state. Alexander Arthur had to return to try to remedy this difficult situation.

After various attempts to re-establish himself in business, Alexander took an appointment with a company in Birmingham. By this time the family was living at Kings Norton in Birmingham. In 1921 following his retirement, he and his wife moved to Godshill in the New Forest. They then moved to Upper Parkstone, near Bournemouth and lived in a house which they called 'Montrave', situated in Vale Road, Parkstone. Their grand-daughter, Freda Aileen Anderson, lived with them.

A letter still exists from this time, sent by Alexander Arthur to his son, Alexander William, and dated 3rd January 1925, just a few months before he died.[2] An extract from this letter concerns early radio and is of some interest, as it illustrates the excitement and problems created by the new development. He wrote:

> As I write to you, your mother is busy listening in to an address on music. She now spends most of her evening on the headphone. The set was put in on Xmas Eve, but owing to haste is not yet the success it should be. The man who fixed it up has promised to put in a vulcanite board instead of the wood one temporarily fixed and he then expects better results as the studs will be more regular in height, giving a better adjustment for contact.

Alexander Arthur Anderson died on 26 April 1925 at the age of 71 and was buried at the main cemetery in Bournemouth. His wife and grand-daughter remained in Upper Parkstone until 1929. They then moved to Quinton, near Birmingham, to live with Dorothy Winifred Anderson. Ada Catherine died on 3 October 1932 and was buried in Bournemouth with her husband. A memorial headstone marks the grave.

It is understood that from an early age Alexander Arthur had been a member of the Plymouth Brethren. Indeed, the nature of the marriage ceremony at the home of his future wife suggests that he may have been a member before the age of twenty-four. This is most surprising since, as has been noted earlier, Alexander John Anderson, his father, had wished his sons to be brought up as members of the Church of England, despite the long family connection with the Church of Scotland.

Some details concerning the life of Alexander William Anderson and his family are given in the next chapter. The following notes briefly outline something of the lives of his sisters.[3] It appears that in 1907 the three sisters received bequests under the will of Margaret Home who was one of the daughters of Susan Anderson and Abraham Home — see Chapter Six.

Dorothy Winifred Anderson was a pupil at King Edward's Grammar School, Birmingham. She spent two years in Switzerland with her parents. She then took a teachers' training course but found she did not like teaching and arranged to enter Birmingham University. However, she was unable to complete her course due to health and other problems. Instead, she took a secretarial course which apparently was a great success. It is believed that for a time she was secretary to Mr. George Cadbury. Eventually, she worked for Henry Hope & Son Ltd., the window frame manufacturers, later to become part of Critall Hope Ltd. After retirement, she lived for some time in Bournemouth. Later Dorothy moved to Frolesworth, near Rugby. She died at Cheltenham on 1 January 1968.

Olive Frances Elise Anderson was at the Birmingham College of Art for five years and worked on jewellery design. During World War I she worked in the drawing office at the Austin Motor Works (Longbridge). In 1922 she married Reginald Augustus Baker (born 1 March 1890 in South Wales), the son of John Robert Baker and Alice Baker, formerly Power. R. A. Baker was the manager for Thomas Cook in Shanghai, China. They lived in China until the outbreak of World War II and then returned to live in Birmingham. Two sons were born:

1. David Alexander Baker, L.D.S., who was born on 24 December 1922. D. A. Baker is now a dental surgeon for the City of Birmingham Schools Authority.

2. Roderick John Baker, M.P.S., was born on 15 August 1930 in Shanghai. He was baptised in Shanghai Cathedral and in due course was confirmed in Lichfield Cathedral, having attended St Chad's Cathedral Choir School. Roderick married at Wells Cathedral on 28 September 1957, Joan Marion (born 4 February 1936), the eldest daughter of Gerard Arthur Ingalton Sanders, formerly of the Indian Army. Their children are:

    a. Stephen Roderick Baker, born 14 November 1958.
    b. Frances Claire Baker, born 25 February 1961.
    c. James Thomas Baker, born 29 June 1964.
    d. Catherine Louise Baker, born 4 March 1966.

Roderick Baker is now the principal pharmacist at Yeovil District Hospital.

Reginald A. Baker died on 17 April 1961 and his widow, Olive Frances, lived with her elder son in Birmingham until her death on 6 June 1981.

Anne Marjorie Anderson attended Kings Norton Grammar School after her return from Switzerland. She became ill and was in hospital for some time.

Towards the end of World War I Anna Marjorie married Norman Vinson Jones (born 9 January 1894), the son of William Henry Jones and Eliza Jones, formerly Vinson. N. V. Jones was an automobile consulting engineer and the family lived in Nottingham. He died at Nottingham on 6 December 1955. Anna Marjorie died at Bristol on 14 October 1964.

Two sons were born:

1. Derrick Vinson Jones was born in 1923 but died at Nottingham in 1931.

2. Alexander Vinson Jones was born on 20 March 1925 at Nottingham. Alexander married Marjorie Evans of Wolverhampton on 18 August 1951. He is a Chartered Architect (R.I.B.A), now with Lloyds Bank in London.

CHAPTER TEN

Alexander William Anderson (15 September 1880–10 May 1971)

THE SON OF ALEXANDER ARTHUR ANDERSON and Ada Catherine, Alexander William was born in Camberwell, Surrey, on 15 September 1880. He died in his 91st year in 1971. It is known that he attended a boarding school at Bexhill-on-Sea. His subsequent early education and training is not certain but it is understood that he entered business with his father and received training in engineering. As mentioned in the preceding chapter, he was active in his father's business in Doncaster. With his sisters, he received a very strict home discipline and was a member of the Plymouth Brethren for some years, although eventually he was confirmed into the Church of England.

In 1904, at the age of 24, Alexander William decided to take an appointment in India. It is known that he was very aware of the family connections with that sub-continent. In his youth he met a number of the people mentioned in earlier chapters, many of who had served in India, including Major-General Hadow. Although Alexander William does not appear to have obtained any formal qualifications in engineering his practical training and experience must have equipped him to take an engineering appointment.

While in India, he met and married Aileen Florence, the daughter of Alexander Niblett. She was born on 29 December 1882.[1] Her father held a senior appointment in the Indian Civil Service, being the head clerk of the Treasury in Agra. Her mother was Florence Evelyn Matilda Niblett. Alexander William and Aileen Florence married in India on 23 February 1910 when he was in his thirtieth year and she was twenty-eight. Later, presumably in 1910, they returned to England and lived for a time in Yorkshire. There, early in 1911, their daughter, Freda Aileen Anderson (Ann) was born. Unfortunately, after such a short marriage, Aileen Florence died at the same time. Lacking the care of her own mother, Freda Aileen was brought up by her grandparents, Alexander Arthur and Ada Catherine Anderson. They were as parents to her and she lived with them until their death.

In order to develop his career, Alexander William obtained another overseas appointment. This time he went to Sierra Leone in West Africa where he

68

worked on railway construction. On the outbreak of World War I in 1914 he joined the army, seeing service mainly in the Middle East. There is a certificate signed by Winston Churchill as Secretary of State for War recording that Alexander William Anderson was mentioned in a dispatch from Lieutenant-General W. R. Marshall, dated 11 November 1918 'for gallant and distinguished services in the field'.[2]

It seems that in the turmoil which followed the war, Alexander William returned home to England to be with his family. Then, in about 1919, he met Winifred Ann(ie), the daughter of John Charles Pusill, an engineer who was the son of Alfred Pusill, a captain in the Merchant Naval Service. Her mother was Margaret Jane May Pusill, the daughter of Samuel Foyle and his wife, Anne Knill, formerly Coleman, who came from Devon.

Alexander William and Winifred Ann married early in 1920 when he was 39 and she was twenty-four. Their first son, Alexander Norman, was born in November 1920. In 1921, Alexander William took another appointment overseas in the Colonial Service. He returned to West Africa but this time to the Gold Coast. He was again engaged on railway construction duties, including the building of bridges. Winifred accompanied Alexander William on at least one of his overseas tours and at other times maintained the family home in Kings Norton, Birmingham. A second son, Donald, was born on 4 June 1924 in England. Alexander William's appointment in the Gold Coast continued until 1927. During the leave of the Chief Resident Engineer, he was acting Chief Resident Engineer.[3] At the end of his contract in September 1927, he and Winifred returned to England and took up temporary residence at Watlington, near Oxford. Here, on 23 March 1928 their third son, Michael Arthur, was born. Alexander William obtained a further short appointment with the Colonial Service, again in West Africa, this time in Nigeria. He was appointed to the position of district engineer, Capital Works, with the Nigerian Railways. Following the contraction of overseas investment and the completion of his contract, Alexander William returned home finally in July 1929. For a time, the family lived in Birmingham and then they moved to Swanage in Dorset before moving to Bedfordshire.

During the early 1930s, Alexander William tried to obtain further overseas appointments but the widespread recession reduced opportunities. Although Alexander William had gained very good civil engineering experience, in common with many others of his era, he had not obtained formal qualifications and by this time he was over fifty years of age. For a time, the family lived at Stagsden, near Bedford. From here, Alexander William obtained an appointment as a survey engineer with the authority responsible for the catchment area of the River Ouse. He remained with this authority, holding various appointments, until his eventual retirement in his late sixties.

From Stagsden, Alexander William and his family moved to Sutton in the Isle of Ely. While they lived at Sutton, a daughter was born. She was named

Mary Frances and was born on 7 February 1935. At around this time, Alexander William was engaged in another engineering construction project. This was the building of a new lock system on the River Ouse, known as Brownshill Lock. This lock was at the end of the tidal reach and formed a part of the flood control system for the River Ouse. Alexander William was the resident engineer responsible for the construction.

In 1937, the family again moved, this time to the village of Over, about ten miles from Cambridge and within a mile of a section of the River Ouse. Alexander William Anderson became a well-known figure in the village and in a wide area associated with the river. He was responsible for survey and other works connected with the River Ouse. He employed a small number of men from the area on survey, drainage, maintenance and construction schemes concerning the fens and the flood control systems for the river and associated waterways.

During World War II Alexander William took an active part in the Local Defence Volunteers and subsequently the Home Guard. He and Winifred continued to live in Over until after his eventual and delayed retirement from the River Ouse catchment authority. Alexander William was a very active man who would walk great distances in the course of his survey work. It seems that even in the earlier heat of West Africa he had found it necessary to walk considerable distances on surveys before the railways were built. This walking ability remained with him until a very late age. Some time after his eventual retirement, Alexander William and Winifred went to Canada for a year. There they lived with their second son, Donald, and his wife Sylvia and their children. Alexander William's final years were spent living in Stanmore, Middlesex, not far from his eldest son and family. Although his eyesight had been impaired by a tropical eye complaint, he remained alert, taking a great interest in the affairs of the world and his family until the end of his life. He died at Edgware Hospital on 10 May 1971 in his ninety-first year.

Winifred Ann Anderson moved from Stanmore to live in an hotel in Sidmouth, Devon. Devon had been the home of her parents and her mother's family. After an illness, Winifred Ann moved to a nursing home in Torquay where she died on 2 September 1978.

Alexander William had two daughters, one by his first marriage and one from his second. The first daughter, Freda Aileen Anderson, known as Ann, was born in 1911 when, as already mentioned, her mother died. She was subsequently brought up by her grandparents. At this time, her father's youngest sister, Marjorie, was only sixteen.[4] She lived in Birmingham until 1920. After the family moved to Bournemouth, Ann attended the High School until 1929. During this time she had developed an interest in art and subsequently became interested in dress and fashion. In due course she attended Birmingham College of Art Fashion at Handsworth. Subsequently, Ann was appointed to the Domestic Science College in Manchester where she spent the next six years. During the war, her next appointment was with Walker Crosswellers, responsible for their advertising department. From there, Ann moved to Cheltenham to take up a position at the Cheltenham College of Art. This became the Gloucester College of Art and Design running diploma (subsequently B.A.) courses in painting, sculpture and fashion. Freda Aileen Anderson was appointed head of the Fashion and Textile Department. Following her retirement, she continued to live in Cheltenham at 'Spring Hill', The Crippetts, until 1983 when she moved to Borth-y-Gest in North Wales.

His second daughter, Mary Frances Anderson, was born on 7 February 1935. She was educated at the Cambridge High School for Girls. On 9 March 1957 she married Tom Willingham Turnill, born 22 July 1934 and educated at Stamford, who was a pilot in the Royal Air Force and is now a Squadron Leader. He is the son of Leslie Gordon Turnill (born 7 July 1900, died 27 February 1977) and his wife, Dorothy Margaret Catherine Richardson (born 13 December 1898 and died 27 July 1980).[5]

They have two children:

1. Nicholas Willingham Turnill, B.A., born 30 December 1958. He married on 28 June 1980, Sian Cecilia Cumming, B.A., who was born 16 January 1957. They are both graduates from Keele University. Their sons are:

   a. Peter Trevor Willingham Turnill born on 16 July 1981.

   b. Jonathan William Alexander Turnill born on 16 July 1981.

   c. Timothy Nicholas Gordon Turnill born on 16 February 1984.

2. Claire Frances Turnill, born 15 September 1962 (which was the date her grandfather, Alexander William Anderson, was 82).

In addition to his two daughters, as noted earlier, Alexander William Anderson had three sons. A brief outline of their lives so far is given in the next chapter.

CHAPTER ELEVEN

Alexander Norman Anderson (born 1 November 1920)
Donald Anderson (born 4 June 1924)
Michael Arthur Anderson (born 23 March 1928)

ALEXANDER NORMAN ANDERSON, who is usually known by his second name, is the eldest son of Alexander William Anderson and Winifred Ann Anderson. His early years were mainly spent in the Birmingham area during the time when his father was working in West Africa. When the family moved to Bedfordshire, he was educated at Bedford Modern School. He entered the Royal Air Force as an aircraft apprentice and undertook his early training at R.A.F. Halton. Later, after training as an engineer and with the approach of war, Alexander Norman was posted overseas. First he was engaged in the Ethiopian campaign and then later in the North African campaigns. He spent some four years in Africa, finally being engaged in the Italian Campaign. He was then posted back to England and obtained some home leave for the first time since the start of the war. Alexander Norman remained in the regular Air Force for some years after the war. However, over the years he had been developing an interest in art and eventually left the Air Force to develop his career in this subject. He attended Harrow College of Art to undertake full time training and then completed a teachers' training course. Subsequently, he taught at Harrow County Grammar School and in due course was appointed first, Head of the Art Department and then Deputy Headmaster of the School.

In his paintings, the medium he uses is egg tempera on gesso panels. He has had five one-man shows, four in London and one in Toronto. In addition he has exhibited in mixed shows, including the Royal Academy. Works have been purchased by private collectors in several countries and by the Philadelphia Museum of Art, U.S.A. Two paintings were reproduced in a book about the work of young artists in 1957.[1] A painting from his second one-man show at the Trafford Gallery was reproduced in *The Times* on 12 October 1960 which was entitled 'Orthodox Youths'.

On 25 July 1950 Alexander Norman married Beryl Margaret, a state registered nurse, the daughter of Newling Doveton Lawton (born 23 November 1896 and died 1930) and his wife, Annette Dorothea Parker (born 1894 and died 1936). Beryl Margaret was born on 8 July 1923 and lived in South Africa for eight years. Her paternal grandfather married Anne Beatrice Doveton. An interesting and comprehensive study of the Doveton family has been published called *The Dovetons of St Helena*.[2]

Alexander Norman and Beryl Margaret have three sons:

1. Alexander John Anderson, B.A., born 4 January 1954.

2. Peter David Anderson, B.A., born 20 July 1956.

3. Christopher Colin Doveton Anderson, born 22 May 1963.

In early planning for his retirement from teaching, Alexander Norman and Beryl moved from the Harrow and Pinner area where they had lived for many years and now live at Cott Farm, Dartington, near Totnes in Devon. There he has a studio from which it is hoped he will be able to produce many more paintings in the years to come.

Donald Anderson, the second son of Alexander William Anderson, was born in Kings Norton, Birmingham, on 4 June 1924. After attending a number of schools due to the movement of his parents to various parts of the country, Donald chose a career in engineering. This was interrupted briefly by service in the Royal Air Force. After suffering a knee injury, he was unable to continue training for active flying duties and was discharged from the Air Force with a disability pension at the age of nineteen.

Donald married on 4 November 1944 at South Kensington Sylvia Margaret, the daughter of Robert William Sparrow (born 15 December 1896 and died in 1941). Her mother was Margaret Charlotte Elise Buckingham (born 15 May 1896 and died 12 May 1938). Sylvia Margaret was born on 14 December 1921. Donald and Sylvia, with their three young children, emigrated to Canada in 1949. He pursued his career in engineering, specialising in mechanical engineering for thermal power projects and related works. Donald read for the examinations of the Association of Professional Engineers of Ontario and was placed first in the final examinations which he took in 1966. His wife, Sylvia, is a fine soprano singer and her musical talents are shared by her children. Members of the family, all resident in Canada, are:

1. David Geoffrey Anderson, who was born in Hammersmith, London, on 25 January 1946. He was married on 22 December 1979 in Simcoe, Ontario, to Karen Jay Proctor, B.A., who was born on 9 December 1951 and is the daughter of Howard and Kay Proctor. They have a daughter Bailey Jay who was born on 19 February 1984.

2. Lesley Margaret Anderson, B.A., who was born in Hammersmith, London, on 13 May 1947. She was married on 3 July 1971 in Toronto to Peter Allan Bennett, B.A., who was born on 27 February 1945, the son of Allan and Helen Bennett. Their children are:

    a. Rosemary Margaret Bennett, born 18 July 1975.

    b. Nicholas Drew Bennett, born 1 August 1977.

3. Patricia Ann Anderson (adopted) who was born in Hammersmith, London, on 30 January 1948. She was married on 7 May 1972 in Niagara Falls, Ontario, to William Edwards, B.Sc., M.B.A., who was born on 29 March 1948. Their children are:

    a. Tracy Ann Edwards, born 29 September 1977.

    b. Alexander Simon Edwards, born 29 January 1979.

    c. William Conrad Edwards, born 5 June 1981.

4. Karen Elizabeth Anderson, who was born in Niagara Falls, Ontario, on 14 June 1952. She was married on 27 January 1973 in Georgetown, Guyana, to Barry Austin Lynch, a solicitor from London, England. They lived in England and subsequently emigrated to Canada in 1976. After requalifying in Canada, Barry was called to the Bar in Ontario and is a barrister and solicitor registered with the Law Society of Upper Canada. Their children are:

    a. Jacqueline Marie Lynch, born 22 March 1975.

    b. Julia Deborah Lynch, born 5 March 1978.

    c. Heather Kelly Lynch, born 5 January 1980.

Michael Arthur Anderson, the third son of Alexander William Anderson, was born at Watlington, near Oxford, on 23 March 1928. No doubt the name Arthur was included because Alexander Arthur Anderson (see Chapter Nine) had died in 1925. His marriage took place on 27 March 1954 to Anne, the daughter of Joseph Beynon, formerly of Carmarthenshire (born 13 August 1903 and died on 5 January 1965) and his wife, Kate (born 5 December 1901) the daughter of Frank Hawkins of Pontypridd. Anne Benyon was born at Cardiff on 23 December 1931.

There are four children:

1. Michael Graeme Anderson, born 5 January 1956, educated at Ellesmere College. He married on 9 December 1976 Jane Elizabeth (born 31 March 1957) the daughter of Leonard Herbert Browning and his wife, Rose Helen Smith.

Their children are:

a. Matthew Ged Anderson who was born 6 July 1980.

b. Emma Kate Anderson who was born on 15 October 1982.

2. Richard Charles Anderson, born 4 July 1959, was educated at Ellesmere College and the King's School, Chester. He is a graduate from The London School of Economics in the University of London and is a Chartered Accountant.

3. Sarah Anne Anderson, born 28 June 1962, was educated at The Queen's School, Chester and Westfield College in the University of London.

4. Deborah Jane Anderson, born 11 October 1968 is a pupil at The Queen's School, Chester.

In 1980 a cadet matriculation of arms was obtained with a suitable difference based on the arms matriculated in 1780. This involved making a petition to Lord Lyon, King of Arms, with proofs of descent from James Anderson (see Chapter Five). The matriculation of arms, which covers 200 years from 1780 to 1980, reads as follows:

Michael Arthur Anderson, Holder of the Degree of Bachelor of Science (Economics) of the University of London, Fellow of the Institute of Chartered Accountants of England and Wales, Fellow of the Institute of Cost and Management Accountants, Company Director residing at Kintrave, Meadow Court, Mollington, Chester, having by Petition unto the Lord Lyon, King of Arms of date 20th June 1979 shewn that he, the Petitioner, born Watlington in the County of Oxford, 23rd March 1928 (who married 27th March 1954 Anne, daughter of Joseph Beynon, and has with other issue an elder son and heir apparent Michael Graeme Anderson, born 5th January 1956) is the third son of the late Alexander William Anderson, civil engineer, formerly in the Colonial Service, and his wife Winifred Annie, daughter of John Charles Pusill; that the Petitioner's said father (born Camberwell in the County of Surrey 15th September 1880 and died 10th May 1971) was the only son of Alexander Arthur Anderson, architect and his wife Ada Catherine Seaton; that the Petitioner's said grandfather (born 6th September 1854 and died 26th April 1925) was the third son, but eldest son with issue of Alexander John Anderson, Captain in the late 38th Native Infantry, Honourable East India Company Service, and his wife Anna Eliza daughter of John Landon Jones; that the Petitioner's said great-grandfather (born 7th October 1826 and died 9th March 1858) was the eldest son of Alexander Anderson of Montrave, in the County of Fife, sometime Major in the Madras Engineers of the Honourable East India Company Service, and his wife (married 22nd November 1825) Mary Margaret, eldest daughter of John Hampton Hampton of Henllys, Anglesey, North Wales; that the Petitioner's said great-great grandfather (born 17th March 1794 and died 25th June 1855) was the eldest son of Patrick Anderson, writer to His Majesty's Signet, and his wife (married 14th September 1786) Susan, daughter of the Reverend Gilbert Hamilton, Doctor of Divinity, Minister of Cramond; that the Petitioner's said great-great-great-grandfather (born 1741 and died 24th December 1809) was the second son of James Anderson of Newbigging, Kingask and Monthrive, Advocate, and his wife Janet, daughter of Patrick Lindsay, Lord Provost of Edinburgh and a descendant of Patrick,

4th Lord Lindsay of the Byres; that Alexander Anderson of Montrave aforesaid succeeded his uncle Alexander Anderson of Newbigging and Kingask (who married at Edinburgh 18th October 1794 Janet, daughter of Patrick Lindsay of Eaglescarnie and died without issue 26th November 1818),[3] eldest son of the said James Anderson of Newbigging, Kingask and Monthrive aforesaid; that certain Ensigns Armorial were recorded in the Public Register of All Arms and Bearings in Scotland (Volume 1, Folio 243) of date 5th October 1780 in the name of the said James Anderson of Newbigging; and the Petitioner having prayed that the foresaid Ensigns Armorial might be matriculated of new in his own name with a suitable difference The Lord Lyon King of Arms by Interlocutor of date 5th February 1980 Granted Warrant to the Lyon Clerk to matriculate in the Public Register of All Arms and Bearings in Scotland in the name of the Petitioner the following Ensigns Armorial, videlicet:

> 'Argent, on a chevron Gules between three stars in chief and a crescent in base Azure, a mullet Or. Above the Shield is placed an Helm befitting his degree with a Mantling Gules doubled Argent, and on a wreath of the Liveries is set for Crest a Star Azure, and in an Escrol over the same this Motto "NIL CONSCIRE SIBI".

> Matriculated the 30th day of April 1980. Extracted furth of the 57th page of 64th volume of the Public Register of All Arms and Bearings in Scotland this 26th day of April 1980.'

The matriculation detailed above can be compared with the original entry detailed in Chapter Five dealing with the life of James Anderson of Newbigging.

In the preface to this book, the comment is made that genealogy is a live and continuing subject. Since 1979, when the original petition upon which the above matriculation is based, was submitted to Lord Lyon, some additional facts have been established which amend or slightly add to the details shown in the matriculation. First, the date of birth of Patrick Anderson, W.S., was not 1741 as shown, but approximately 1755. The difference arose from a note made at some time in the past on a family record which incorrectly showed him as having died at the age of 68 on 24 December 1809. The memorial record at the Greyfriars burial ground in Edinburgh shows that in fact he was only 54 when he died. Secondly, information is now available concerning the father (and mother) of Ada Catherine Seaton, the wife of Alexander Arthur Anderson, and this is detailed in Chapter Nine, although the information was not known when the Petition was submitted. It is also interesting to note that the artist who prepared the extract of matriculation has spelt Provost as Provest which was the style of the 18th century.

So far an attempt has been made to show the genealogy and some biographical details about members of a series of Anderson and other related families over several centuries. This is an instalment in a continuing story. From the details already shown there are many living members of these families to continue the story into the future. One of the exciting things about the study of family pedigrees is the discoveries that can be made about family relationships when viewed over a number of centuries. The next chapter outlines the genealogy of what is believed to be another related series of Anderson families who shared the same family origins in the 15th and 16th centuries from the north east of Scotland.

CHAPTER TWELVE

Other Anderson families and their descendants from the
16th century to the present time

IN THE PREFACE to this book and in Chapter Five, it was explained that Reverend James Anderson, who was born in approximately 1535, was described in the 1780 matriculation of arms used by his descendants as being the grandson by a younger son of the family of Anderson of Westertown in the County of Banff. The preface also discusses very similar Anderson arms described by Jervise in his book as seen by him on a memorial in the burial ground at Dumbennan, near Huntly in Aberdeenshire. [1,2] He refers to this memorial as bearing the date 1627 and the name Jacobus Andersone (or James Anderson). As a result of information discovered in 1982, copies of two connected Anderson family trees have been obtained from Aberdeen University library. These were compiled by Francis James Anderson in the period 1911 to 1916 and I am indebted to him for the detailed research he put into these charts. It is believed that the Anderson family outlined by him descends from the same Anderson family of Westertown as Rev. James Anderson and his descendants. This has not been proved conclusively but a number of factors are sufficiently strong to give the suggestion a good degree of probability.

F. J. Anderson's charts detail the Anderson family of Wester Ardbrake (Banffshire) and the descent of the family of Anderson of Grace Dieu, County Waterford in Ireland. These two charts have been combined with additional information from Burke's Irish Family Records and information obtained from current members of the family. [3] The outline chart based on these sources is shown as Chart No. 2.

One of the notes by F. J. Anderson concerning James Anderson of Dummoys, which was near Strathbogie (Huntly), Aberdeenshire, was that in 1627 he erected a monument to his parents in Dumbennan churchyard. It seems reasonable to believe that this is the same memorial bearing the Anderson Arms described by Andrew Jervise in his book. Although James Anderson is described as being of Dummoys, it may be that he acquired this property following his marriage as his wife's father, Andrew Haliburton, is described as being of Dummoys. The chart notes that James Anderson was a Notary Public and tenant of one half of the lands of Dumbennan in 1600. He was 'Servitour' (factor or man of business) to George, 1st Marquis of Huntly, 1603. He acquired Dummoys prior to 5 July 1620. He acquired Wester Ardbrake (Banff-shire) in 1630 and transferred it to his eldest son, John, in 1633. He was appointed a J.P. for Aberdeenshire in 1636. James married Agnes Haliburton who died prior to 2 October 1657. It will be noted that Rev. James Anderson had earlier married a member of the Haliburton family and her name was also Agnes. Rev. James Anderson died in 1603 and his wife at some time after that.[4] James Anderson died in about 1646 and his wife in about 1657.

The connection between Westertown, Wester Ardbrake and Westerton is shown by a number of the entries on the charts by F. J. Anderson. On a copy of one of his charts he has added the names of two of the earlier generations of the Andersons from Westerton. He shows John Anderson of Westerton who was living in 1537. His son is shown as Alexander Anderson of Westerton who was living in 1562 and probably died between 1625 and 1627. One of his sons was James Anderson who was born in 1575. See the next chapter for a theory concerning another and probably elder son.

James Anderson and his wife, Agnes Haliburton, are shown to have had a number of sons. The eldest was John Anderson who was probably born in about 1610. Entries on the charts show references to John Anderson of Wester-town. His eldest son was another James and there are various references to him as being of Westertown or of Westerton (both are near Huntly). He and his wife built a new house of Westertown (Wester Ardbrake). Their names are appa-rently shown on a stone built into the gable of a farmhouse adjoining the site. His son, John Anderson, is described as being of Westertown. These notes tend to suggest that the same Anderson family have been connected with Wester-town and the surrounding area for many years, maybe going well back into the 16th century and possibly the 15th century.

Having concluded that the series of Anderson families shown on the charts prepared by Francis James Anderson are part of the same family grouping shown in the earlier chapters of this book, it is appropriate to give at least a brief outline of these families through to the present time. Their story is obviously full and varied and it is not possible to do sufficient justice to them without extensive further research. This must follow when more time is avail-able. For now, the notes which follow are based on the work undertaken by F. J. Anderson, supplemented by some more recent sources.

James Anderson and his wife, Agnes Haliburton, as mentioned above, appear to have had three sons. In his earlier chart dated 1911, F. J. Anderson lists these as:

1. John Anderson, born c. 1610 and died c. 1690. See below for further notes.

(2) Patrick Anderson who was living in 1696. However, in his later chart
     dated 1913-16, F. J. Anderson has deleted the reference to Patrick.
     Possible reasons for this are discussed below and in the next chapter.
     In place of Patrick, the later chart shows:

2. Alexander Anderson who was living in 1641 when he witnessed documents for his elder brother. He appears to have been an advocate in
   Edinburgh.

Both charts show as the third son

3. George Anderson who was living in 1641 and is believed to have died
   after 1700. He married Jean Stewart and they had at least three children.
   These were:

   a. John Anderson who was probably born in about 1680.

   b. Thomas Anderson who was born in 1682.

   c. Marjorie Anderson who was born in 1687.

The dates of birth of Thomas and Marjorie are known with reasonable accuracy
because they were listed in the poll book of 1696 as being aged 14 and nine
years respectively. F. J. Anderson concluded that John was probably away at
college in 1696. George Anderson was described as being 'in Dumbennen' and
as a gentleman tenant in 1696. He apparently had two men servants and two
women servants and one herd. It is hoped that someone who reads about
Alexander and George or their descendants can offer further information about
them. In the case of Patrick, some consideration has been given to why he was
deleted from F. J. Anderson's later chart. It is concluded that it may be
possible that he was a cousin to the above three brothers. The reasons for this
theory are discussed in the next chapter.

   Returning to John Anderson, the eldest of the three brothers, much more is
known about him and his descendants. In 1634, John married Anne, the eldest
daughter of Alexander Gordon of Merdrum. In 1649, he failed to subscribe to
the League and Covenant (see Chapter Two) and had to make repentance
in Botriphnie Kirk. In 1650 he is described as scandalising the minister of
Botriphnie who was Mr. Alexander Fraser.[5] In 1651 he is even accused of
encouraging witchcraft, yet later that year he asked the Presbytery to appoint
a minister to Botriphnie. The minister, Alexander Fraser, was in fact deposed
on 26 June 1650 for subscribing a paper against the Covenant. He had to make
repentance in his own kirk on 16 February 1651. The parish remained vacant
for four years, although attempts were made to fill it by the appointment of
James Petrie, a schoolmaster from Banff.[6]

   In 1652 John Anderson became Laird of Ardbrake. In 1657 he proved his
title to Dummoys and then transferred it and Wester Ardbrake to his eldest

son, James, and Katharine Leslie, at the time of their marriage. His own wife, Anne Gordon, died on 19 November 1670. Katharine, the wife of his son, James, died in 1671 and so father and son erected a monument to their wives in the south aisle of Botriphnie kirk. F. J. Anderson must have seen this in 1911 as he states that it was quite legible, having been protected by an overhanging yew tree. The church apparently went out of use in about 1879. John Anderson lived until after 1688 as he was present at the baptism of his great-grandchildren, James in 1684, Katharine in 1686 and Alexander in 1688.

John Anderson and Anne Gordon, his wife, had five children and some information is available about each of them:

1. James Anderson was probably born in 1635 — see below for more details about him.

2. Alexander Anderson was probably born in 1636 and died around 1685. He attended Aberdeen University and is described as having laureated in 1658 at the University and King's Colleges of Aberdeen. He then trained in the law because he was admitted as an advocate on 9 January 1666. Although details of his marriage have not yet been traced, his children were:

   a. John Anderson.

   b. Mary Anderson, who married her cousin, William Smithwick, and they had a son named Alexander.

3. Arthur Anderson was born in 1648. He too attended Aberdeen University and in 1670 laureated at University and King's College, Aberdeen. He is described as the Rev. Arthur Anderson, LL.D. and as chaplain to William III. He must have gone to Ireland as he died without issue in 1714 and was buried in the churchyard of The Rower, County Kilkenny. His tombstone bears the Arms granted to his elder brother. This was still to be seen in 1912.

4. Susannah Anderson. Her dates of birth or death are not known but she married a William Smithwick of Cranavaby, County Kilkenny. They had a son

   William Smithwick. He married Mary Anderson, his cousin, and had a son, Alexander.

5. Margaret Anderson. Again her dates of birth or death are not known. She married Angus McPherson of Dalradie in Banff. They had at least two children:

   a. John McPherson who was baptised at Botriphnie on 25 April 1689.

   b. Aeneas McPherson who married Katharine Field.

Reverting to the eldest son, James Anderson, who was born in about 1635, he married in 1657, Katharine, the fourth daughter of Robert Leslie of Findrassie, whose wife was Isobel, the daughter of Abraham Forbes of Black-ford. Katharine Leslie was apparently a great-great-grand-daughter of George, the 4th Earl of Rothes. In 1664, James Anderson and his wife built the new house of Westertown (Wester Ardbrake). This is shown by a stone built into the gable of the farmhouse adjoining the site. A few years later, on 9 March 1667, Katharine died, aged thirty-nine. Details of her children are given below. Later in the same year, James married Isobel, the daughter of Doctor Alexander Douglas of Downies, Kincardineshire and the widow of Rev. Alexander Cant.

At an unspecified date between 1672 and 1678, James Anderson registered Arms in the Public Register maintained by Lord Lyon, King of Arms.[7] He was described as being of Westerairbreck. James probably died in about 1704. He and his first wife had the following children:

1. Elizabeth Anderson was probably born in 1658. She married on 16 October 1675 John Gordon of Carroll in Sutherland who was Sheriff Depute of Sutherland. He died in 1701. They had three sons and two daughters:

   a. John Gordon, who died in about 1737, having had two sons.

      i. Hugh Gordon.

      ii. John Gordon who became a surgeon.

   b. Robert Gordon.

   c. William Gordon.

   d. Katherine Gordon.

   e. Elizabeth Gordon.

2. John Anderson of Westertown was probably born in about 1659. See below for further details about him.

3. Anna Anderson, whose date of birth and death are not known, married on 5 August 1684, Robert Gibson of Linkwood, Elgin. Their children were:

   a. Jean Gibson, baptised 28 February 1689.

   b. James Gibson, baptised 29 January 1693.

4. Alexander Anderson of Grace Dieu, Waterford in Ireland, was probably born in about 1662. He was a captain in the Grenadier Company of Sir John Hill's Regiment and promoted major on 18 November 1696. In 1699 King William III granted to Alexander Anderson the 'escheat' of all goods etc. belonging to James Anderson the elder, of Westertown and John Anderson, his eldest son, 'put to the horn for debt 3.2.1698'.

He does not appear to have married but had a son, George Anderson, who served in the Scotch Royal Dragoons. Alexander died in about 1733.

5. Mary Anderson, whose dates of birth and death are not known, married Thomas Baker of Ballytobin, County Kilkenny. They had a son named Anderson Baker.

John Anderson married on 8 February 1683 at New Machar, Jean, the daughter of Robert Gordon, 8th Laird of Straloch. She had been born at Pitlurg on 19 November 1659 and was therefore 23 when she married. John Anderson was imprisoned in the Tollbooth at Edinburgh 'for treasonable discourses'. It should be noted that this was on 16 March 1687 when King James VII of Scotland was on the throne, better known in England as King James II. In the following year, 1688, the king was forced to leave the country with the arrival of William and Mary. However, it appears John Anderson incurred forfeiture and had his Arms riven on 26 July 1687.[8] In 1690 he was one of a great number of people included under the Act rescinding the forfeitures and fines since the year 1665. For a fuller discussion about these times and events, see Chapter Three which discusses the life of his namesake, Rev. John Anderson. It is not clear when John Anderson died but references have not been traced about him after 1704 which was about when his father died. It is not clear either what were the circumstances of the debts which gave problems in 1698.

John Anderson and his wife, Jean Gordon, had seven children, as follows:

1. James Anderson, baptised on 26 March 1684 at Botriphnie — see below.

2. Katherine Anderson, baptised on 19 May 1685 and died prior to 27 September 1704.

3. John Anderson, baptised on 30 September 1686, but nothing else is known.

4. Alexander Anderson, baptised 4 July 1688 — see below for discussion concerning the question of his descendants.

5. Jean Anderson, baptised 2 September 1689, died unmarried on 25 March 1710 in Edinburgh.

6. Isobell Anderson, baptised 13 October 1690, died later than 1710 but nothing else is known.

7. Elizabeth Anderson, baptised 24 March 1690 and died prior to 27 September 1704.

8. Anna Anderson, baptised 26 June 1693 but died before 27 September 1704.

It appears from Burke's Irish Family Records that the youngest son, Alexander, succeeded his uncle, Major Alexander Anderson, to the estate of Grace Dieu. Burke also shows that Alexander married on 2 February 1721, the daughter of William Brewster and had issue. However, an addition typed on to the Wester Ardbrake chart prepared by F. J. Anderson indicates that it was James, the eldest son, who married Jane Brewster on 2 February 1721.[9] The chart shows him as being of Grace Dieu, although he was a Doctor of Medicine from Aberdeen. Evidence to support the marriage between James Anderson and Jane Brewster is perhaps to be found by an entry which F. J. Anderson notes from the will of Major Alexander Anderson of Grace Dieu. He refers to 'my brother John Anderson' and to 'my nephew James Anderson and his wife Jane'. The note on the Wester Ardbrake chart states that in 1721 James Anderson married Jane, daughter and co-heiress of William Brewster of Shandon Park, County Cork, son of Sir William Brewster, Lord Mayor of Dublin. Jane is shown as having died in 1754 but James Anderson died before her as his widow administered his estate in 1737.

It appears that James and Jane Anderson left three children:

1. James Anderson — see below.

2. Jane Anderson who married Robert Carew and had a son, Robert Carew, who married a Miss Robins of County Tipperary and a daughter, Jane, who married someone named Wogan.

3. Catherine Anderson married someone named Dobbyn of Ballinakill, Waterford.

As already implied by the earlier comments concerning who married Jane Brewster, a slight mystery affects the records about James Anderson. F. J. Anderson records that when James was a minor he was robbed by his trustee, who is said to have destroyed the tombstones of his father and mother in the graveyard at Innistiogne, to prevent proof of descent. This may well be why there is a question concerning whether his father was James Anderson or his brother, Alexander. If, however, James was born in say 1722, he will have been about fifteen years of age when his father died in about 1737. His mother lived until 1754 when James was in his early thirties, so it is not clear what dispute arose concerning the proof of his descent or why his parents' tombstones would have been destroyed.

The younger James Anderson married twice. First he married in 1756 Henrietta Boyd who died before 1762. Secondly he married Susanna, the youngest daughter of Christmas Paul and Ellen, the daughter of Robert Carew, M.P. of Ballinamona. She was born in 1748, married in 1764 and died in 1816. She and James Anderson were buried at Clifton parish churchyard, having left Ireland in 1798. They had a number of children:

1. James Anderson, probably born in about 1765 and died without issue in 1838.

2. Paul Anderson, born on 29 March 1767. He became a lieutenant-general and the Colonel of the 78th Highlanders. He was Chief of Sir John Moore's staff at Corunna.[10] Later he became the Governor of Pendennis Castle. He died without issue at Widcomb, Bath, in 1851. He was awarded a C.B. and K.C.H.

3. Alexander Anderson was probably born in about 1768 and died without issue in 1833.

4. Henry Anderson was probably born in about 1769 and died without issue.

5. Joshua Anderson was born on 8 December 1770 — see below for further information about him.

6. Robert Anderson died without issue 21 March 1801.

7. Ellen Anderson died unmarried in 1861.

Joshua Anderson of Grace Dieu became the Rev. Joshua Anderson, M.A. and the rector of Myshall, County Carlow. He married on 1 October 1807, Anne, the eldest daughter of Captain William Perceval of Temple House, Ballymote, County Sligo. She died 24 March 1854, having been born in 1787. Rev. Joshua Anderson died on 6 April 1859. He and his wife had 11 children as follows:

1. Anne Anderson, born in 1809 and died in September 1884. She married on 4 February 1845 Charles Newport Bolton of County Waterford who died on 2 April 1884. They left issue.

2. James Anderson, born 4 August 1810 — see below for further details.

3. William Anderson, born in 1813 — see below for fuller information.

4. Robert Carew Anderson, born in 1815 — see below for details of his descendants.

5. Paul Christmas Anderson was born in 1816 or 1817 and died without issue on 24 February 1907.

6. Alexander Anderson was probably born in about 1818. He served in the Royal Navy and was in command of H.M.S. *Cressy* on which he died in August 1854 without issue.

7. Jane Ellen Anderson was born in 1820 and died on 14 March 1906.

8. Ellen Anderson was probably born in about 1822. She married on 13 December 1859 George Bevan Russell, M.D., of Fermoy, County Cork. She died on 9 February 1902 leaving issue. One of her daughters,

Ellen Katherine Russell, married her cousin, Charles Alexander Anderson — see below for details of their issue.

9. Catherine (Kate) Anderson, who was probably born around 1824, died on 18 February 1855.

10. Henrietta Anderson died on 22 January 1927.

11. Susanna Anderson died on 14 September 1911.

From the 11 children made up of five sons and six daughters, it is known that two of the daughters married and had children and three of the sons married, leaving children as follows.

James Anderson married on 25 April 1842, Margaret, the daughter of Robert Carew of Ballinamona. She died on 29 February 1864 and James died on 22 October 1867. Their issue was:

1. Jane Margaret Anderson who was probably born in about 1845. She married on 15 December 1868, Michael Clare Garsia who was with the 30th Regiment. He was subsequently the Inspector General of Prisons and died on 20 April 1903. Jane Margaret lived until 9 October 1936 when she died, leaving issue.

2. James Paul Anderson, born 21 January 1850 and died on 26 September 1860.

3. Thomas William Anderson was born on 26 June 1852. He married on 10 November 1879 Constance Agnes Jane, the daughter of Rev. Anthony Latouche Kirwan. They had a daughter, Susan Alice Anderson, who was born in 1881. Constance died in that year on 9 August. Susan Alice Anderson lived at Grace Dieu until she died unmarried on 19 December 1941. T. W. Anderson married a second time on 2 October 1907 when he married Ellen Blanche Carew Blacker Kirwan, the sister of his first wife. They did not have any children. He died on 5 September 1925 and his wife died on 6 April 1944. Thomas Anderson was a J.P. and a deputy lieutenant.

4. Alexander Carew Anderson was born on 6 May 1856. He married on 24 August 1880 Margaret Winifred Alicia, the youngest daughter of Nicholas Power of Belle Vue, County Kilkenny. They had two children:

a. Paul Alexander Anderson who was born on 5 January 1883. He married on 14 June 1921, Aileen Anne, the younger daughter of John Ulick Bourke. She died on 13 January 1944. He died on 10 October 1942. They had a son:

    William Alexander Anderson who was born on 22 September 1922. He served with the Royal Navy and was lost on active service on the Submarine *Trooper* on 17 October 1943.[11]

b. Muriel Louise Anderson was born on 31 March 1894 and died on 18 January 1923.

William Anderson married on 24 August 1859, Elizabeth Paul, the daughter of Samuel Wallis Adams. William was in the Civil Service. He died on 20 November 1904 and his wife died on 20 December 1910, leaving issue:

1. Wilhelmina Elizabeth Anderson who married Albert Alexander McCall of the 76th Regiment, with issue.

2. Joshua Alexander Anderson was born on 19 January 1867. He became the Rev. Canon, rector of Aborfield, from 1898 to 1945. He was also Proctor of Convocation for Oxford, 1922 and Hon. Canon of Christ Church College, Oxford, 1930. In 1896, he married Edith Constance, the daughter of Henry Hainsworth. She died in 1945 and he died without issue on 5 November 1947.

3. James William Anderson was born on 2 March 1869. He became a doctor (M.R.C.S., L.R.C.P.) and died unmarried on 15 June 1913.

Robert Carew Anderson who was born in 1815 became a doctor. He was a Surgeon Major with the 13th Light Dragoons and became Deputy Inspector General of Hospitals. He married on 13 October 1853 Jane Wallis, the daughter of Rev. Henry Bolton. Robert Anderson died on 2 February 1885 and his wife died on 6 April 1904, leaving issue:

1. Robert Henry Anderson who was born on 7 August 1854 and died without issue on 31 December 1896.

2. Charles Alexander Anderson was born on 10 February 1857 — see below for fuller information about him and his descendants.

3. William Paul Anderson was born on 16 June 1858. He became a major in the Indian Army and died unmarried on 27 November 1935.

4. Francis James Anderson, born 17 February 1860. See below for fuller information about him and his descendants.

5. Frances Ann Grace Anderson was born on 3 December 1861 and died unmarried in 1941.

6. Joshua Perceval Anderson was born on 4 May 1863 and died unmarried on 9 October 1905.

7. Katherine Jane Henrietta Anderson was born on 1 August 1864. On 28 January 1902 she married Harry Mervyn Kemmis-Betty of the Royal Navy who became a vice-admiral. He died on 22 December 1940 and she died without issue on 18 August 1948.

Charles Alexander Anderson had a distinguished and gallant military career.[12] He was born on 10 February 1857 and entered the army in 1876. He was appointed captain in 1884, major in 1893 and lieutenant-colonel in 1901. Charles Anderson served with the Jowaki–Afridi Expedition 1877–8 and was awarded a medal with clasp. From 1878–80 he served in the Afghan War, during which time he was mentioned in dispatches and gained a medal with two clasps. He served with the Burmah Expedition 1885–6, and then at the North-West Frontier, India 1897–8, being mentioned in dispatches on three occasions and gaining a medal with clasp. In 1908 he commanded the 1st Brigade Bazaar Valley Expedition and then the 1st Brigade Mohmand Field Force, after which he was promoted major-general for distinguished service in the field. He commanded troops in South China 1910–13 and then served in World War I, being mentioned in dispatches twice and being created a K.C.B. His last command was in India 1917–19, and then in 1920 Sir Charles retired.

Charles married on 11 January 1893 Ellen Catherine Russell who was his cousin, being the younger daughter of Ellen Anderson and George Bevan Russell. He died on 20 February 1940 and his wife died on 2 January 1956, leaving issue as follows:

1. Charles Bevan Carew Anderson who was born on 12 April 1894. See below for fuller details and descendants.

2. William Perceval Anderson was born on 9 July 1895 and died unmarried on 11 August 1912.

3. Noel Maurice Anderson was born on 30 November 1896. He became a major in the 2nd/5th Maharatta Light Infantry of the Indian Army and served in World War I. He married on 22 August 1922, Sheila Lyle, the daughter of Lieut.-Colonel David Simpson of Elgin, and died on 28 March 1940, leaving issue:

   a. Rosemary Shelagh Anderson, born 13 September 1923. She is an artist who married on 9 January 1946 Denis Higbee, a painter, and has a daughter:

      Sarah Tamsyn Higbee who was born on 20 October 1952.

   b. Mary Dawn Anderson, born 19 November 1935, married on 1 April 1960, Norman Stewart McNaughton. They have issue:

      i. Richenda Jane McNaughton, born 11 March 1962.

      ii. Charlotte Ann McNaughton, born 5 May 1964.

      iii. James Alexander Noel McNaughton, born 6 May 1970.

Charles B. C. Anderson, who was born in 1894, read Medicine at Edinburgh University. He served with the R.A.M.C. in World War I, the Afghan War in 1919 and in World War II. He succeeded to Grace Dieu following the death of

William Alexander Anderson in 1943. On 26 April 1924 he married Alice Grace Mary, the daughter of John Ralph Barkley. She died on 13 February 1976 and he died on 17 July 1979.[13] Their issue is:

1. Charles William Michael Anderson was born on 30 June 1925. On 6 February 1960 he married Daphne Holt, the daughter of H. Benson of Salisbury, then Rhodesia.

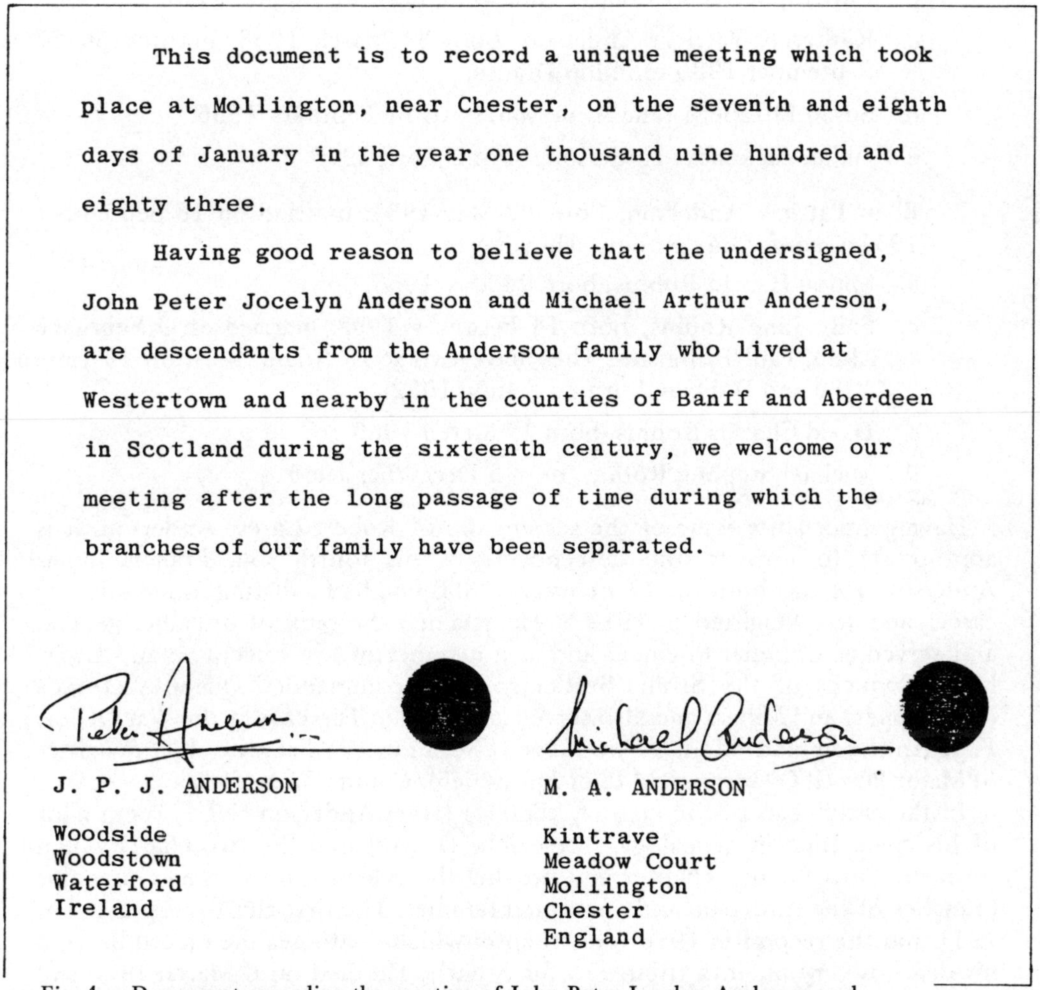

> This document is to record a unique meeting which took place at Mollington, near Chester, on the seventh and eighth days of January in the year one thousand nine hundred and eighty three.
>
> Having good reason to believe that the undersigned, John Peter Jocelyn Anderson and Michael Arthur Anderson, are descendants from the Anderson family who lived at Westertown and nearby in the counties of Banff and Aberdeen in Scotland during the sixteenth century, we welcome our meeting after the long passage of time during which the branches of our family have been separated.

J. P. J. ANDERSON   M. A. ANDERSON

Woodside   Kintrave
Woodstown   Meadow Court
Waterford   Mollington
Ireland   Chester
                                     England

Fig. 4   Document recording the meeting of John Peter Jocelyn Anderson and Michael Arthur Anderson in January 1983.

2. John Peter Jocelyn Anderson who was born on 5 November 1926. He married 31 December 1953 Nanette, the daughter of Walter Percival Knight of Rhodesia. They have issue:

   a. Jonathan Michael Paul Anderson, born 31 January 1955, married on 12 April 1980, Susan Frances Butler and they have a daughter, Victoria Frances, born on 13 September 1981 and a son Timothy Paul born on 6 February 1984.

   b. Christopher Peter Charles Anderson, born 27 August 1956.

   c. Katherine Patricia Anderson, born 31 March 1958, married on 27 September 1980 to Philip Dranse.

   d. Susan Elizabeth Jane Anderson, born 21 February 1966.

   e. Julian Alexander Anderson, born 2 April 1969.

3. Ellen Patricia Anderson, born 27 May 1931, married on 18 September 1954, George Gray Robins. They have issue:

   a. Simon Harold Robins, born 24 May 1956.

   b. Sally Jane Robins, born 14 February 1958, married on 9 February 1980, Paul Robinson. They have two sons, Adam, born on 13 June 1980 and Duncan, born on 3 June 1982.

   c. David Charles Robins, born 12 March 1960.

   d. Michael Stephen Robins, born 3 December 1963.

Having traced the issue of the second son of Robert Carew Anderson, it is appropriate to turn to the descendants of his fourth son, Francis James Anderson. He was born on 17 February 1860 and had a distinguished military career and was knighted in 1919.[14] He attained the rank of brigadier general and served as Colonial Engineer and as a member of the Executive and Legislative Councils of the Straits Settlements. He commanded Queen Victoria's own Sappers and Miners and also served as Assistant Director at the War Office. F. J. Anderson married on 3 November 1886, Frances Alice, the elder daughter of Major Purcell O'Gorman, M.P. of Springfield, County Waterford.

In the early years of this century, Francis James Anderson clearly spent a lot of his spare time in genealogical research. He prepared the two charts which form the basis for this chapter and provide the evidence for linking two major branches of the Anderson and associated families. The first chart was printed in 1911 and the second in 1916. This chapter which continues the record beyond his death is very much a tribute to Sir Francis. He died on 6 March 1920 and his wife died on 8 January 1947 leaving issue as follows:

1. James Carew O'Gorman Anderson was born on 22 July 1893. He married on 27 September 1921 Stella, the younger daughter of Ralph

Beaumont Benson. She died on 6 December 1933 without issue. He married a second time on 21 September 1935 Veronica Beatrice, the elder daughter of Hon. Sir (Frank) Trevor Roger Bigham. He died on 19 November 1946, leaving issue:

a. Richard Benedict O'Gorman Anderson, born 26 August 1936, Professor of Political History, Cornell University.

b. Francis Rory Peregrine Anderson, born 11 September 1938, married 1976 Gyongy Vir from Hungary.

c. Melanie Catherine Sainthill Anderson, born 28 January 1943, who is with Amnesty International.

2. Francis Sainthill Anderson was born on 22 November 1894. He entered the army in 1915 and won a Military Cross. Shortly before the end of the war he was killed in action on 25 August 1918.

3. Blanche Marguerite Anderson was born on 27 November 1889, but died on 28 February 1893, being buried at Penang.

4. Mary Frances Walton Anderson was born on 13 April 1891. She married on 27 March 1916, Robert Woodhouse who died on 21 December 1966, leaving issue:

a. Francis Swinburne Woodhouse, born 25 May 1920.

b. Alice Cynthia Sainthill Woodhouse, born 29 July 1918. She married on 4 February 1941, Sir Ernest William Davis-Goff Bt. Their issue is:

  i. Annabel Clair Davis-Goff, born 19 February 1942, married Michael Nichols of Bridgewater, Connecticut, U.S.A. They have a son Max and a daughter Jennie.

  ii. Julia Christian Davis-Goff, born 18 August 1943, married John Godfrey Barker of Castletownbere, County Cork and they have a son Christian and a daughter Andrea.

  iii. Alice Maria Davis-Goff, born 15 March 1948, married Christopher Quarry of Sittingbourne in Kent. They have a son Andrew and a daughter.

  iv. Robert William Davis-Goff, born 12 September 1955, married Sheelagh Chadwick. They have a son William and a daughter Sarah.

  Alice Cynthia married again on 21 October 1961 Hector O'Connor, sculptor, who died in 1970.

c. Vivian Anne Woodhouse who was born on 17 May 1925. She married on 15 October 1947, Patrick de Cruce Grubb. Their issue is:

i. Richard de Cruce Grubb who is a member of The Institute of Chartered Accountants in England and Wales, born on 5 July 1948. He married Elizabeth Johnson on 23 July 1976. They have a daughter Charlotte born 20 January 1979, a son Thomas born 3 October 1980 and another daughter Edwina born 25 July 1982.

ii. Nicholas de Cruce Grubb, born on 28 November 1950, married Barbara Villiers Stuart on 18 August 1979. They have two daughters, Georgina Elizabeth born 17 June 1980 and Natasha Jane born 16 January 1983.

As already explained, much of the information in this chapter has been obtained from the research work undertaken by Sir Francis James Anderson who died in 1920. It is greatly hoped that further and fuller information about the members of this series of Anderson families and their descendants can be obtained in due course. However, in the belief that sufficient evidence is available to show the likely common origins of these families with the other Anderson families from Westertown dealt with earlier in the book, a meeting between some members of two of the current families was arranged. This took place in January 1983, and is recorded in a short signed statement which is reproduced on page 89 as evidence of a practical achievement resulting from the study of genealogy.

The next chapter considers a number of other Anderson families and explores grounds for believing there may be connections between them and the two groups of families recorded in this and earlier chapters.

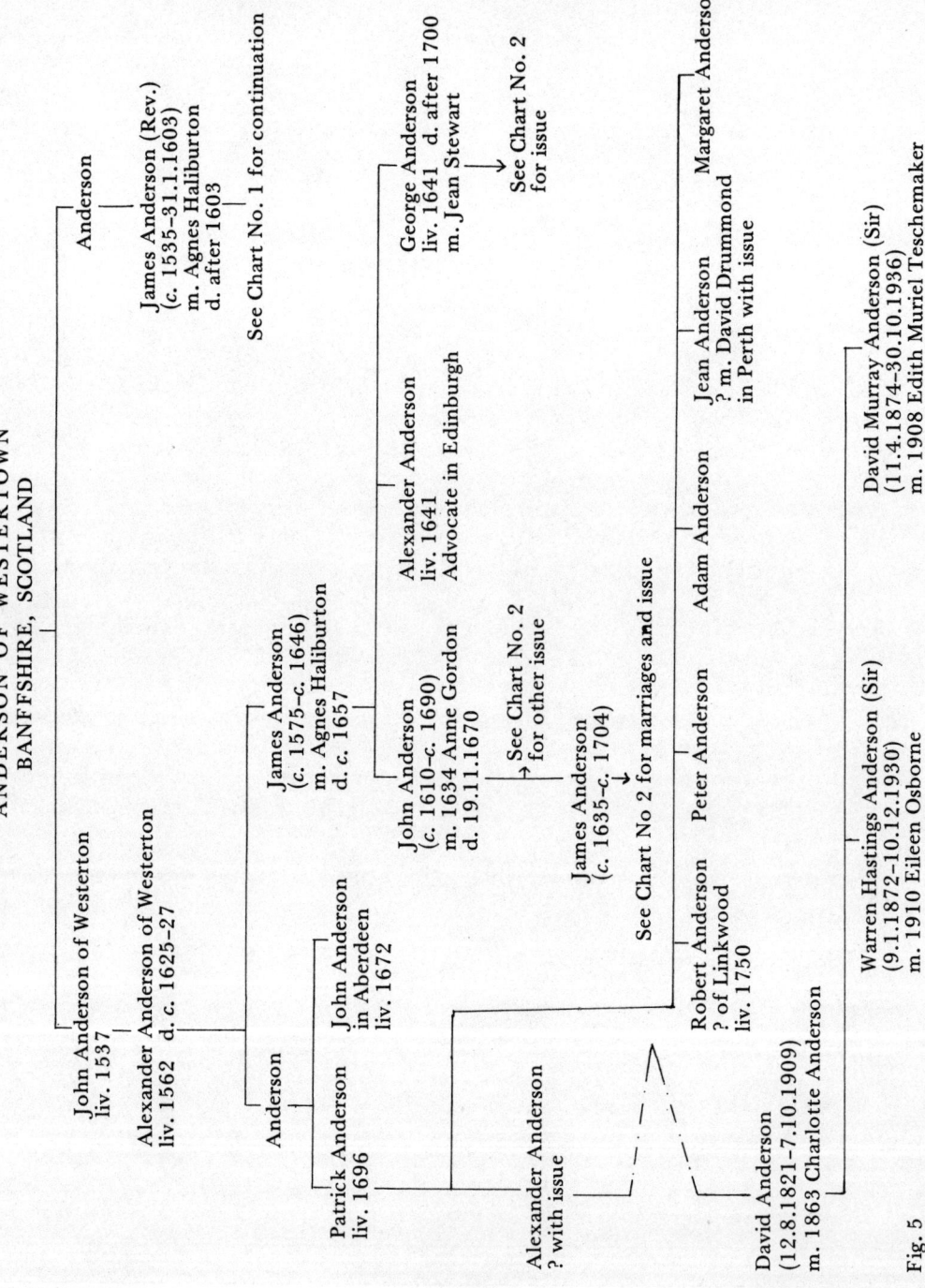

ANDERSON OF WESTERTOWN
BANFFSHIRE, SCOTLAND

John Anderson of Westerton
liv. 1537

Alexander Anderson of Westerton
liv. 1562 d. c. 1625–27

Anderson

Anderson

James Anderson (Rev.)
(c. 1535–31.1.1603)
m. Agnes Haliburton
d. after 1603

See Chart No. 1 for continuation

James Anderson
(c. 1575–c. 1646)
m. Agnes Haliburton
d. c. 1657

Patrick Anderson
liv. 1696

John Anderson
in Aberdeen
liv. 1672

John Anderson
(c. 1610–c. 1690)
m. 1634 Anne Gordon
d. 19.11.1670

See Chart No. 2
for other issue

Alexander Anderson
liv. 1641
Advocate in Edinburgh

George Anderson
liv. 1641 d. after 1700
m. Jean Stewart

See Chart No. 2
for issue

Alexander Anderson
? with issue

James Anderson
(c. 1635–c. 1704)

See Chart No 2 for marriages and issue

Robert Anderson
? of Linkwood
liv. 1750

Peter Anderson

Adam Anderson

Jean Anderson
? m. David Drummond
in Perth with issue

Margaret Anderson

David Anderson
(12.8.1821–7.10.1909)
m. 1863 Charlotte Anderson

Warren Hastings Anderson (Sir)
(9.1.1872–10.12.1930)
m. 1910 Eileen Osborne

David Murray Anderson (Sir)
(11.4.1874–30.10.1936)
m. 1908 Edith Muriel Teschemaker

Fig. 5

CHAPTER THIRTEEN

Anderson Heraldic Links

IN THE PREVIOUS CHAPTER it was explained why it is believed that the Anderson families discussed were descended from the same Anderson family from Westertown as the Rev. James Anderson and his descendants outlined in the first 11 chapters.

Based on information received from Lord Lyon, King of Arms and a certain amount of other research, it is now suggested that James Anderson, the earliest known member of the family, outlined in Chapter Twelve, may not have been the eldest son. His elder brother may have been the father of Patrick Anderson who was listed, together with his children, in the earlier chart compiled by F. J. Anderson but deleted by him when making revisions. This suggestion is made following an examination of coats of arms which were in use at various times. The key set of arms from 1627 appears not to have been officially recorded in the Public Register maintained by Lord Lyon and certainly to this extent the study is incomplete. However, in his book printed in 1910 entitled *The Andersons in Phingask and Their Descendants*, J. M. A. Wood lists in an appendix a number of arms of certain Anderson families of Scotland. One of these entries reads as follows:

ANDERSONS OF DUNBENNAN, ARDBAKE
and MELLINSIDE

Azure, a Saltier, Argent, between three Mullets Or and a Crescent in Base of the third; Crest, a fir tree seeded proper, issuant from a Mount in Base.

Motto: Stand Sure

Fig. 6

In his book mentioned in the introduction to this book and in the previous chapter, Jervise refers to a set of Anderson Arms on a memorial in Dunbennan.

These are described, although the colours are not known, as: 'A saltire between three stars (or mullets) and a crescent in base'. In view of the identical configuration of the two sets of arms and the reference to Dunbennan, it seems likely that the arms used on the memorial are those detailed by J. M. A. Wood, although no record of these arms has been found in the Public Register. It is not known where J. M. A. Wood obtained the reference to the arms detailed above. It will be noted that, with the inclusion of a chevron in place of the saltire, the Dunbennan arms are very similar to the arms matriculated by James Anderson of Newbigging in 1780 but which had been in use for more than a hundred years earlier (see Chapters Two and Five). F. J. Anderson found evidence that the memorial erected in 1627 was built by James Anderson of Dummoys to his parents. The coat of arms used would presumably have been the arms of his father. If James Anderson had been the eldest son, he would have borne the same arms on his father's death and his eldest son and grandson would have borne them also in their turn. This grandson was James Anderson who matriculated arms in about 1672. The arms matriculated by him, however, were not the arms found on the Dunbennan monument erected in 1627. They were in fact as follows:

James Andersone of Westerairdbreck Bears argent a saltire engrailed betwixt two mollets in chief and base gules and as many boar heads erased in fess azure. Above ye shield ane helmet befitting his degree mantled gules doubled argent. The motto in ane Escrol 'stand sure'. The crest is ane Oak-tree growing out of ane torse proper.

Public Register Volume 1 Folio 239.[1]

Fig. 7

These arms are so different to the arms used in 1627 as to suggest that they were created by someone not directly entitled to the earlier arms, which would be the position with the descendants of a younger son. However, the motto is the same and the crests are similar, although the fir tree has become an oak tree.

It is interesting to note that J. M. A. Wood records further sets of arms which include similar characteristics. Some of these are as follows:

ANDERSONS OF CANDACRAIG

Argent, a Saltier, Sable, surmounted with another Azure, between two Mullets Gules and as many Boars' Heads couped of the third;

Crest, on a wreath, Argent and Or, a fir tree seeded proper

Motto: Stand Sure

ANDERSONS OF MILTOUN OF NOTH, EARLSFIELD, and NEWTOUN OF PREMNAY

Azure, a Saltire Argent, between two Mullets Or in Chief and Base, dexter a ploughshare, sinister a Lochaber Axe both of the third;

Crest, on a wreath, a fir tree seeded proper issuant from a Mount

Motto: Stand Sure

ANDERSONS OF BOURTIE

Argent, a Saltier, Azure between four Mullets Gules Crest a fir tree seeded proper issuant from a Mount in Base

Motto: Stand Sure

Fig. 8

It will be seen that the location of the second of the holders of the above arms is very similar to the description for Patrick Anderson in 1696 which is given below.

Reverting to the arms on the Dunbennan memorial (Fig. 1), it is interesting to speculate about the circumstances under which it fell to James Anderson in 1627 to erect the monument to his parents, bearing the Anderson Arms, presumably of his father, as described by Jervise. F. J. Anderson states that James Anderson erected the monument and Jervise refers to Jacobus (or James) Anderson as being named on the stone but does not specify the context so it could well have been as the person who erected the memorial as distinct from being one of those commemorated. James Anderson may have built the memorial jointly with an elder brother, although there is no known record of this. His elder brother may have died before 1627, but after he had married and left children. The theory now being advanced is that the eldest of these children may have been the Patrick Anderson detailed by F. J. Anderson on the chart he prepared in 1911 and originally thought by him to have been the son of James Anderson. He had clearly found some evidence to change this view by the time he prepared his revised chart a few years later. Some support for the suggestion that James Anderson had an elder brother is to be found from the heraldic links which are outlined below. The following details concerning Patrick Anderson and his family were supplied by F. J. Anderson on his earliest chart.

Patrick Anderson was Commissioner for the Poll in 1696. In that record he is described as being the principal tenant of MyIntoune of Noth and Heretor of the lands of Newtoune of Premney, the valuation of which was £100. The poll book records that he had a wife but does not name her. He is also shown as having four manservants, three womanservants and two herds. His children are detailed as being four sons and two daughters as follows:

1. Alexander Anderson — see below.

2. Robert Anderson — see below.

3. Peter Anderson.

4. Adam Anderson.

5. Jean Anderson — see below.

6. Margaret Anderson.

Although no dates of birth or death are known at this stage, if all these children were alive in 1696, some of them could have been alive to beyond the middle of the next century. The significance of this will be more apparent when reference is made to Robert Anderson and Jean Anderson after first considering an intriguing theory concerning the possible descendants of Alexander Anderson.

If the general rules of heraldry apply, Alexander Anderson shown above would have inherited his father's arms without any difference and could in turn pass them on through a succession of eldest sons. On this basis, he may have been the forebear of David Anderson who was born on 12 August 1821 and appears, from a memorial in Chester Cathedral associated with his name, to have been entitled to these arms. David Anderson entered the army in 1839 and progressed to the rank of General in 1888. For some time he served in the North Western Frontier of India and was Governor of the Royal Military College, Sandhurst, from 1886 to 1888.[2] He was Colonel of the Cheshire Regiment from 1894, an honour subsequently also to be held by his elder son. In 1863, David Anderson married Charlotte, the second daughter of another David Anderson from St Germains in Haddingtonshire. David Anderson died on 7 October 1909, leaving at least two sons:

1. Warren Hastings Anderson, born on 9 January 1872 — see below.

2. David Murray Anderson, born on 11 April 1874 — see below.

Warren Hastings Anderson had a most distinguished military career which is outlined in the *Dictionary of National Biography*.[3] He was born at Aldershot and educated at Marlborough. He went to Sandhurst and in 1890 into the Cheshire Regiment. He served in the South African War and then, after attending the Staff College, was with the War Office. In 1914 he became an instructor with the rank of lieutenant-colonel at the Staff College. He then saw extensive service in France during the war and was awarded the C.B. in 1918. In 1919 he became commandant of the Staff College. This appointment continued for three years and in 1922 he was created a K.C.B. He had further senior appointments in Asia Minor and then in India. In 1927 he returned to England and was appointed quartermaster general of the forces.

The National Dictionary records:

> Hastings Anderson was a born soldier, reared amongst soldiers, yet he had none of the insular outlook which sometimes accompanies the innate loyalty of the British Officer. He had high ideals and a definite conception of the dignity of a British General and the duties required of that dignity, yet he never lost the grace which led him to observe a gentle and chivalrous attitude towards others. He was very fair-minded and although he held strong opinions and expressed them with force and complete clarity, no one could be more whole-hearted and loyal in carrying out decisions of a higher authority which were contrary to his views . . . He was extremely proud of his own regiment (the Cheshire). He was the author of an *Outline of the Development of the British Army* (1930).

W. H. Anderson married in 1910 Eileen, the only daughter of Hamilton Osborne, but there were no children from the marriage.[4] He died in London on 10 December 1930. Sir Warren Hastings Anderson became Colonel of the Cheshire Regiment in 1928 and his decorations are in a special display case in the Regimental Museum at Chester Castle. It is the memorial in Chester Cathedral to him and his father and to members of the Cheshire Regiment who fell in the Great War which bears the same coat of arms as the memorial of 1627 described above.

David Murray Anderson, who was born on 11 April 1874 at Newton-by-Chester, also had a distinguished service career.[5] He, however, was in the Royal Navy from 1889. He became a captain in 1911, rear-admiral in 1922, vice-admiral in 1927 and admiral in 1931. He was created a K.C.B. in 1930. From 1929 to 1931 he was the Admiralty representative on the League of Nations advisory commission. He was appointed Governor and Commander-in-Chief of Newfoundland until 1936. In November 1935 he was appointed Governor of New South Wales. On the journey out there, he was taken ill and spent six weeks in hospital in Perth. He was sworn in at Sydney on 6 August 1936. Because of his recurring illness, his wife ably undertook many official duties on his behalf. On 29 October 1936 he collapsed suddenly and died of a cerebral haemorrhage on 30 October. After a memorial service in Sydney, his body was shipped to England and buried in Fittleworth cemetery, Sussex. He had married in 1908 Edith Muriel, the daughter of W. H. Teschemaker. No details are available as to whether they had any children. Lady Anderson was appointed a Dame of the British Empire in 1937.

Information as to whether David Murray Anderson and his wife had any children or information about any other issue from General David Anderson or earlier members of the same family would be very welcome. Research to confirm the hypothesis that David Anderson was descended from Alexander Anderson, as suggested above, will depend upon more time being available to complete the necessary searches. The Armorial Bearings, however, suggest most strongly that this could very well have been the case.

Having discussed these possible descendants from Patrick Anderson, an interesting point may be noted which might refer to his second son, Robert. If he wished to use arms based on his father's, a suitable difference would have to be made. It transpires that a Robert Anderson of Linkwood recorded arms in about 1750 which are very similar to the arms described earlier. The entry in the Public Register reads:

Robert Anderson of Linkwood Esquire in the County of Elgin and Forres Bears vizt. Argent a saltier ingrailed sable betwixt a rose in chief two Mullets in the flanks Gules and a Crescent in base. Crest a hand holding a pen proper.

Motto: Honesty is the best Policy.

Volume 1 Folio 116.

Fig. 9

The similarity in the arms in this case, although clearly not conclusive, supports the view that there may well have been the family connection suggested. The saltire shown on the arms in Chester Cathedral is also sable as in the above case.

Although there may be no connection with the Jean Anderson listed above as the daughter of Patrick Anderson, another memorial has been seen bearing this name. In Greyfriars burial ground in Perth, there is a memorial stone to David Drummond, a wright in Perth, and to his wife who was Jean Anderson. The names of their children are also detailed on the stone, with dates from 1741 to 1769. The interesting point about this memorial is that in one half it shows the same Anderson arms that Jervise refers to as being on the memorial stone erected in 1627 in Dunbennan churchyard and which can also be seen in Chester Cathedral today. A daughter could have used her father's arms without difference and her husband in this case may not have borne arms.

Lord Lyon has very kindly drawn my attention to one further set of arms which are very similar to those being discussed. They are recorded in the Public Register, very close to the arms of James Anderson of Westerairdbreck, being on the next folio and also c. 1672. (See entry at top of page 101).

One wonders whether this John Anderson was perhaps the younger brother of Patrick Anderson as Lord Lyon suggests that it is possible that the wavy saltire was a cadency difference.

The chart on page 94 shows how the line from the earlier generations of the Anderson family from Westertown may possibly have descended. This chart is

John Andersone in Aberdein Bears Argent a saltyre waved betwixt three mollets and a crescent in base gules: Above ye shield ane helmet befitting his degree mantled gules doubled argent. Next is placed on ane Torse for his crest a cross-staff erected marked with the degrees of Latitude.

The motto in ane Escroll Per Mare.

Volume 1 Folio 240.

Fig. 10

based on the heraldic links suggested and discussed above. It is also founded on the information left by Francis James Anderson in his chart dated 1911. Clearly more work will be necessary to develop the theory outlined above and information from any reader who can help by adding to this outline would be greatly appreciated. However, one further set of arms have been identified which may fit into the outline pedigree suggested above. The following arms were also listed by J. M. A. Wood in his book and they have been identified by Lord Lyon as follows from the Etherington Martyns manuscript.

James Anderson   Writer to the Signet

Azure, a saltire Argent between three Mullets in chief and flanks and a crescent in base Or.

Crest A crescent or increscent Or

Motto: Graditim

Fig. 11

This James Anderson was the son of Rev. Patrick Anderson and the following information concerning father and son has been obtained from published sources. Patrick Anderson was born in approximately 1629. He graduated from St Andrews in 1648 (M.A.). He was then admitted as the minister of Walston in 1655 but was deprived of his living in 1662 under the actions taken against Presbyterian ministers (see Chapter Three dealing with the life of Rev. John Anderson). He lived in Edinburgh for some years but was charged before the Privy Council for having held conventicles at Boghall, Biggar and his house during the years 1674–8. He was ordered to be imprisoned on the Bass or to pay a fine of 2,000 merks. A merk is not a coin but a measure of value. One merk is about two-thirds of a pound. He managed to pay the fine and agreed to move away from Edinburgh and retire to Dalkeith. He was restored to his ministry at Walston in 1689 after the Revolution. He married Margaret, the second daughter of James Threipland, the Chamberlain of Biggar. They had a number of children, although at this stage information is only known about one. Patrick Anderson died on 22 July 1691 at about sixty-three years of age.

James Anderson, a son of Patrick Anderson, was born on 5 August 1662. He obtained a degree as an M.A. and subsequently became a Writer to the Signet after being apprenticed to Robert Richardson. He married Jean, the daughter of John Ellis of Elliston who was an advocate. They had a daughter, Mary, who married David Pitcairn of Dreghorn. In turn they had a daughter who married someone named Robertson and they had a son who became Principal Robertson. In each of these cases it is likely that there were additional children also.

James Anderson, M.A., W.S., was an author, genealogist and antiquary. He was the author of *Selectus Diplomatum Numismatum Scotiae Thesaurus* and of *Collections relating to the history of Mary Queen of Scots* in four volumes published in 1727. He was Fiscal, 5 December 1689, and Postmaster-General for Scotland from June 1715 until 29 November 1717. He died on either 2 April 1728 or 3 April 1729. James Anderson matriculated the arms recorded earlier. It will be noted that although the crest and motto are different, the shield is identical to that of the arms described earlier for the Andersons of Dunbennen and others, including that used by Sir Warren Hastings Anderson, although the colours on the arms in Chester Cathedral are different, being as follows:

Argent, a saltire sable between three mullets (or stars) in chief and flanks and a crescent in base Gules.

Fig. 12

Lord Lyon has suggested that these arms may have been recorded at the College of Arms in London but enquiries to confirm this have not yet been finalised.

Having outlined various coats of arms which may suggest family relationships, it is fascinating to note some other sets of arms which bear certain similarities. Direct family relationships have not been proved in any of these further examples, but one has to bear in mind that the object of heraldry is to provide identification of a specific individual. On the basis that these are all authentic arms matriculated and recorded in the Register of Arms, then a reason for granting the particular arms is likely to have existed and been proved to Lord Lyon before the arms would have been matriculated. These examples provide a possible basis for future research and it would be very interesting to hear from anyone who is currently entitled to these arms or has any further information about the connection between the various branches of the Anderson family.

ANDERSON OF MILL HILL[6]

Apparently the second son of William Anderson of Dantzic was John William Anderson who was born in Dantzic in 1735-6. He was created a baronet on 14 May 1798 but died without issue in 1813. His arms were:

> Azure on a saltire ermine between three mullets and in base a crescent argent, an antique key, or, and a sword ppr hilted in gold, in saltire transfixed through the collar of the city chain.

ANDERSON OF FERMOY, CO. CORK, created a baronet in 1812

> Quarterly or and argent a saltire engrailed per saltire gules and sable between a mullet pierced in chief two boars' heads erased respecting each other in fesse of the fourth and in base a trefoil slipped vert.

> Crest A tree ppr surmounted by a saltire numettee sable

> Motto: Stand Sure.

The above arms incorporate many of the features of the arms matriculated by James Anderson in 1672.

ANDERSON – MAYOR OF LIVERPOOL IN 1860[7]

Gules a saltire between three mullets in chief and flanks and a crescent in base argent on a chief of the second a stag's head cabossed of the first between two martlets sable.

Crest An oak tree and equally pendent therefrom two weights ppr.

Motto: Pro Deo certo.

Fig. 13

These arms belonged to Thomas Darnley Anderson who, in addition to being the Mayor of Liverpool in 1859-60, was a founder member of Mersey Docks and Harbour Board. He was a member of the board from 1858 to 1866.

WILLIAM ARCHIBALD ANDERSON — 1860

Gules a saltire between three mullets in chief and flanks and a crescent in base argent within a bordure ermine, on a chief of the second a stag's head cabossed of the first between two martlets sable.

W. A. Anderson was a merchant in Glasgow and clearly connected with Thomas Darnley Anderson. As both sets of arms were matriculated in 1860, they were probably brothers.

ANDERSON OF NOTGRAVE (LO 20.2.1961)[8]

Argent a saltire engrailed sable between a crescent in chief and three mullets in the flanks and base all gules, on a chief azure a Maltese Cross of eight points between two crosses patee fitchy of the first within a bordure gules.

Crest A stag lodged sable attired and gorged of a coll. argent

Motto: Providentia Providebit.

Note in this case the reversal in the arrangement of the crescent to some of the other examples. The same feature is to be found in the next example.

ANDERSON OF DOWHILL

Argent a saltire engrailed sable between a crescent in chief and three mullets in the flanks and base gules all within a bordure azure.

Motto: Providentia et industria

Fig. 14

There are likely to be a number of other sets of arms containing similar characteristics connected with Anderson families and information about them and those who have current rights to use such arms would be gratefully received. This is an area which will be fertile for future investigation. It is hoped that the range of information about many families contained in this book will serve to stimulate others to participate in the absorbing world of genealogical research.

The members of a number of other Anderson families have provided me with family history outlines and this is greatly appreciated. For example some genealogical information is available concerning the following families:

1. The families descended from William Anderson *c.* 1446 from Perthshire to the present families who are descendants from John Lindsay Anderson who was born in 1870 and died in 1943.

2. Joseph Anderson *c.* 1575 whose daughter Margaret was married to Donald Armstrong by John Knox.

3. Robert Haddon Anderson of Greenock who was born in 1822 and one of the families descended from him is that of Sir Kevin Victor Anderson, Q.C., in Australia.

4. Much early Anderson family research was also carried out by Sir Francis James Anderson in addition to the material already extensively used in this and the previous chapter.

Any attempt to collate and develop all this interesting material would lead to delay in completing this book. It is hoped that much more work can be undertaken subsequently for publication at a later date. There may be considerable advantages to be gained from a joint research project undertaken with others interested in Anderson families.

The final two chapters deal in much fuller detail with two other family groupings; the Lindsay family and the Hampton family. In a sense, they fit earlier into the narrative, the Lindsays around Chapters Five and Six and the Hamptons with Chapters Seven and Eight. However, in order not to break the sequence of the Anderson families being discussed, they have been given separate chapters at the end of the book, although both families deserve attention in much fuller detail than it has been possible to provide here.

CHAPTER FOURTEEN

Patrick Lindsay (1686–1753)
and The Lindsay Family from *c.* 1050 to the present time

BECAUSE OF THEIR LONG HISTORY of service in Scottish affairs, a great deal has been written concerning the Lindsay families.[1] From these published sources it can be seen that the main family descent passes through the years as the Earls of Crawford, Earl of Balcarres, Lord Lindsay of Crawford and Balniel or the Earls of Lindsay, Lords Parbroath, Viscount Garnock and others and in particular the old title of Lords Lindsay of the Byres. As an introduction to other sources of information, the following paragraphs give a brief summary of the Lindsay family. This is followed by more detailed information about the branch of the family leading to Janet Lindsay, wife of James Anderson of Newbigging, discussed in Chapter Five. In addition, information is shown about other known descendants from the same branch of the Lindsay family. The name is often spelt Lindesay but the more modern form, omitting the 'e', is adopted here for consistency, although the older form of spelling may be more attractive.

The Lindsay family is understood to have been of Norman descent, originating with N. de Lindsay who was living in 1050. It is assumed that they became established in England and then Scotland after the Norman Conquest in 1066. The first ancestor in Scotland was Sir Walter de Lindissi, described as a noble and knight of the early 12th century. It may be found useful to refer to chart 3 as this shows the subsequently line of descent to Sir David Lindsay, Lord of Crawford 1314–55. He married Maria, daughter of Sir Alexander de Abernethy, and had four sons. The first son, David, died without issue. The second, Sir James Lord of Crawford, died in 1397 without male issue. The third son, Sir Alexander of Glenesk, died in 1382 leaving a son, David, created Earl of Crawford in 1398. As indicated on the chart, the present Earl of Crawford is descended from this family line, although for a number of years the title was held by the Earls of Lindsay. The fourth son was Sir William Lindsay of the Byres who obtained the Barony by charter on 17 January 1365 or 1366 on the resignation of his brother, Sir

Alexander of Glenesk. Sir William was a celebrated knight who died before 1393. His son was Sir William Lindsay of the Byres and his son, Sir John Lindsay, became 1st Lord Lindsay of the Byres in 1444. He died on 6 February 1482, leaving three sons and a daughter:

1. David, 2nd Lord Lindsay, died in 1490 without issue.

2. John, 3rd Lord Lindsay, died without male issue after 25 December 1496.

3. Patrick, 4th Lord Lindsay, married Isabella, daughter of Pitcairn of Feothon, and died 1526 having had three sons.

A most interesting account of a famous trial involving David, the 2nd Lord Lindsay, and his defence by his brother, Patrick who became the 4th Lord Lindsay, is to be found in Chapter 8 of the *Lives of the Lindsays*.[2]
The three sons of Patrick, 4th Lord Lindsay of the Byres, were:

1. Sir John Lindsay of Pitcruvie who had three sons. Sir John, however, died before his father, Patrick.

2. William of Pyotstone from whom the recent Earls of Lindsay are descended, as explained later.

3. David of Kirkforthar who was killed at Flodden in 1513.

Sir John Lindsay had three sons:

1. John 5th Lord Lindsay of the Byres.

2. Patrick of Kirkforthar who died without issue.

3. David of Kirkforthar who married Helen Crichton and died at a great age in 1592.

The descendants of John 5th Lord Lindsay of the Byres provided the subsequent descendants and holders of the title until the death of the 15th Lord Lindsay of the Byres in 1808. During this time the title of Earl of Lindsay was created and for a long time this branch of the family also held the title of Earls of Crawford. For a fuller explanation of the complicated history of these titles, reference should be made to the standard works on the peerage.
From David of Kirkforthar came descendants who were later recognised to be the 7th and 8th Earls of Lindsay and also the 16th and 17th Lords Lindsay of the Byres, respectively. David of Kirkforthar had a son, John Lindsay of Kirkforthar, who died on 4 December 1599. His son, Patrick died before him in 1584, having had two sons:

1. David of Kirkforthar who died before his father but his issue descended to David, 7th Earl of Lindsay, 6th Viscount of Garnock and 16th Lord Lindsay of the Byres. The latter died without issue on 5 May 1809. The

titles then passed over to the descendants of the second son, James, as described later in this chapter.

2. James Lindsay had a son, Patrick, who lived at St Andrews.

The last named Patrick Lindsay was apprenticed to William Williamson, wright in St Andrews, on 9 January 1639. He was admitted as a burgess on 10 February 1646. Patrick Lindsay became Deacon of the wrights in St Andrews and died before 21 January 1663. On 26 June 1645 he married Beatrix, the daughter of William Daes, merchant burgess of St Andrews. She died in October 1681. They had issue:

1. Hugh who was baptised in St Andrews on 13 September 1649 but died as an infant.

2. Patrick, his heir, baptised in St Andrews, 8 February 1652 — see below.

3. James who was baptised in St Andrews on 3 February 1659 but died before his father.

4. Beatrix who is mentioned in her father's will but died before him on 11 August 1660.

Patrick Lindsay, who was born in 1652, became a schoolmaster. He is recorded as having been the schoolmaster at Pittenweem. Afterwards he became rector of the Grammar School at St Andrews. Some references show him as Rev. Patrick Lindsay but he does not appear to be listed in Hew Scott, so this title may be incorrect and could at some time have arisen from the use of the term rector for the headmastership of the Grammar School in St Andrews, even though the term rector is usual in Scotland.[3] He was cognosced heir to his father before the bailies of St Andrews on 9 February 1687. He was admitted as a burgess of St Andrews on 13 June 1698 and he died in about 1722. Patrick Lindsay married Janet, the daughter of John Lindsay of Newton of Nydie. This John Lindsay was descended from Norman Lindsay who in 1627 was Chamberlain to John, 10th Lord Lindsay of the Byres, who became the 1st Earl of Lindsay and 17th Earl of Crawford.

Norman Lindsay had a son, John Lindsay of Newton, burgess of Anstruther, who died in 1676. His son was Alexander Lindsay of Newton who died in 1685, leaving a son, John Lindsay of Newton of Nydie, who was still living c. 1720. He had three sons who died without issue and a daughter named Janet. She married Patrick Lindsay as shown above.

Patrick and Janet Lindsay had the following children:

1. Patrick Lindsay, baptised on 10 March 1686. He and his family are discussed more fully in the rest of this chapter.

2. John Lindsay—born at St Andrews on 21 July 1692, but he died in infancy.

3. Alexander Lindsay who was born in St Andrews on 29 March 1702, but again he died young.

4. Beatrix, the eldest daughter, received a disposition from her grandmother, Beatrix Daes, on 3 August 1681.

The eldest son, Patrick Lindsay, was heir to his father and mother. Since he became prominent in the affairs of Edinburgh, quite a lot of information is available concerning his life.[4] In due course, his daughter Janet married James Anderson of Newbigging, so it seems very worthwhile to give a fuller account of his life. As a young man Patrick Lindsay apparently served with Sir Robert Riche's regiment of foot, seeing service in Spain until the Treaty of Utrecht in 1713. This series of treaties brought temporary peace to a greatly divided Europe which had involved the campaigns of the great Duke of Marlborough. Shortly after this time, Great Britain was involved with its own problems connected with the Jacobite uprising in 1715.

Following the Treaty of Utrecht, Patrick Lindsay returned to his home town of St Andrews and married on 22 June 1715. He was admitted to the freedom of the city on 10 September 1722. Although his father had been the rector of the Grammar School at St Andrews, Patrick must have inherited some of the skills of his grandfather who had been a joiner, for after leaving the army he established himself as an upholsterer. He moved to Edinburgh to set up his business, which prospered. He was also appointed as one of the magistrates of the city. He became the Dean of Guild and subsequently Lord Provost of Edinburgh. He was first elected Lord Provost in 1729 and he remained in office until 1731. He was again elected Lord Provost in 1733, remaining until 1735. It is reported that while he was serving as Dean of Guild in 1728, his shop was entered by thieves who murdered his apprentice and stole his cash box.

Whilst still Lord Provost of Edinburgh, Patrick Lindsay entered parliament in 1733. He was brought into parliament by Lord Islay. At about this time he wrote a book called *The Interest of Scotland, considered with reference to its Police, Agriculture, Trade, Manufacture and Fishery*. This was published in Edinburgh in 1733 with a second edition in London in 1736. The Duke of Argyle, hero of the 1715 Jacobite uprising, and his brother, Lord Islay, were two of the most powerful men in Scotland at this period. It appears that Lord Islay was very successful in ensuring that his nominated candidates were returned to parliament.

In 1736, Patrick Lindsay became involved in an unfortunate event which became known as the Porteous Riot.[5] Apparently, two notorious smugglers named Robertson and Wilson were captured at Pittenweem on the Fife coast. They were taken to the Tolbooth of Edinburgh and sentenced to death. Before the day of execution they attempted to break out from prison in company with others. Wilson, a bulky man, became stuck in a window frame and

Robertson was prevented from escaping. On the Sunday before their execution, the two were taken to church as was the custom at the time. Some of their comrades attacked the guards and Robertson managed to escape. Wilson, however, was foiled in his bid to escape but he delayed the guards so that they could not recapture Robertson. As a result, Wilson became something of a hero and martyr.

On 14 April the execution was due to take place and the city guard was under the command of a Captain Porteous who, because of both his duties and his temperament, was not popular. However, the execution of Wilson was completed but no sooner was the body taken down than the crowd became restive. Missiles were thrown at the executioner and the guard. Captain Porteous was somewhat out of temper and as a result acted rashly. It is said that he ordered the guard to fire on their assailants. His men obeyed but fired above the heads of the crowd. Unbelievable as it may seem, as a result they shot a number of people who had been viewing the scene from upper windows.

There was an outcry for Captain Porteous to be brought to trial. On 20 July he was found guilty by an Edinburgh jury and sentenced to death. A petition was presented to Queen Caroline, then acting as regent for the king, her husband, who was abroad. She granted a respite for six weeks which was made known five days before the date fixed for the execution. The announcement was greeted with considerable indignation in the city. An unsettled atmosphere prevailed in Edinburgh as 8 September approached, which was the original date set for the execution. On the 7th, an organised crowd started to assemble in the suburb known as Portsburgh. After various efforts had failed, the crowd broke into prison and carried the unfortunate Porteous to the Grass Market, the usual place of execution. There was a delay while a rope and a temporary gallows (a dyer's pole) were found. With makeshift arrangements, Porteous was clumsily hung by a means which could only be described as crude murder. The crowd disappeared leaving the suspended body of Porteous.

This outrage to the authority of the capital of Scotland caused a great deal of anger on the part of the government. Part of this wrath was directed towards the magistrates of the town. Patrick Lindsay was, of course, one of these magistrates. When the riot broke out they were assembled in a tavern in the Parliament Close. According to their enemies, they were engaged in merry-making. The magistrates claimed to be deliberating on measures to restore order in the town. Patrick Lindsay was sent by the magistrates to seek help from the Welsh Fusiliers who were on duty in the city. He took a verbal message from the magistrates to General Moyle and the Commander of the Castle asking them to deal with the rioters. Because of some previous problems, the officers refused to act without written instructions. They also refused to act 'because Lindsay evidenced signs of conviviality'. In a letter to the great statesman Walpole, Lord Islay wrote:

I have had great difficulty to prevent mischief between General Moyle and Mr. Lindsay. Moyle says that Lindsay was drunk and never asked for his assistance. Lindsay says that he told him he came from the magistrates to ask for assistance.

The Porteous riot was followed by a rigorous enquiry which failed to reveal who was responsible. Parliament, however, decided to take action against the City of Edinburgh. In February 1737 a Bill of Pains and Penalties was brought in for the 'chastisement of the offending city'. The bill was passed by the Lords but its passage through the Commons was much more difficult. One of the terms was that the Lord Provost was to be declared incapable of public office and condemned to a term of imprisonment. A number of other drastic measures against the city were proposed. Patrick Lindsay was one of the Scottish members in parliament who opposed this course of action as an 'insult to their nation'. As someone who had twice been Provost of Edinburgh, his speech on the matter must have commanded considerable respect. It is reported that 'Lindsay delivered a convincing speech against the proposal'. The end result of the Bill was only to impose a fine of £2,000 on the city for the benefit of the widow of Captain Porteous and to depose and disqualify the Provost.

The above account of the Porteous Riot was written before reading the very much fuller description of the events given by Sir Walter Scott in his book *The Heart of Midlothian*. Anyone who is interested will find that account most fascinating.

After he had retired from parliament, Patrick Lindsay was appointed Governor of the Isle of Man by the Duke of Atholl. Patrick Lindsay had married on 22 June 1715 Margaret, the daughter of David Monteir. They had five children:

1. Mary Lindsay, born in about 1716, who died unmarried.

2. Janet Lindsay, born in 1717, married James Anderson of Newbigging and Monthrive, Fife (see Chapter Five). They had three children:

    a. Alexander Anderson — see Chapter Six.

    b. Patrick Anderson — see Chapter Six.

    c. Margaret Anderson who married Alexander Nairne, an accountant in Edinburgh.

3. Patrick Lindsay, born in 1718 — see below for further details.

4. John Lindsay, born in approximately 1720 — see below for further details.

5. James Lindsay who was probably born in about 1722. He was a captain in the Navy of the East India Company Service who died in Bombay in India, unmarried.

After the death of his first wife, Patrick Lindsay married twice more. His second wife was Janet, the daughter of James Murray of Polton, but they had no children. Next he married Lady Catherine Lindsay, the youngest daughter of the 18th Earl of Crawford and Lindsay, and again there was no issue.[7] Patrick Lindsay died in his 67th year on 20 February 1753, having been served heir to his father on 10 May 1744 and heir to his mother on 30 August 1748. He died at the Cannongate in Edinburgh.

Turning to the descendants of Patrick Lindsay, two lines of consanguinity through female descent continue to the present day. The descendants of his daughter, Janet Lindsay, are to be found in the Anderson family and others descended from James Anderson, as detailed in the earlier chapters of this book.

The other line descends from the third child but eldest son who was also named Patrick Lindsay. He was probably born in about 1718 as he is reported to have died on 20 October 1801 in his 83rd year. In 1741 he was appointed Deputy Secretary of War. On 7 July 1747 he married Margaret, the only child of Thomas Haliburton of Eaglescairnie, near Haddington, Lothian. She died on 20 August 1819 at the age of ninety. Patrick Lindsay and Margaret inherited Eaglescairnie and it remained in the possession of the family for many years. As explained in Chapters Six and Seven, members of the Anderson family were frequent visitors to Eaglescairnie. It is understood that Eaglescairnie House still exists, being the property of Mr. Robin S. Salvesen. Patrick and Margaret Lindsay had three daughters, Catherine, Janet and Jean. The second daughter, Janet, married on 18 October 1794, her cousin, Alexander Anderson of Kingask (son of Janet Lindsay). She was born in about 1757 and was therefore 37 when she married Alexander Anderson. She died on 17 December 1825 without issue. See Chapter Six for further information concerning the life of Alexander Anderson. Jean died unmarried on 14 September 1821 aged sixty-three.

The first daughter, Catherine Lindsay, married on 23 July 1773 Alexander Stuart, the 10th Lord Blantyre. She died at Lennoxlove on 29 December 1822, three years before her sister and some thirty-nine years after the death of the 10th Lord Blantyre who had been the third of the sons of the 7th Lord Blantyre to hold the title. Catherine Lindsay and the 10th Lord Blantyre had issue as follows:[8]

1. Robert Walter, 11th Lord Blantyre, born 26 December 1775 — see below.

2. Patrick Stuart of Eaglescairnie, born 10 June 1777 and married 20 July 1810, Catherine Henrietta, daughter of the Hon. John Rodney. They had six sons and six daughters. Apparently none of the sons had surviving issue, although some of the daughters did.

3. William Stuart, born 1778, died unmarried in 1837.

4. Charles Francis Stuart, born 1780, died 2 December 1858.

5. Margaret Stuart, married 5 October 1809 and died without issue 20 October 1839.

Robert Walter Stuart, the 11th Lord Blantyre, also married a daughter of the Hon. John Rodney, namely Fanny Mary, the 2nd daughter, whom he married on 20 February 1813. They had issue:[9]

1. Charles Stuart, who became the 12th and last Lord Blantyre, born 21 December 1818 — see below.

2. William Stuart, born 3 March 1824 and married 6 September 1866, Georgina, the eldest daughter of Lieutenant-General G. B. Tremenheere, but died without issue 1 April 1896.

3. Walter Rodney Stuart, born 16 July 1826, and died 13 September 1838.

4. James Stuart, born 28 July 1827, died 11 April 1870 unmarried.

5. Henry, born 30 June 1830 and died 13 April 1842.

6. Catherine Stuart, married 23 March 1843 W. Rashleigh and died 8 November 1872.

7. Fanny Mary married 10 August 1847 to W. B. Ferrand and died 18 December 1896, leaving issue.

8. Georgina Eliza, married 27 May 1857, Rt. Hon. Sir Andrew Buchanan 1st Bt.

9. Caroline Henrietta married 12 August 1850, John Charles 7th Earl of Seafield and they had issue.

Robert Walter, the 11th Lord Blantyre, was accidentally killed during a conflict at Brussels on 23 September 1830.

Charles Stuart, the 12th Lord Blantyre, married 3 October 1843, Lady Evelyn Leveson Gower, the 2nd daughter of George Granville, the 2nd Duke of Sutherland. She was born 8 August 1825 and died at Nice, 24 November 1869. He died on 15 December 1900. They had issue:

1. Mary Stuart, born 15 September 1845, who died unmarried.

2. Ellen Stuart, born 31 August 1846, and married 15 June 1864, to Sir David Baird, Bt. — see below.

3. Evelyn Stuart, born 24 June 1848, who married 7 March 1871 Archibald, 3rd Marquess of Ailsa, and died 26 July 1888, leaving issue — see below.

4. Gertrude Stuart, born 11 November 1849, married 30 September 1875, W. H. Gladstone of Hawarden — see below.

5. Walter Stuart, born 17 July 1851 but died unmarried 15 March 1895 about five years before his father, so that the title of Lord Blantyre became extinct on his father's death.

6. Blanche Stuart, born 6 March 1867, died 7 September 1868.

Ellen Stuart and Sir David Baird had six children of whom two had issue who are still living.[10] These were:

1. Hilda Baird who was born on 22 April 1875, and married on 7 July 1908, Curtis Walter Lampson.

2. William Arthur Baird who was born on 20 March 1879 and married on 28 January 1908, Lady Constance Evelyn Conyingham. Their children include the 5th Baronet Sir David Baird, who was born on 6 July 1912.[11]

The descendants of Evelyn Stuart and the 3rd Marquess of Ailsa included three sons who became in turn the 4th, 5th and 6th Marquess of Ailsa. They also had two daughters, one of whom had issue. The 6th Marquess of Ailsa was born on 28 October 1882. He married on 28 January 1922 and died 31 May 1957, leaving issue. Archibald David Kennedy, the 7th Marquess of Ailsa, was born 3 December 1925 and married 7 April 1954 to Mary the youngest daughter of John Burn.[12] Their children are:

1. Elizabeth Helen Kennedy, born 23 February 1955, married in 1976 to Rev. Norman Walker Drummond. Their issue is:

   a. Andrew Drummond born in 1977.

   b. Margaret Drummond born in 1980.

   c. Marie Clare Drummond born in 1981.

2. Archibald Angus Charles Kennedy, the Earl of Cassillis, born 13 September 1956. He married in 1979 Dawn Leslie Anne the daughter of David Keen. Their children are:

   a. Rosemary Kennedy, born in 1980.

   b. Alicia Jane Kennedy, born 11 July 1981.

3. David Thomas Kennedy, born 3 July 1958.

Gertrude Stuart (died 25 April 1935) and William Henry Gladstone (born 3 June 1840, died 4 July 1891) the eldest son of the famous statesman had three children.

1. Evelyn Catherine Gladstone was born on 2 January 1882 and she died unmarried on 11 December 1958.

2. Constance Gertrude Gladstone was born on 2 May 1883 and she died unmarried on 11 March 1963.

3. William Glynne Charles Gladstone was born on 14 July 1885. After many years in public service including being an M.P. from 1911 to 1915, William joined the 3rd Battalion of the Royal Welch Fusiliers. He was killed in action on 13 April 1915. He had not married and his death in terms of the Gladstone family had wide repercussions. The effect on the village of Burton in Wirral a few miles from the family home at Hawarden was also very far reaching. The situation is well described in an excellent book published in 1984 by The Burton and South Wirral Local History Society called *Burton in Wirral*. The book describes how the death of this descendant of the Lindsay family led to the sale of the extensive Gladstone estate in Burton by Henry Neville Gladstone (later Baron Gladstone of Hawarden). William Glynne had made his uncle his heir in the event of his death without issue. Problems connected with this arrangement led to the need to reorganise the affairs of the Gladstone estates.

The above paragraphs outline the descendants of Patrick Lindsay from the elder daughter of his eldest son. They show that in addition to a number of Anderson families, many other families can trace their descent from present generations back to him.

To complete this review of the life and descendants of Patrick Lindsay, it is appropriate to consider the descendants of his second son, John Lindsay. He married in 1776 Margaret Maria, the daughter of Charles Hackett Craigie. John Lindsay who was a lieutenant-colonel in the Army died on 8 April 1780, only four years after his marriage. He had a daughter, Anne, who died unmarried on 7 January 1851. His son was named Patrick after his grandfather. He was born on 24 February 1778 only two years before his father's death. He became a distinguished general, having started a career in the Army just before his 16th birthday. In 1794 he was involved in operations in Holland with actions in November and December 1794 and January 1795. He was wounded in the leg on 30 December 1794. From 1797 to 1802 he served in the West Indies. This was followed from 1805 to 1808 by service in Naples, Malta and the Mediterranean. From 1809 he was engaged in the Peninsular War under the command of Arthur Wellesley, later the Duke of Wellington. The records show that in spring 1810 he was officially thanked by the Duke of Wellington for his exertions in the removal of upwards of 5,000 sick from hospitals when they were in danger of being overrun by a division of the advancing French army when it moved into Badajoz. He was in action at the battle of Bussaco on 27 September 1810 and at the siege of Badajoz in 1811. He saw further actions in 1811 and was with the forces which finally repulsed the French army in November and December 1813. As the French were forced back into France, Patrick Lindsay was engaged in the action under the walls of Bayonne on 13 December 1813. After that he was involved in the skirmish on the advance to Toulouse and was in the battle at Toulouse on 11 April 1814 which marked the final end of the Peninsular war and Napoleon's departure for Elba.

A large part of the successful army, including Patrick Lindsay, was despatched to Canada to repulse the American incursion which had been taking place since 1812. He saw service in Canada and U.S.A. from 1814 to 1815 including the affair of Plattsburgh in New York State. After the Treaty of Ghent which marked the conclusion of this campaign, Patrick was with the forces which returned to Europe to help recover the position in France. It is not certain whether he was in the Battle of Waterloo but he served in France from 1815 until 1818. After a time spent at home he served in New South Wales from 1827 to 1829. This was followed by service in India from 1832 to 1836. During this time, as Brigadier Lindsay, he was in command of the forces engaged in the campaign for the reduction of Coorg.[13] As a result of his success in this major operation, Patrick Lindsay was invested with the Order of the Bath and became Sir Patrick Lindsay.

Sir Patrick Lindsay started making his claim to the titles as 8th Earl of Lindsay, 7th Viscount Garnock and 17th Lord Lindsay of the Byres, by virtue of his descent from Patrick, 4th Lord Lindsay of the Byres. The 7th Earl of Lindsay had died in 1809 without male issue and subsequently Sir Patrick Lindsay has been recognised as the next holder of the titles from that time until his death on 14 March 1839, aged 61. As outlined above, he had an outstanding military career and his death was universally regretted.[14] He was the last direct male descendant from the eldest son of Patrick, 4th Lord Lindsay of the Byres. As has been shown already, there are many descendants from his cousin, Catherine Lindsay, and from his other cousin, Patrick Anderson, details of whom have been shown in Chapters Seven to Eleven.

Following the death of Sir Patrick Lindsay, the various titles have been recognised as passing to the descendants of William Lindsay of Pyotstone who was the second son of Patrick, 4th Lord Lindsay of the Byres. Fortunately, this male line of descent still continues through to the present time.[15] The current Earl is the 14th Earl of Lindsay and 23rd Lord Lindsay of the Byres. His elder son holds the title of Viscount Garnock and his son is the Master of Garnock. He was married on 2 March 1982 to Diana Chamberlayne Macdonald and one of the guests at their wedding was the Princess of Wales.

CHAPTER FIFTEEN

The Hampton and Lewis families of Anglesey, North Wales 1460–1968

IN CHAPTER SEVEN, it was seen that Alexander Anderson married Mary Margaret Hampton from Henllys Hall, Beaumaris, Anglesey. Very little appears to have been written concerning the history of the Hampton family which is curious, as they had a long history of public service in Anglesey and must have been very well known ever since the early days of their arrival in Beaumaris. A comprehensive pedigree is shown in the large book by John Edward Griffith *Pedigrees of Anglesey and Caernavonshire Families.*[1] Chart 4 shows an abridged family tree to which it may be found helpful to refer whilst reading this chapter. For the origins of the Hampton family, it seems one would have to study old records in Lancashire. William Hampton of Lancashire was appointed to Beaumaris Castle before the reign of Edward IV (1461–1483). It is reported that he was one of the garrison at Beaumaris Castle even in 1460. He appears to have held the rank of Deputy Governor but is likely to have been responsible for the castle as he and his descendants all remained at Beaumaris. William Hampton apparently received a grant of Henllys, originally the home of the Welsh Princes of Gwynedd.

William Hampton's association with Henllys Hall is still indicated in the house by a carved inscription over a large fireplace. With some other initials and a replica of the early coat of arms appears the name HAMPTON 1460. A long list of members of the Hampton family buried in nearly Llanfaes Church burial ground is given in a memorial roll in the church itself. This starts with William and shows the date 1460 but it is possible that this may not have been the year of his death. Members of the family were interred in a private mausoleum situated in the grounds of the church in an area set aside for the family.

Henllys Hall is situated on a high viewpoint above Beaumaris overlooking the Menai Straits with fine views of the North Wales mountains. It is reputed that Prince Llewelyn Madoc lived at Henllys.[2] He is supposed to have ruled the old Welsh town at Llanfaes whilst the Hamptons, resident at the castle, governed the English town of Beaumaris. Later the family moved from the castle to Henllys Hall.

According to Griffith, William Hampton was succeeded by Jenkin Hampton and in turn by Harry Hampton and again by a further Jenkin Hampton. Little is known at present about the early generations of the family until one comes to Richard Hampton. He was High Sheriff of Anglesey 1545 to 1547 and married Elin, daughter and heiress of William ap Gruffydd of Conway. They are buried at Llanfaes and the memorial roll shows the date of Richard's death as 1590. The roll also shows two earlier Richard Hamptons, one of 1495 and the other 1546, but they are not listed by Griffith. Richard and Elin (or Elyn) appear to have had some thirteen children of whom many died in infancy. A number of others married and may have had families. Some details are shown in the work by Griffith. Their heir however was another William Hampton who was Mayor of Beaumaris in 1562 and who died in 1609. He married twice. First, he married Gaynor, daughter of William Lewis of Presaddfed. They had five children, including Edward Hampton, most of whom lived to become adults but apparently none left issue. Secondly, in 1561, he married Elin, daughter of Rowland Griffith of Plas Newydd, the widow of Edward Holland of Plas Bern. They had seven children, the eldest of whom, William, succeeded to the Henllys estate after the death, without issue, of his eldest half-brother, Edward Hampton. William Hampton married first Margaret, the daughter of Robert Wynn of Voelas and had a daughter, Ellen. He married secondly, Grace, the daughter of William Glynn of Lleuar. He died in 1639 and was succeeded by their eldest son, again named William Hampton, who was Mayor of Beaumaris 1623-4. He died in 1665, being succeeded by his son, Robert Hampton. He was succeeded in turn by his son, also named Robert Hampton. This Robert Hampton had a son, Richard, and a son, Robert, in addition to four daughters.

Richard Hampton married Mary, the daughter of Rev. Hugh Humphreys, but died in 1728 (or 1725 according to the church roll) without issue. The roll does list a Richard who died in 1728 but the former entry is coupled with the name of his wife. The younger son, Robert Hampton, succeeded his brother to the estate and by his second wife, Mary Morris of Denbighshire, had a daughter and a son. Richard Hampton had been High Sheriff of Anglesey in 1722 and his brother, Robert, was High Sheriff in 1732. Robert Hampton's second wife, Mary, is shown by Griffith as having been buried on 16 July 1729, at Beaumaris. This, however, seems unlikely unless there was an unusual delay in the christening of their children. Mary, the daughter, is shown to have been christened on 28 November 1729 and William as being christened on 2 January 1731 but he died and was buried on 28 February 1731. Robert Hampton died in 1738 and this left his daughter, Mary Hampton, as his heiress. On 11 April 1746, when she was only about seventeen years of age, she married John Jones of Trefollwyn. From here starts an interesting attempt to keep the Hampton name alive. John Jones was High Sheriff of Anglesey in 1750. They had three children:

1. John Hampton Jones, born 24 February 1747 and died 12 September 1806.

2. William Jones, born 10 June 1748, but died in the same month.

3. Mary Jones, born 2 November 1749 who married William Lloyd of Rockville, County Roscommon.

John Hampton Jones was High Sheriff of Anglesey in 1770, having been appointed a Deputy Lieutenant in 1768. In 1770 on June 25 he married Emma, the daughter of Rev. John Lewis, M.A., the rector of Beaumaris, and Elizabeth Roberts of Bodior, Rhoscolyn, Anglesey. Griffiths shows in his book that the Roberts (linked with the Owen family) and then Lewis family pedigrees can be traced back in outline to the early ruling families of Wales. This is also shown by a pedigree roll chart dated 1851 which starts with an early Welshman named Beli Mawr who lived about twenty years before the Roman invasion of Britain.[3] The chart traces Beli Mawr's descendants, many of whom became the ancient rulers of different parts of Wales. It also shows their relationship to various British royal families over the years. It then relates the various lines of descent to a wide range of people living in the middle of the 19th century, including the Marquess of Westminster and John Lewis Hampton Lewis — see below.

Rev. John Lewis had several children and his eldest surviving son, John, was High Sheriff of Anglesey in 1764 and, although married, died without issue. This left the children of the marriage between Emma and John Hampton Jones as the heirs to the Lewis family line and tradition, including the Owen and Roberts pedigrees. Emma Lewis was born at Bodior on 26 January 1743 and died 31 August 1768. She and John Hampton Jones had two sons and two daughters. The daughters both died unmarried but the sons both married and left children.

Dealing first with the second son of John Hampton Jones and Emma Lewis; he was Robert Edward Hampton who was baptised on 14 May 1779. In due course he obtained a degree of Bachelor of Arts. On 22 January 1812 he married Susannah Dorothy, the daughter of John Williams of Penlarth Ucha, County Merioneth. They had a son, Henry Berkeley Hampton, and a daughter. The daughter was named Maria Dorothea Wilhelmina Sydney Hampton and she married a Robert Webster, described as being of the 99th Regiment. It would be of great interest to know if there were descendants from this marriage or if Henry Berkeley Hampton married and had children.

The eldest son of John Hampton Jones and Emma Lewis was John Hampton who was born on 21 November 1775. From an early age he had assumed the surname of Hampton, not Jones. His maternal grandfather, Rev. John Lewis, had a son, John Lewis, who was High Sheriff for Anglesey in 1764. He married Margaret, the daughter of Richard Hughes of Bodrwyn but they had no children. In his will, dated 21 October 1807, John Lewis left his estate in trust to his wife, Margaret, for her life and then to his nephew, John Hampton Hampton, or failing him, to his other nephew, Robert Edward Hampton Jones, for life.

The will provided that within one year after becoming entitled, he should 'take upon himself, herself and themselves and use in all deeds and writings where to etc. the surname of Lewis together with his, her own family name and shall quarter the arms of the Bodior Family (Roberts) and Lewis with his or their own family arms'. John Lewis died in April 1810 and his wife, Margaret, died in July 1829. John Hampton Hampton then became entitled to the estates with the condition that he assumed the name of Lewis also. He therefore made a petition in 1830 to the sovereign to be able to do this in the following terms:

> The Petitioner prays Our Royal Licence and Authority that he may continue to use the surname of Hampton and henceforth take, use and bear the surname of Lewis in addition to and after that of Hampton and that he may also bear the Arms of Lewis and the Bodior family quarterly with those of Hampton that his issue may also bear the arms of Hampton and that such of his issue may hereafter succeed to the said devised estates may — take, use and bear the said surname of Lewis and bear the arms of Lewis and the Bodior family.

This was granted by Royal Licence by King George IV on 1 June 1830.

It transpired however that the Hampton arms had been in use for a long time but not registered and recorded by the College of Arms. In order to be able to comply with the terms of the will, the arms were granted to John Hampton Hampton Lewis in 1832, based on his petition of 1830. The arms were not really used by themselves as this grant was immediately followed by the new grant of quartered arms. These arms must be unusual in that they bear two crests. Details of these interesting arms are given at the end of this chapter.

On 19 December 1796 John Hampton Hampton married Mary, the daughter of Richard Chambers of Whitbourn Court and Cradley Hall, Hereford, and the widow of Thomas Harris Freeman of Gains in Herefordshire. John Hampton Hampton was High Sheriff of Anglesey in 1813 and was appointed a Deputy Lieutenant for the county. He died 22 January 1843, his wife having died the year before on 3 January 1842. They had two sons and four daughters as follows:

1. John Lewis Hampton (subsequently Lewis), born 18 October 1798 — see below.

2. Joseph Hampton Hampton was born on 2 February 1800 and baptised at Twyning in Gloucestershire on 30 October 1802. He became a cadet in the East India Company Service in 1822 and was appointed an ensign on 11 July 1823. He arrived in India on 5 September 1823 and may have met Alexander Anderson who left India in 1824. He married at

Bareilly on 21 April 1824, Ellen, the daughter of Major Hall, also of the East India Company Service. Having been in the 25th Native Infantry, he transferred to the 50th Native Infantry in May 1824. He was appointed a lieutenant on 18 November 1824. He was in operations against the Kolls in 1832–3. From 1836 to 1842 Joseph Hampton Hampton was Adjutant to the 50th Native Infantry. After having leave from 1844 to 1846 he was engaged in the second Sikh war and was in the garrison at Lahore. He was also engaged in the Santhal Revolt in 1855. Appointed a captain in 1842, he became a major in 1854 and was appointed a lieutenant-colonel in 1858. He retired on 31 December 1861 with the rank of Hon. Colonel. Joseph Hampton Hampton died at Brynhyfryd, Beaumaris, Anglesey on 4 October 1878. He and his wife had at least one child, named John Lewis Hampton.[4]

3. Emma Hampton, born 2 February 1801, and died 5 August 1819.

4. Anna Maria Hampton, born 27 April 1802, and died as an infant.

5. Mary Margaret Hampton, born 7 September 1803, married 22 November 1825, to Major Alexander Anderson of Kingask (later Montrave), Fife, Scotland. See Chapter Seven and Chapter Eight for full details of their descendants.

6. Anna Maria Surman Hampton, born 4 January 1811, married 8 June 1835 to Charles Longman of Abbot's Langley, Hertfordshire.

It would be very interesting to learn if there were further descendants from Joseph Hampton Hampton (the second son) or from Anna Maria Surman Hampton, the sixth child.

Information is available, however, concerning the descendants of the first son, John Lewis Hampton-Lewis. He was born on 18 October 1798 and became a major in the 5th Dragoon Guards. He was a J.P. and a Deputy Lieutenant and High Sheriff of Anglesey in 1846. He married on 2 September 1833 Frances Elizabeth, daughter and heiress of Thomas l'Anson of Prior House, Richmond, Yorkshire. John Lewis Hampton-Lewis died on 5 September 1871 and his wife died on 30 January 1878 aged seventy-two.[5] Their children were:

1. Thomas Lewis Hampton-Lewis — see below.

2. John Vivian Hampton, born on 18 June 1835, married on 2 June 1868 to Lady Laura Elizabeth Phipps, daughter of Constantine George Augustus Phipps, 2nd Marquess of Normanby. He died 18 August 1890 leaving issue:

    a. Constance Laura who married in 1892 Brigadier General George Warren Biddulph, R.A., of Brandon, Suffolk, and had issue but details are not known.

3. Fanny Mary Hampton, born 4 April 1838, married on 2 January 1872 William G. Griffith of Llas Llanfair, Caernarvonshire. She died on 26 June 1908 leaving issue named J. L. Griffith, but any details of subsequent descendants are not known.

4. Mary Grace Freeman Hampton, born 11 June 1842 and died 20 October 1927.

Thomas Lewis Hampton-Lewis was born on 9 August 1834. He too became a J.P. and a Deputy Lieutenant and also High Sheriff of Anglesey in 1869. He was the Colonel commanding the Royal Anglesey Engineer Militia 1878 to 1891. In 1891 he became Honorary Colonel of that Corps, late of H.M. Hon. Corps of Gentlemen-at-Arms and formerly captain, 5th Dragoon Guards. He was educated at Sandhurst, entered the Army in 1852 and served in the Crimean War 1854 to 1856. A collection of his posessions are now on display in the military museum at Chester Castle.

He married 20 February 1872 Lettice Martha, the daughter of Henry Pritchard of Trescawen and died at Bodior, 10 March 1912, having had issue:

1. John Arthur Hampton-Lewis, born 26 March 1874 and died 2 August 1875.

2. Mary Gwendoline (Gwendolen) born 1 April 1875. She reassumed the name of Hampton on succeeding to Henllys. She married 3 October 1914, Lieut.-Colonel Bertie Cunynghame Dwyer, D.S.O. (1917). They assumed by Royal Licence 1915 the additional surname of Hampton. He became a J.P., a Deputy Lieutenant and was High Sheriff of Anglesey in 1929. He was born in 1872, Mary Gwendolen was his second wife and he died 9 June 1967.[6] Mary Gwendolen died in 1946 without issue.

3. John Lewis Hampton-Lewis, born 1 October 1876, died unmarried 6 June 1906. He was in the Royal Artillery and served in the South African War 1900–1901.

4. Dorothy Lettice, born 14 April 1880, married 2 August 1913, Randal, 14th Baron Louth of Louth Hall and The Orchard, Maidenhead, Berks. She died 16 August 1923, having had a son, Randall Patrick Ralph Oliver, Second Lieutenant 5th Inniskilling Dragoon Guards, He was born 9 December 1914 and married 13 February 1936 Gwendoline Mary, daughter of E. A. Cowling, but died shortly afterwards on 14 July 1936, as a result of an accident.

5. Sisili Myfanwy, born 11 March 1883, married 26 February 1908 Arthur Charles Davies, youngest son of Richard Davies of Treborth, Lord-Lieutenant of Anglesey. He was killed in action in 1915. She married secondly on 2 August 1921 Cyril Panton Vivian (born 12 September 1885) of Plas Llandayfran, Llangefni, Pentraeth, Anglesey, third son of

Hon. Claud Hamilton Vivian. By deed poll in 1947 following the death of Mary Gwendolen in 1946, Cyril Panton Vivian and Sisili Myfanwy assumed the additional surname of Hampton.[7] He died without issue on 23 November 1960. Sisili Myfanwy died on 2 February 1968 aged 84 years.

6. Thomas Herbert Richard Hampton-Lewis, born April 1885 and died 29 October 1911.

It would appear from the above that despite great family endeavours to keep the name Hampton alive, it may not have been possible. Some of the earlier branches of the family, for example Joseph H. Hampton, may have descendants bearing the name of Hampton as he had a son, John Lewis Hampton. It is not known however whether there were any subsequent descendants.

It appears that after long centuries of Henllys belonging to the Hampton family, it was finally sold around 1950. First it became a college used by Franciscan Friars. It was sold again in 1971 and is now used as an hotel. It is called Henllys Hall Hotel and hopefully this will enable the house to be maintained in use for many years to come. Anyone interest in the Hampton family history will find a visit to Henllys very worthwhile as is a visit to the nearby church of Llanfaes. In the porch of Henllys Hall are a number of stones set in the wall with family inscriptions and dates covering many years. Outside the house are inscriptions no doubt marking various times when the house was extended or altered. A booklet dealing with the History of the Post Service at Beaumaris interestingly contains a photograph taken from a sketch of Henllys dating from around 1830. In addition to the early date on the fireplace already mentioned, the main staircase in the Hall shows the family arms and the date 1852.

The coats of arms of the Hampton and Lewis families were combined with suitable quartering in 1830 and are particularly fascinating in drawing on their family origins as follows:

Quarterly: 1st and 4th, quarterly, 1st and 4th Argent a chevron sa. between three Cornish choughs ppr., in the beak of each an ermine spot (LEWIS); 2nd and 3rd gules, on a chevron between three bucks' heads cabossed argent a crescent of the field for difference (ROBERTS OF BODIOR); 2nd and 3rd gules, on a fess or, between a mullet in chief and an escallop in base argent, three martlets sable (HAMPTON). Crests 1st a Cornish chough ppr. in the dexter claw a fleur-de-lis (LEWIS); 2nd A wyvern amidst bulrushes ppr. (HAMPTON) Motto A Deo et Rege (HAMPTON).

Any further information concerning the Hampton and Lewis families would be welcomed and it would also be interesting to hear from or receive information about others who can trace descent from these families.

APPENDIX ONE

The Home family of Wedderburn and Paxton

In Chapter Six, it was shown that Susan Anderson married Reverend Abraham Home. This appendix deals with some additional information concerning the Home family and refers to problems experienced by Abraham before he met Susan. It also notes what happened concerning the Home family estates of Paxton and Wedderburn.

Abraham Home was descended from Alexander Home of Kennetsidehead who was put to death as a covenanter in 1682. He and his wife Jean who died on 5 October 1755 had at least two sons. The second of these was George Home of Broadhaugh, the minister of Chirnside, who married on 19 August 1706, Catherine (who was baptised on 20 January 1678 and died in 1745), the daughter of John Home of Ninewells and aunt of David Home, the historian. Their issue was:

1. Alexander Home, minister of Stichill.

2. Abraham Home who was baptised on 22 February 1711 — see below.

3. Rachel Home, baptised 11 January 1713.

4. Joseph Home, baptised 26 February 1714.

5. George Home, who became a baker in Edinburgh, was baptised on 7 June 1716.

6. Margaret Home, who was baptised on 25 March 1718, married on 23 November 1743, Robert Robertson of Prenderguest and died 30 July 1786. Her issue included Margaret Robertson — see below.

The second son, Abraham Home, married on 4 November 1748, Elizabeth Hay who died on 12 February 1790. He died on 2 October 1768. Their issue was:

1. George Home who was born on 12 December 1749 — see below.

2. Alexander Home, surgeon of 26th Foot, who was born 23 March 1752, and was put to death by order of Tipu Sultan in the Third Mysore War in 1792.

127

3. Margaret Home, born 18 August 1754.

4. Robert Home, born 8 April 1757.

5. Abraham Home, born 28 May 1763.

George Home (Rev.), born on 12 December 1749, died at Gunsgreen on 1 September 1836. He married on 7 October 1774 his cousin Margaret, the daughter of Robert Robertson of Prenderguest and Brownsbank and his wife Margaret Home. Margaret, the wife of George Home, died on 2 December 1828 aged eighty-one. Their issue was:

1. Abraham Home was born on 25 December 1775 — see below.

2. Margaret Ann Home.

3. Elizabeth Home, born 6 May 1778, married Rev. George Tough, minister of Ayton.

4. Hay Home, born 13 November 1779, died unmarried.

5. Jean Home, born 25 May 1782, married in January 1811 William Forman Home of Wedderburn. See below for details of the marriage of their daughter, Jean.

Details about the marriage of Abraham Home to Susan Anderson have been outlined in Chapter Six. Before he met Susan, Abraham Home had reason to expect that he was going to become the heir of George Home of Paxton — see below. In view of this he gave up his living as the minister of Ayton on 29 March 1814 and lived with George Home. However, unsuccessful attempts were made to persuade Abraham Home to marry the niece of George Home. She was named Nancy Stephen and was the adopted daughter of Ninian Home, Governor of Grenada. Following a disagreement about this matter, Abraham Home returned to the ministry. Apparently he was able to retain the annuity of £300 per annum given to him by George Home of Paxton at the time he had resigned from Ayton.

It appears that later, after the death of Susan, his wife, Abraham Home may have been the author of *Memoirs of an Aristocrat*, London 1838. Apparently this was a very controversial book which was banned for some time.[1] It appears to be an attack on certain members of the Home family. Although the reasons for this attack are not clear, they may have been connected with the earlier disagreement and the fact that he did not become heir to George Home of Paxton. Instead, Paxton and other properties passed on in the Home family through Abraham's sister, Jean, as follows.[2] George Home of Wedderburn died in 1720 but had married Margaret, the eldest daughter of Sir Patrick Home Bt. of Lumsden. They had issue:

1. David Home of Wedderburn who died without issue in 1762.

2. George Home of Culpeper, Virginia, U.S.A., who was born 30 May 1697 and died in 1760 leaving issue in America.

3. Patrick Home of Wedderburn died unmarried in 1766.

4. Francis Home died unmarried in 1732.

5. John Home, a captain in the Royal Navy, died unmarried in 1758.

6. James Home, a captain in the Royal Navy, was killed in action in 1758 and was not married.

7. Margaret Home married in 1732 Ninian Home of Billie. They had issue, Patrick Home of Wedderburn and others, who all died without issue.

8. Isabella Home married Alexander Home of Jardinfield. Their issue was:

   a. Ninian Home of Paxton who became Governor of the island of Grenada and was murdered there in 1795.

   b. George Home of Wedderburn and Paxton who presumably did not marry or, if he did, had no issue, thus raising the question of who should be his heir.

9. Jean Home married Reverend John Tod, the minister of Ladykirk. Although they had three sons and three daughters, only one daughter married. She was Margaret Tod who married in 1779 John Forman. She died in 1820 and their issue was:

   a. John Tod Forman who succeeded to Wedderburn as heir under the entail. He then assumed the name of Home and, although he married, he did not leave any children.

   b. William Forman Home was born on 24 April 1782. He married in 1811 Jean, the daughter of Rev. George Home of Gunsgreen and the sister of Rev. Abraham Home. They had a daughter named Jean Home who became the heiress of Wedderburn, Billie and Paxton. She married in 1832 David, the eldest son of Admiral Sir David Milne, G.C.B., and died on 14 April 1876.

Remembering that Rev. Abraham Home had refused to marry the adopted daughter of Ninian Home named Nancy Stephen, it is interesting to note that a member of the Milne family did marry someone named Stephen. Sir David Milne, who was born on 25 May 1763 and died on 5 May 1845, married firstly, on 16 April 1804, Grace, the daughter of Sir Alexander Purves Bt. and had two sons. One was David Milne who was born on 22 January 1805. He became an advocate and died in 1890. He married, as above, Jean, the daughter and heiress of William Forman (or Foreman) Home. David Milne then seems to have taken the name of Home. Their first son was David Milne-Home of Wedderburn, Paxton and Billie, who was born on 25 September 1838. He married firstly on 1 August 1867 Jane, the daughter of Sir Thomas Buchan-Hepburn Bt. They had four sons and four daughters. His second marriage was in 1889 to Mary Pamela, the eldest daughter of Charles David Cunyingham Ellis, and they had a son.

On 19 September 1819 Sir David Milne married his second wife, Agnes, the daughter of George Stephen of Grenada. She died on 27 August 1862.

It would be interesting to find fuller information about Agnes and Nancy Stephen; whether they were sisters or even the same person, what their relationship was to the Home family and whether the marriage of Agnes had any influence on the fact that the daughter of Jean Home became heir to Paxton rather than Abraham Home as had been expected.[3]

APPENDIX TWO

The Jones and Landon families

Much of the information about the Jones and Landon families included in this Appendix has been abridged from information left by Anna Eliza Jones. Fuller details can be made available to anyone specially interested in research into these families.

As already explained in Chapter Eight Anna Eliza Jones was the daughter of John Landon Jones and Sarah Jacques. The family of John Landon Jones can be traced from John Jones of Shepton Mallett, as follows. John Jones of Shepton Mallett married in 1710 Elizabeth Albin who died in 1749. They had eight children of whom the fifth was William Jones who was born in December 1722 and who died 1 April 1795. He married in 1755 Jane Kendall who was born 9 March 1721 and died 20 October 1817. They had five children:

1. John Jones who was born on 11 September 1756 — see below.

2. Edward Kendall Jones, born 8 October 1757 and died 14 November 1812. He married in 1784 Anna Kendall who died 20 October 1817, leaving Edward Henry Jones and other issue.

3. Charles Henry Jones.

4. Anna Jones, born in 1760 and died in 1827, married John West and left issue.

5. William Albin Jones, married Amelia Peak and had issue.

John Jones married Anna Landon — see below — who was born on 17 December 1761 and died 27 August 1858. He died on 6 January 1845 leaving issue:

1. Maria Jones who died in 1881.

2. John Landon Jones — see below.

3. Anna Brooman Jones who died on 13 January 1849.

131

4. Louisa Jones who died in 1868.

5. William Palmer Jones who died in 1869.

John Landon Jones married Sarah Jacques. He died on 20 April 1843 and she died in 1848, having had the following children:

1. William Landon Jones who was born in India on 18 April 1823. He was educated in England at St Paul's School, Southsea, near Portsmouth. In 1840 he entered Addiscombe and on 1 August 1842 proceeded to India as an ensign. He returned to England on leave in April 1858 and must have visited Scotland to see his younger sister, Anna Eliza. There he met Louisa Margaret Anderson and married her on 16 August 1859 when she was 19 years of age. They departed for India on board the steam vessel *Delta* sailing from Southampton on 4 December 1859. Their first child was born in India in 1860. After two years they came back from India, landing at Brighton on 4 March 1862. W. L. Jones died in 1878. He and Louisa Margaret had the following children (see also Chapter Seven).

    a. Margaret Julia Jones, born 20 June 1860.

    b. Edward Palmer Jones, born in 1865.

    c. James Alexander Landon Jones, born 5 March 1866.

2. Sarah Louisa Jones who was born (probably in India) on 2 November 1824. After living in England for some years, after the death of her parents she returned to India in 1849. She married on 2 June 1851 Lieutenant John R. Coombs of the 42nd Regiment (H.E.I.C.S.). While on leave in 1854 and 1855, they visited Scotland and he sketched 'Montrave House'. They returned to India and finally left in 1877. J. R. Coombs died in 1892 and his wife died in 1894. In addition to two sons who died as infants, their family were:

    a. Annie Louisa Coombs, born in 1853 and died in 1948.

    b. Mary Alice Coombs, born in 1856 and died in 1888.

    c. Alfred Coombs, born in 1862 and died in 1930.

    d. Edward Coombs, born in 1865 and died in 1943.

3. Ellen Jones who died on 9 June 1842.

4. Anna Eliza Jones who was born on 19 January 1833 and married Alexander John Anderson — see Chapter Eight.

5. Henry Albin Jones who was born on 23 November 1843 and died in 1883.

Information concerning the Landon family lineage includes the following: Philip Palmer of Richmond, Surrey, was the second son of Charles Palmer who was the fourth son of Sir Philip Palmer Bt. Philip married Jane Thompson of Nettleden, Bucks. He died in 1780 and she died in 1782. They had a daughter, Anna Palmer who was born in 1738 and died in 1819. She married in 1758 James Landon of Cheshunt, Herts, who was born in 1728 and died in 1812. They had issue:

1. James Landon, born in 1760 and died 1794, who married M. Dent, who also died in 1794.

2. Charles Richard Landon, born in 1766, became rector of Vange in Sussex and died on 11 February 1834, having married in 1802 C. M. Harrop, who died on 12 March 1844, leaving issue.

3. John Landon, born in 1767, painted in oils and water-colours. He married in 1806 and died in 1847.

4. Philip Landon who married in 1797 S. C. Harrop (possibly a sister of C. M. Harrop).

5. Harry Landon who died as an infant.

6. Samuel Landon was born in 1775 and married in 1812 Elizabeth Maud of Hillingdon in Middlesex. He died on 5 August 1844 but his wife lived until 1877.

7. Anna Landon, born 17 December 1761 and married John Jones — see above.

8. Jane Landon, born in 1764 and died 1838, married Joshua Collier of Tottenham who died on 13 March 1844, having had eight children, some of whom also had issue — see below.

9. Louisa Landon, born in 1774 and married in 1801 Charles Mayo of Cheshunt, who died on 10 December 1858 at the age of ninety-one. She died on 22 September 1852.

It is interesting to note that in addition to Anna Landon, two other descendants of Anna Palmer and James Landon also married members of the Jones family. The first of these was Mary Emma Collier, the daughter of Jane Landon and Joshua Collier. She married in May 1818 Edward Henry Jones who was born on 6 November 1790 and died on 12 October 1865. He was a wine merchant in London. She was born on 12 August 1795 and died 20 January 1869, having had issue:

1. Jane Anna Jones, born 1818 and died 1899.

2. Edward Kendall Jones, born 1820, died in 1903, was also a wine merchant in London.

3. James William Jones, born 1822, died 1896.

4. Caroline Mary Jones, born 1823 and died in 1919, having married someone named Jackson.

5. Henry Parr Jones, born in 1825 and died in 1909, married on 13 August 1863 Louisa Littler, the daughter of J. Littler and Anna Louisa Collier. Anna Louisa who was born in 1801 and died in 1851 was the sister of Mary Emma Collier.

6. Ellen Louisa Jones, born in 1827 and died in 1884.

7. Louisa Mayo Jones died as a child.

8. Charles Collier Jones, born in 1832 and died in 1882.

9. Frank M. Jones, born in 1834 and died in 1911.

10. William West Jones (D.D.), born in 1838 and died on 21 May 1908, became Archbishop of Capetown in 1897. He married Emily, the daughter of John Allen of Altrincham, Cheshire, and they had two sons.

NOTES AND SOURCES

Preface

1. Additional information may also be obtained in due course by following up a lead indicated by the catalogue of the British Museum Library. This records 'Answers for Alexander Duff of Braico to the Petition drawn up, printed and given in to the Parliament against him by John Anderson Younger of Westertoun (1687)'. Unfortunately, the original copy in the library was destroyed.
2. *Epitaphs and Inscriptions from Burial Grounds and Old Buildings in the North West of Scotland* by Andrew Jervise.
3. A similar coat of arms, but incorporating a different colouring, can be seen in the Great Hall of Edinburgh Castle not connected with the name of Anderson, but this must be exceptional.
4. In particular *History of Scotland* in three volumes by P. Hume Brown, Cambridge University Press, 1911.

Introduction

1. In particular, reference should be made to *Mary Queen of Scots* by Antonia Fraser.

Chapter 1

1. Matriculation of Anderson Arms in 1780 — see Chapter Five.
2. *Fasti Ecclesiae Scoticanae*, Hew Scott, Oliver & Boyd, Edinburgh.
3. Copy of letter from F. S. Ferguson to Mr. Bancroft, British Museum Reading Room (date 17 November 1960) in the possession of M. A. Anderson.
4. Hume Brown.
5. Mitchells — see also William Sievwright Greyfriars Burying Ground, Perth, 1893.

Chapter 2

1. Hew Scott.
2. Ibid.

3. *The Diocese and Presbytery of Dunkeld* by John Hunter, 1918.
4. *Historic Scenes in Perthshire* by William Marshall, 1880.
5. Ibid, also Mitchells *North Perthshire Monumental Inscriptions*.
6. Marshall.

Chapter 3

1. Hew Scott, and Catalogue of Edinburgh Graduates.
2. Register of the Privy Council.
3. Hunter.
4. Hume Brown.
5. Hunter.
6. Ibid.
7. *The Place-Names of Cumberland* by A. M. Armstrong and others, C.U.P., 1950.
8. Hunter and Hew Scott.
9. *The East Neuk of Fife* by Rev. Walter Wood, Edinburgh, 1887 and *Fasti Ecclesiae Scoticanae* by Hew Scott.

Chapter 4

1. Hew Scott.
2. *The Moderators of the Church of Scotland from 1690 to 1740* by Rev. John Warrick, Edinburgh and London 1913.
3. Warrick.
4. Ibid.
5. Ibid.

Chapter 5

1. *Scottish Land Names* by Sir Herbert Maxwell, 1894.
2. *A Hand Book of Mottoes* by C. N. Elvin, 1963. *Elvin's Mottoes Revised*.
3. *The East Neuk of Fife*, Walter Wood.

Chapter 6

1. The memorial can still be seen in the eighth division of tombs by the private road leading to Heriots Hospital. See also *Monumental Inscriptions in Greyfriars Churchyard, Edinburgh*, by J. Brown.
2. *Fasti Ecclesiae Scoticanae* and *A History of the House of Hamilton* by George Hamilton.

3. At No. 71 Princes Street according to the autograph book compiled by their son, Alexander Anderson.
4. *Sources for Scottish Genealogy and Family History* by D. J. Steel, Phillimore.
5. In the possession of Miss F. A. Anderson (see Chapter 10).
6. Hew Scott's *Fasti.*

Chapter 7

1. *Addiscombe: Its Heroes and Men of Note* by H. M. Vibart, Constable, 1894.
2. The autograph book is in the possession of Alexander Norman Anderson.
3. Warrick; also *Dictionary of National Biography*, Benjamin Bell.
4. *Eminent Men of Fife* by M. F. Conolly and *Addiscombe* by Vibart.
5. India Records, Orbit House, Blackfriars Road, London. L/MIL/II/38f. f. 463.
6. For details of this campaign see *Military History of the Madras Engineers from 1743* by H. M. Vibart 1883. Reference is made to the wound received by Alexander Anderson.
7. Notice in *The Scotsman* dated 30 November 1825.
8. *Old Parish Registers* 456/4 p. 63. Register House Edinburgh.
9. The Statistical Record, Fife.
10. The original is in the possession of Miss F. A. Anderson.
11. *Fife Pictorial and Historical* Vol. 2 A. H. Millar 1895; also books by A. S. Cunningham *Rambles in the Parishes of Scoonie* etc.
12. *Eminent Men of Fife* by M. F. Conolly.
13. *Addiscombe* by Vibart.
14. Recollection in notebook in the possession of M. A. Anderson made by Alexander William Anderson.
15. Ibid.
16. India Office Records — Cadet applications.
17. Ibid.
18. *Who Was Who 1897-1916.*
19. Letter from A. W. Anderson to M. A. Anderson dated 25 October 1959.
20. According to his death certificate — one of the 1855 issue showing very full details.

Chapter 8

1. Statement re birth in cadet application papers, India Record Office L/MIL/9/204 f. f. 151-159.
2. *Addiscombe* by Vibart.
3. Outline details left by Anna Eliza Anderson (formerly Jones) — originals in the possession of Miss F. A. Anderson.
4. Subsequently sold — whereabouts of originals unfortunately not now known but photographs are available.
5. A copy is in the family papers in the possession of M. A. Anderson.
6. Ibid.
7. Ibid.
8. The Edinburgh Academy Register 1824-1914.

9. *Addiscombe* by Vibart and India Office Records L/MIL/9/220 f. f. 248–256.
10. *The Times* and *Who Was Who*.
11. Cheltenham College Register — early years.
12. *Addiscombe* by Vibart.
13. India Office Records L/MIL/9/228 f. f. 717–22.
14. He also had at least one son — John Augustus Barron, born 1850, died 8 January 1936. *The Macmillan Dictionary of Canadian Biography.*

Chapter 9

1. Now in the possession of A. N. Anderson.
2. Family papers in the possession of M. A. Anderson.
3. These notes are based on information from Miss F. A. Anderson and descendants from Mrs. Baker and Mrs. Jones.

Chapter 10

1. Birth Certificate — A. F. Niblett.
2. Family papers in the possession of A. N. Anderson.
3. Ibid.
4. See Chapter Nine.
5. L. G. Turnill was a photographer and well known sportsman, the son of Willingham Turnill (born 1866, died 1947) and Rhoda Richardson who was well known as a water diviner in the Stamford area.

Chapter 11

1. *Young Artists of Promise* by Jack Beddington 1957, The Studio Publications.
2. *The Dovetons of St Helena* by Edward Carter, Cape Town, 1973.
3. Eaglescarnie should have read Eaglescairnie and refers to Eaglescairnie House near Haddington which still exists.

Chapter 12

1. *Epitaphs and Inscriptions from Burial Grounds and Old Buildings in the North West of Scotland* by Andrew Jervise.
2. Dumbennan is used here as F. J. Anderson spelled the name in this form on his chart. It is likely to be an old form for what is more generally spelt as Dunbennan.
3. In particular from J. P. J. Anderson.
4. See Chapter One.

5. *Fasti Ecclesiae Scoticanae*, Hew Scott.
6. Ibid.
7. For details of the matriculation see Chapter Thirteen.
8. There is no entry concerning this event on the Register of Arms according to Lord Lyon in a letter dated 27 May 1982.
9. This is also shown by a manuscript entry made by F. J. Anderson on a copy of Wester Ardbrake chart in the possession of J. P. J. Anderson and lent by him to me.
10. He was present at the death of Sir John Moore and was apparently his close friend. A number of books refer to these events, e.g. *Corunna* by Christopher Hibbert, also *Moore of Corunna* by Roger Parkinson, 1976.
11. Burke's *Irish Family Records*.
12. *Who Was Who 1929-1940*.
13. Information from J. P. J. Anderson on this and a number of other more recent events.
14. *Who Was Who 1916-1928*.

Chapter 13

1. Letter from Lord Lyon dated 27 May 1982.
2. *Who Was Who*.
3. A briefer note is in *Who Was Who*.
4. Without issue according to the *Dictionary of National Biography*.
5. *Who Was Who* and *Australian Dictionary of Biography*.
6. Burke, *Extinct and Dormant Baronetcies*.
7. Burke, *The General Armory*.
8. Burke, *Landed Gentry*.

Chapter 14

1. In particular *Lives of the Lindsays* by Lord Lindsay, 2nd ed., 1849, 3rd ed., 1858.
    Burke, *Peerage*.
    Douglas, *Baronage of Scotland*.
2. See also *The East Neuk of Fife* by Walter Wood.
3. Burke, *Peerage and Baronetage*.
4. *Dictionary of National Biography* and *Lives of the Lindsays* etc.
5. Hume Brown.
6. *The House of Commons 1715-54* by Romney Sedgwick, Vol. 2.
7. *The Scots Peerage*.
8. Burke, *Peerage and Baronetage*, 1901.
9. Ibid.
10. For fuller details see Burke, *Peerage and Baronetage*, current edition.
11. Ibid.
12. Ibid.
13. For details about the campaign see *Military History of the Madras Engineers* by H. M. Vibart 1883.

14. See *Lives of the Lindsays* for an extract from the *Fifeshire Journal* of 23 May 1839.
15. Details of the family lineage can be seen in Burke, *Peerage and Baronetage* Debrett, etc.

Chapter 15

1. *Pedigrees of Anglesey and Caernarvonshire Families*, J. E. Griffith, 1914.
2. Notes in Henllys Hall Hotel brochure.
3. By J. J. H. Harris of St John's College, Cambridge, and the College of Preceptors, London. Headmaster of the Grammar School, St Asaph, 21 July 1851. The chart is in the possession of M. A. Anderson.
4. *Officers of the Bengal Army 1758-1834*, V. C. P. Hodson.
5. *Landed Gentry*, Burke, and memorial in Llanfaes Church.
6. *The Times* 10 June 1967. *Who Was Who 1961-1970*.
7. Burke, *Peerage*.

Appendix I

1. *Memoirs of an Aristocrat and Reminiscences of the Emperor Napoleon by a Mid-shipman of the* Bellerophon *1837*, contains various particulars regarding the family of Home in Berwickshire.
2. *Landed Gentry*, Burke, 1898.
3. More information may be found in the Historical Manuscripts Commission Report on the manuscripts of Colonel David Milne Home, H.M.S.O. 1902.

BIBLIOGRAPHY

Anderson, John: *Historical and Genealogical Memoirs of the House of Hamilton*. Edinburgh, 1825.
> Gives an interesting account of the Hamilton family.

Brown J.: *Monumental Inscriptions in Greyfriars churchyard, Edinburgh*.
> Gives details of memorial for Alexander Anderson of Kingask, his brother and families.

Carter, Edward: *The Dovetons of St Helena*, Cape Town, 1973.
> Shows family connection between families of Doveton, Lawton and Anderson.

Cheltenham College Register (early years) refers to Charles Joseph Anderson.

Conolly, M. F.: *Eminent Men of Fife*, Cupar, 1866.
> Includes references to Major Alexander Anderson and to Captain Alexander John Anderson, his eldest son.

Cunningham, Andrew S.: *Rambles in the Parishes of Scoonie and Wemyss* (two separate but overlapping books).
> References to the history of Montrave, including a photograph.

Dickinson, W. Croft, revised by A. A. M. Duncan: *Scotland from the Earliest Times to 1603*, Oxford, 1977.
> This gives a very readable account of early Scotland. It may be regarded as additional to volume 1 of *The Edinburgh History of Scotland*.

Donaldson, Gordon, general editor: *The Edinburgh History of Scotland* in 4 volumes.
> Vol. 1. *The Making of the Kingdom* by A. A. M. Duncan.
> Vol. 2. *The Later Middle Ages* by Ranald Nicholson.
> Vol. 3. *James V – James VII* by Gordon Donaldson.
> Vol. 4. *1689 to the Present* by William Ferguson. Oliver & Boyd.
> These four volumes must form essential reading for anyone who wishes to obtain a comprehensive understanding of the history of Scotland. However, the three volumes by Professor Hume Brown still have many features of value.

Edinburgh Academy Register refers to Patrick Charles Anderson.

Edward, Michael: *Red Year*, Hamish Hamilton, 1973.
> A detailed account of the Indian Mutiny.

Ferguson, A. D. and Anderson, C. F.: *Records of a Family of Andersons of Peterhead from 1560*, 1936.
> A valuable compilation covering many Anderson families but mainly in outline only.

Forbes-Mitchell, William: *The Relief of Lucknow*. The Folio Society, London, 1962.
> W. Forbes-Mitchell was a member of the 93rd Sutherland Highlanders sent out to India in 1857. His account of the mutiny campaign makes fascinating reading. He recounts the battle experiences of Cawnpore as well as Lucknow.

Fraser, Antonia: *Mary Queen of Scots*.
> Gives a very detailed account of the life of the Queen and includes references to some members of the Lindsay family who were involved.

—— *Cromwell Our Chief of Men*.
> A very detailed but readable study which includes many references affecting Scotland.

—— *King Charles II*.
> Again an excellent book for anyone wishing to gain a fuller understanding of the period.

Gilbert, W. M.: *Edinburgh in the Nineteenth Century*, 1901, J. & R. Allan.
   A most interesting record of major events in Edinburgh right through the century.
Griffith, J. E.: *Pedigrees of Anglesey and Caernarvonshire Families*, 1914.
   A most valuable and detailed study which includes the Hampton Family.
Hamilton, George, Lt.-Col.: *The House of Hamilton*, J. Skinner & Co. Ltd., Edinburgh 1933.
   A very useful detailed study.
Hamilton-Edwards, Gerald: *In Search of Scottish Ancestry*, Phillimore, 1973 (reprinted 1980).
Historical Manuscripts Commission. *Report on the Manuscripts of Col. David Milne Home*, H.M.S.O. 1902.
Hume Brown, P.: *History of Scotland*, in 3 volumes. Cambridge, 1901.
   An excellent work showing the relationship between Church and State with date references detailed on the pages of the books.
Hunter, Rev. John: *The Diocese and Presbytery of Dunkeld 1660–1689*, in 2 vols., Hodder and Stoughton, 1918.
   Has detailed entries concerning Rev. Alexander Anderson of Auchtergaven and his son, Rev. John Anderson.
Innes of Learney, Sir Thomas (Lord Lyon): *Scots Heraldry*, Oliver and Boyd, 1934 and 1956.
   This excellent work has now been revised by his son, the present Lord Lyon.
Jervise, Andrew: *Epitaphs and Inscriptions from Burials Grounds and old Buildings in the North East of Scotland.*
Leasor, James: *Follow the Drum* (a novel).
   Gives a very readable description of some of the horrors of the Indian Mutiny.
Lindsay, A. W. C.: *Lives of the Lindsays or a Memoir of the Houses of Crawford and Balcarres* in 3 volumes, 1858.
Macpherson, Sir Aeneas: 'The Loyall Dissuasive', ed. by Rev. Alexander D. Murdoch, Edinburgh, *Scottish History Society*, vol. 41.
   This book contains a full account of the historical relationship between the Macintosh and Macpherson clans.
—— Alexander: *Glimpses of Church and Social Life in the Highlands in Olden Times*, 1893.
   Includes a number of references to the Macpherson clan.
—— William Cheyne: *The Chiefs of Clan Macpherson*, 1947.
Marshall, William: *Historic Scenes in Perthshire*, W. Oliphant, Edinburgh, 1880.
   Includes some information concerning the life of Rev. Alexander Anderson and information about his tombstone.
Maxwell, Sir Herbert: *Scottish Land Names*, Blackwood, 1894.
Meacham, Ellis K.: *The East Indiaman* (a novel), Hodder and Stoughton.
   Gives some impression of seagoing conditions in the naval service of the Honourable East India Company in the early 19th century. Includes a short bibliography.
Millar, A. H.: *Fife, Pictorial and Historical* in 2 vols., 1895.
   Gives information about Montrave, including a photograph and also has other family references.
Mitchell, J. F. and S. Mitchell: *Monumental Inscriptions in North Perthshire*, Scottish Genealogy Society, 1975.
   Includes details of Auchtergaven and Perth — Greyfriars.
Parkinson, Roger: *Moore of Corunna*, 1976.
   Refers to Paul Anderson who was a close friend of Sir John Moore. A number of other books about Corunna also include references about Paul Anderson.
Paul, Sir James Balfour: *The Scots Peerage* in 9 volumes, 1904–1914.

Scottish Record Society, 'Roll of Edinburgh Burgesses'.
  Refers to James Anderson of Newbigging and his son Alexander Anderson of Kingask.
Scott, Hew: *Fasti Ecclesiæ Scoticanæ*.
  Includes references to all known ministers in the Church of Scotland, in most cases
  with some biographical notes.
Scott, Sir Walter: *The Heart of Midlothian*.
  This novel gives a very full description of the events associated with the Porteous
  Riot in Edinburgh in 1736.
Sedgwick, Romney: *The House of Commons 1715-54*.
  See reference to Patrick Lindsay, M.P.
Sievwright, William: *Greyfriars Burying Ground — its Epitaphs and Inscriptions*, 1873.
  Gives records of tombstones in Perth, a number of which do not now exist.
*Society of Writers to Her Majesty's Signet, History of, with a list of the Members of the
  Society*, 1890, T. & A. Constable, Edinburgh, University Press.
  Includes reference to Patrick Anderson, W.S.
Steel, D. J.: *Sources for Scottish Genealogy and Family History*, Phillimore.
Stuart, Rev. A. Moody: *The Life and Letters of Elizabeth Last Duchess of Gordon*, 1865.
  This work outlines the life of Elizabeth Brodie.
Stuart, Margaret and Sir James Balfour Paul: *Scottish Family History*, Edinburgh 1930.
Vibart, H.M.: *Addiscombe: Its Heroes and Men of Note*, 1894, Constable.
  Lists all cadets who went to Addiscombe and has additional notes about Alexander
  Anderson. The book gives a graphic account of the life led by cadets at the college.
—— *Military History of the Madras Engineers from 1743*, in two volumes, 1883, W. H.
  Allen & Co.
  This large work includes reference to Alexander Anderson being wounded at Talneir
  and also refers to Brigadier Lindsay and the campaign at Coorg in India.
Walford, E.: *County Families of the U.K.*, 1876.
  Includes a reference to Montrave.
Warrick, Rev. John: *The Moderators of the Church of Scotland from 1690 to 1740*,
  Oliphant, Anderson and Ferrier, 1913.
  This work includes information about all the moderators in the above period, includ-
  ing Rev. William Hamilton, Rev. Alexander Anderson and Rev. Lauchlan McIntosh.
Wood, James Mackenzie Anderson: *Andersons in Phingask and their descendants*, 1910.
  A most useful work giving leads to many other Anderson families from the north east
  of Scotland.
Wood, Rev. Walter: *The East Neuk of Fife*, Edinburgh, 1887.
  Contains a number of references to Anderson and Nairne families from whom Walter
  Wood was a descendant.

KEY TO ABBREVIATIONS

ANDERSON FAMILIES

a.	adopted
b.	born
bd.	buried
c.	circa — approximately
d.	died
dsp.	died without issue
dspm.	died without male issue
dvp.	died before his father
fl.	living
kia.	killed in action
m.	married
m.dis.	divorced
ob.coel.	died a bachelor
ob.inf.	died in infancy
ob.inn.	died a spinster
ob.juv.	died in childhood
s.	a son
xd.	baptised
DL	Deputy Lieutenant
JP	Justice of the Peace

Anderson of Westertown in Banff, Scotland

Anderson
see Chart No. 2
Fig. 5, p. 94
for continuation

Anderson

James Anderson (Rev.)
b. (c.) 1535   d. 31.1.1603
m. Agnes Haliburton (d. after 1603)

Henry Anderson
Burgess of Perth
b. (c.) 1560   d (c.) 1627
m. Helen Colt   d. 8.6.1618

Henry Anderson (Rev.)
b. 1850   d. 5.6.1641
m. Marion Redheuch
d. (c.) 1655

William Anderson
d. (c.) 1670

Henry Anderson

Alexander Anderson (Rev.) (M.A.)
b. (c.) 1675   d. 9.11.1737
m. (c.) 1697 Isabel Hay
d. 1720

George Anderson

Jean Anderson

Anne Anderson xd. 14.6.1706	John Anderson xd. 12.5.1709	Anne Anderson xd. 6.5.1711	John Anderson xd. 11.10.1712	Alexander Anderson xd. 8.4.1714	George Anderson xd. 18.11.1716	Robert Anderson xd. 31.10.1717

Margaret Anderson
b. (c.) 1697   d. 17.2.1770
m. (1) Laurence Watson (Rev.)
d. 25.8.1718.

John Watson
b. 1716

Elizabeth Watson
b. 1718

m. (2) Lauchlan McIntosh (Rev.)
b. (c.) 1690   d. 13.5.1744

Jean McIntosh
d. 8.3.1759
m. John Ballingal (Rev.)
with issue

John McIntosh
xd. 17.7.1726
d. 1790

Robert McIntosh
Advocate
xd. 6.8.1727
d. 15.4.1805

Bertha McIntosh
xd. 20.10.1728

Lauchlin McIntosh
xd. 23.10.1730

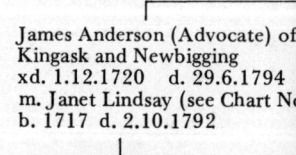

James Anderson (Advocate) of
Kingask and Newbigging
xd. 1.12.1720   d. 29.6.1794
m. Janet Lindsay (see Chart No
b. 1717 d. 2.10.1792

contd. overleaf

Alexander Anderson (Rev.)
b. 1593   d. 30.1.1665
m. Grissal Ballendene
b. 1597 d. 11.7.1665

William Anderson
d. (c.) 1641
Burgess of Perth

John Anderson (Rev.) (M.A.)
b. (c.) 1627   d. Feb. 1708
m. Anna Waugh   d. 1726

ne Anderson
16.1.1729
14.3.1706 James Nairne (Rev.) (M.A.)
b.1680   d. 12.5.1771

Mary Anderson
m. 1718 James Greig (Rev.) (M.A.)
b. 1681   d. 14.5.1727

Margaret Anderson

Ann Greig
b. 1720

John Nairne
ob. inf.

James Nairne
ob. inf.

Janet Nairne
ob. inf.

John Nairne (Rev.) (M.A.)
b. 20.1.1711   d. 15.2.1795
m. 5.4.1749 Elizabeth Gordon

James Nairne
(Rev.) (D.D.)
b. 30.8.1750
d. 15.7.1819
m. 12.1.1778
Helen Kyd
b. 1765
d. 3.2.1836

Helen Nairne
b. 6.1.1752
m. 17.7.1780
George Hall

Alexander Nairne
(Accountant)
b. 27.8.1753
m. 1794
Margaret Anderson
b. 1759
d. 9.12.1838

Ann Nairne
b. 16.2.1755
m. 25.12.1780
Alexander Wood
with issue

Mary Nairne

Jean Nairne
b. 22.1.1759   d. 30.10.1779
m. 27.1.1779 James Forrester
(Rev.)

Peter Nairne
b. 17.6.1761
d. 6.8.1786

hn Nairne
apt.—Navy)
14.10.1778
23.7.1807

Hannah Nairne
b. 29.5.1780
d. 19.10.1849
m. 29.5.1805
John Forman
(W.S.)
with issue

James Nairne (W.S.)
b. 29.8.1782
d. 20.10.1847
m. 9.4.1807
Elizabeth Hill
d. 1869

Alexander Nairne
(Capt. HEICS Navy)
b. 20.2.1785

Elizabeth Nairne
b. 4.11.1787
d. 16.12.1788

Ann Elmsall Nairne
b. 11.1.1791
m. 5.6.1817
William Scott

Charles Nairne
b. 23.12.1794
d. 20.1.1837
m. 20.9.1820
Amelia Forbes
d. 20.3.1874
with issue

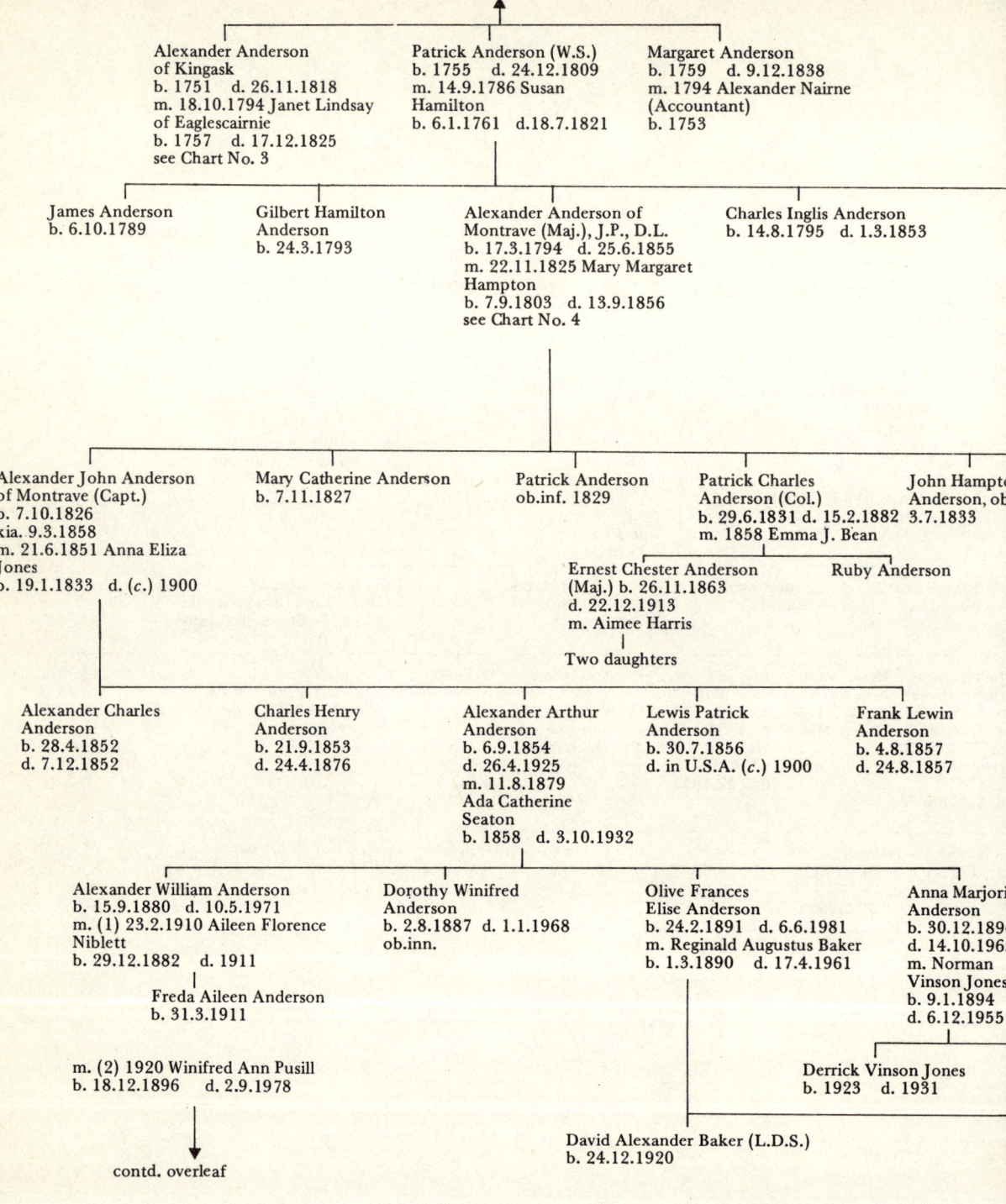

Alexander Anderson
of Kingask
b. 1751   d. 26.11.1818
m. 18.10.1794 Janet Lindsay
of Eaglescairnie
b. 1757   d. 17.12.1825
see Chart No. 3

Patrick Anderson (W.S.)
b. 1755   d. 24.12.1809
m. 14.9.1786 Susan
Hamilton
b. 6.1.1761   d.18.7.1821

Margaret Anderson
b. 1759   d. 9.12.1838
m. 1794 Alexander Nairne
(Accountant)
b. 1753

James Anderson
b. 6.10.1789

Gilbert Hamilton
Anderson
b. 24.3.1793

Alexander Anderson of
Montrave (Maj.), J.P., D.L.
b. 17.3.1794   d. 25.6.1855
m. 22.11.1825 Mary Margaret
Hampton
b. 7.9.1803   d. 13.9.1856
see Chart No. 4

Charles Inglis Anderson
b. 14.8.1795   d. 1.3.1853

Alexander John Anderson
of Montrave (Capt.)
b. 7.10.1826
kia. 9.3.1858
m. 21.6.1851 Anna Eliza
Jones
b. 19.1.1833   d. (c.) 1900

Mary Catherine Anderson
b. 7.11.1827

Patrick Anderson
ob.inf. 1829

Patrick Charles
Anderson (Col.)
b. 29.6.1831 d. 15.2.1882
m. 1858 Emma J. Bean

John Hampto
Anderson, ob.
3.7.1833

Ernest Chester Anderson
(Maj.) b. 26.11.1863
d. 22.12.1913
m. Aimee Harris
|
Two daughters

Ruby Anderson

Alexander Charles
Anderson
b. 28.4.1852
d. 7.12.1852

Charles Henry
Anderson
b. 21.9.1853
d. 24.4.1876

Alexander Arthur
Anderson
b. 6.9.1854
d. 26.4.1925
m. 11.8.1879
Ada Catherine
Seaton
b. 1858   d. 3.10.1932

Lewis Patrick
Anderson
b. 30.7.1856
d. in U.S.A. (c.) 1900

Frank Lewin
Anderson
b. 4.8.1857
d. 24.8.1857

Alexander William Anderson
b. 15.9.1880   d. 10.5.1971
m. (1) 23.2.1910 Aileen Florence
Niblett
b. 29.12.1882   d. 1911
|
Freda Aileen Anderson
b. 31.3.1911

m. (2) 1920 Winifred Ann Pusill
b. 18.12.1896   d. 2.9.1978

Dorothy Winifred
Anderson
b. 2.8.1887 d. 1.1.1968
ob.inn.

Olive Frances
Elise Anderson
b. 24.2.1891   d. 6.6.1981
m. Reginald Augustus Baker
b. 1.3.1890   d. 17.4.1961

Anna Marjorie
Anderson
b. 30.12.1894
d. 14.10.1965
m. Norman
Vinson Jones
b. 9.1.1894
d. 6.12.1955

Derrick Vinson Jones
b. 1923   d. 1931

David Alexander Baker (L.D.S.)
b. 24.12.1920

contd. overleaf

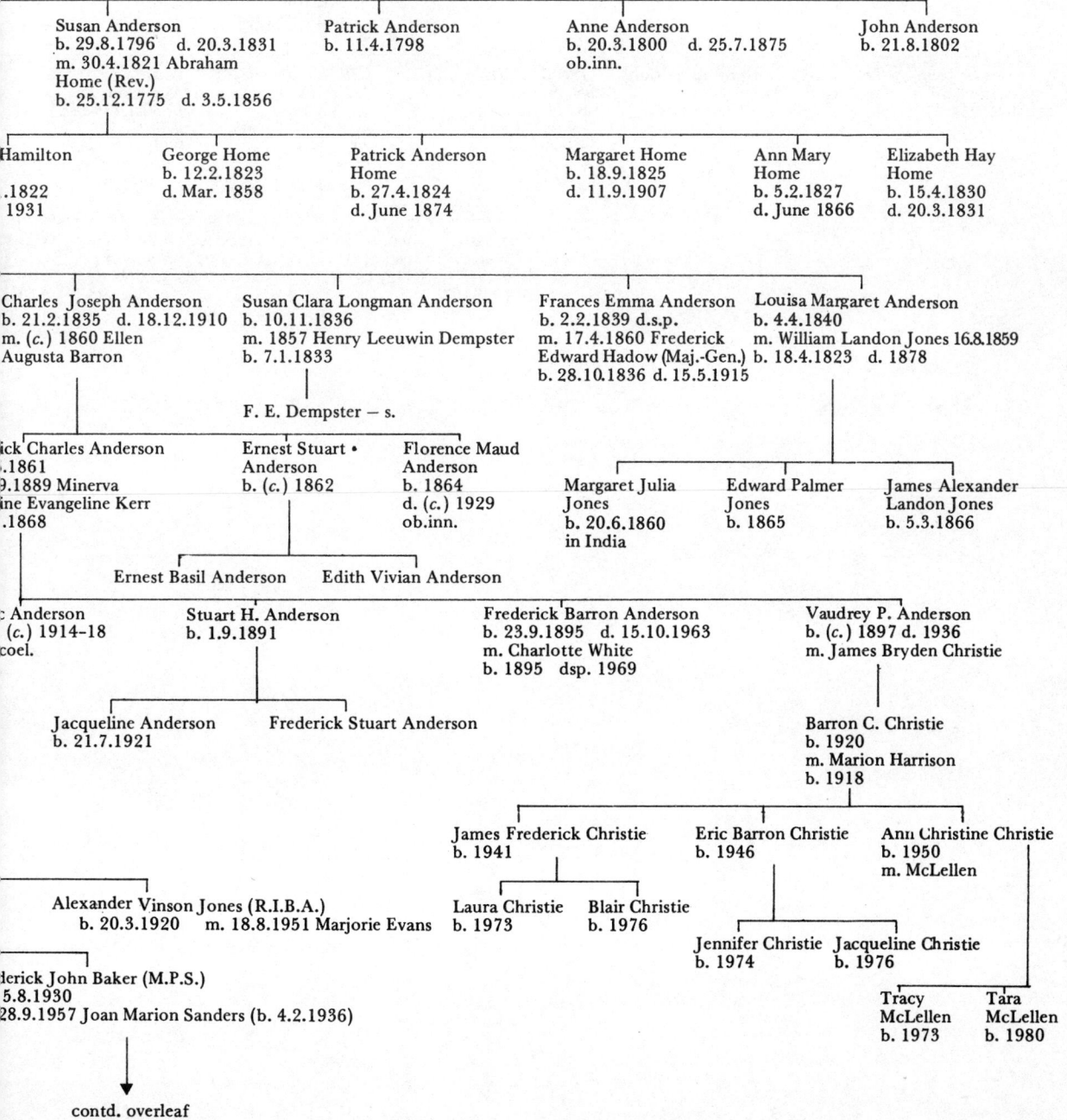

Susan Anderson
b. 29.8.1796 d. 20.3.1831
m. 30.4.1821 Abraham
Home (Rev.)
b. 25.12.1775 d. 3.5.1856

Patrick Anderson
b. 11.4.1798

Anne Anderson
b. 20.3.1800 d. 25.7.1875
ob.inn.

John Anderson
b. 21.8.1802

.Hamilton

.1822

1931

George Home
b. 12.2.1823
d. Mar. 1858

Patrick Anderson
Home
b. 27.4.1824
d. June 1874

Margaret Home
b. 18.9.1825
d. 11.9.1907

Ann Mary
Home
b. 5.2.1827
d. June 1866

Elizabeth Hay
Home
b. 15.4.1830
d. 20.3.1831

Charles Joseph Anderson
b. 21.2.1835 d. 18.12.1910
m. (c.) 1860 Ellen
Augusta Barron

Susan Clara Longman Anderson
b. 10.11.1836
m. 1857 Henry Leeuwin Dempster
b. 7.1.1833

Frances Emma Anderson
b. 2.2.1839 d.s.p.
m. 17.4.1860 Frederick
Edward Hadow (Maj.-Gen.)
b. 28.10.1836 d. 15.5.1915

Louisa Margaret Anderson
b. 4.4.1840
m. William Landon Jones 16.8.1859
b. 18.4.1823 d. 1878

F. E. Dempster — s.

ick Charles Anderson
.1861
9.1889 Minerva
ine Evangeline Kerr
.1868

Ernest Stuart •
Anderson
b. (c.) 1862

Florence Maud
Anderson
b. 1864
d. (c.) 1929
ob.inn.

Margaret Julia
Jones
b. 20.6.1860
in India

Edward Palmer
Jones
b. 1865

James Alexander
Landon Jones
b. 5.3.1866

Ernest Basil Anderson   Edith Vivian Anderson

c Anderson
(c.) 1914–18
coel.

Stuart H. Anderson
b. 1.9.1891

Frederick Barron Anderson
b. 23.9.1895 d. 15.10.1963
m. Charlotte White
b. 1895 dsp. 1969

Vaudrey P. Anderson
b. (c.) 1897 d. 1936
m. James Bryden Christie

Jacqueline Anderson
b. 21.7.1921

Frederick Stuart Anderson

Barron C. Christie
b. 1920
m. Marion Harrison
b. 1918

James Frederick Christie
b. 1941

Eric Barron Christie
b. 1946

Ann Christine Christie
b. 1950
m. McLellen

Alexander Vinson Jones (R.I.B.A.)
b. 20.3.1920   m. 18.8.1951 Marjorie Evans

Laura Christie
b. 1973

Blair Christie
b. 1976

Jennifer Christie
b. 1974

Jacqueline Christie
b. 1976

derick John Baker (M.P.S.)
5.8.1930
28.9.1957 Joan Marion Sanders (b. 4.2.1936)

Tracy
McLellen
b. 1973

Tara
McLellen
b. 1980

contd. overleaf

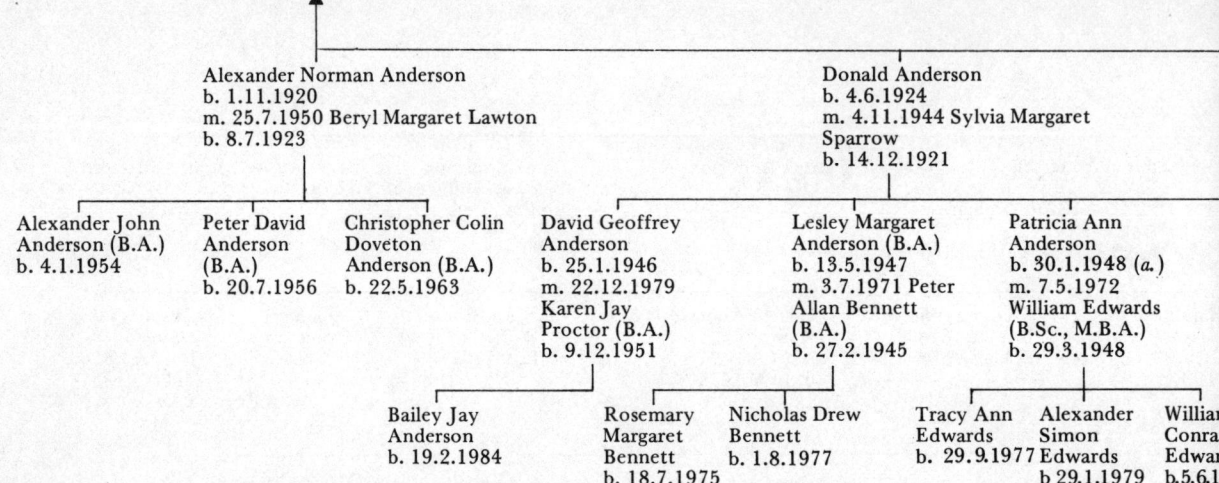

Alexander Norman Anderson
b. 1.11.1920
m. 25.7.1950 Beryl Margaret Lawton
b. 8.7.1923

Donald Anderson
b. 4.6.1924
m. 4.11.1944 Sylvia Margaret
Sparrow
b. 14.12.1921

Alexander John
Anderson (B.A.)
b. 4.1.1954

Peter David
Anderson
(B.A.)
b. 20.7.1956

Christopher Colin
Doveton
Anderson (B.A.)
b. 22.5.1963

David Geoffrey
Anderson
b. 25.1.1946
m. 22.12.1979
Karen Jay
Proctor (B.A.)
b. 9.12.1951

Lesley Margaret
Anderson (B.A.)
b. 13.5.1947
m. 3.7.1971 Peter
Allan Bennett
(B.A.)
b. 27.2.1945

Patricia Ann
Anderson
b. 30.1.1948 (a.)
m. 7.5.1972
William Edwards
(B.Sc., M.B.A.)
b. 29.3.1948

Bailey Jay
Anderson
b. 19.2.1984

Rosemary
Margaret
Bennett
b. 18.7.1975

Nicholas Drew
Bennett
b. 1.8.1977

Tracy Ann
Edwards
b. 29.9.1977

Alexander
Simon
Edwards
b 29.1.1979

Willia
Conra
Edwar
b.5.6.1

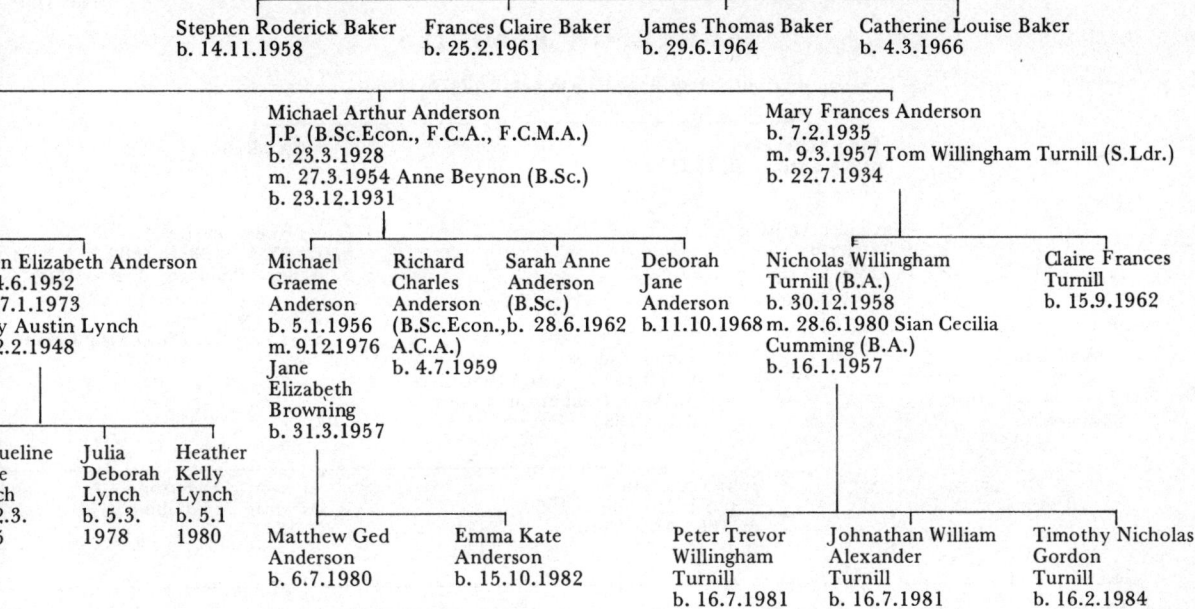

Stephen Roderick Baker
b. 14.11.1958

Frances Claire Baker
b. 25.2.1961

James Thomas Baker
b. 29.6.1964

Catherine Louise Baker
b. 4.3.1966

Michael Arthur Anderson
J.P. (B.Sc.Econ., F.C.A., F.C.M.A.)
b. 23.3.1928
m. 27.3.1954 Anne Beynon (B.Sc.)
b. 23.12.1931

Mary Frances Anderson
b. 7.2.1935
m. 9.3.1957 Tom Willingham Turnill (S.Ldr.)
b. 22.7.1934

ren Elizabeth Anderson
14.6.1952
27.1.1973
ry Austin Lynch
2.2.1948

Michael
Graeme
Anderson
b. 5.1.1956
m. 9.12.1976
Jane
Elizabeth
Browning
b. 31.3.1957

Richard
Charles
Anderson
(B.Sc.Econ.,
A.C.A.)
b. 4.7.1959

Sarah Anne
Anderson
(B.Sc.)
b. 28.6.1962

Deborah
Jane
Anderson
b. 11.10.1968

Nicholas Willingham
Turnill (B.A.)
b. 30.12.1958
m. 28.6.1980 Sian Cecilia
Cumming (B.A.)
b. 16.1.1957

Claire Frances
Turnill
b. 15.9.1962

queline
rie
nch
22.3.
75

Julia
Deborah
Lynch
b. 5.3.
1978

Heather
Kelly
Lynch
b. 5.1
1980

Matthew Ged
Anderson
b. 6.7.1980

Emma Kate
Anderson
b. 15.10.1982

Peter Trevor
Willingham
Turnill
b. 16.7.1981

Johnathan William
Alexander
Turnill
b. 16.7.1981

Timothy Nicholas
Gordon
Turnill
b. 16.2.1984

Compiled by:
Michael A. Anderson

ANDERSON FAMILIES

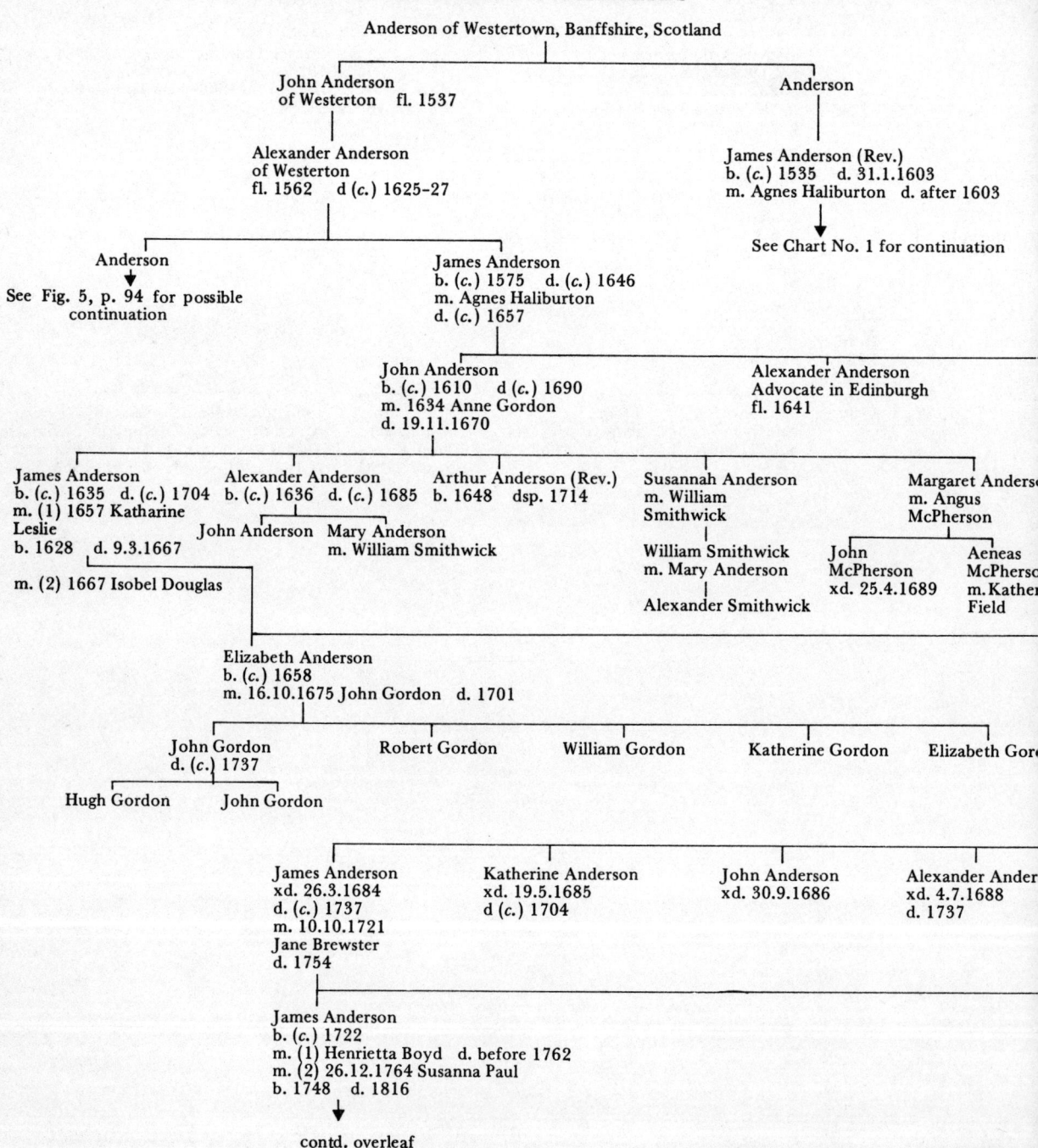

Anderson of Westertown, Banffshire, Scotland

John Anderson
of Westerton   fl. 1537

Anderson

Alexander Anderson
of Westerton
fl. 1562   d (*c.*) 1625–27

James Anderson (Rev.)
b. (*c.*) 1535   d. 31.1.1603
m. Agnes Haliburton   d. after 1603

See Chart No. 1 for continuation

Anderson

See Fig. 5, p. 94 for possible
continuation

James Anderson
b. (*c.*) 1575   d. (*c.*) 1646
m. Agnes Haliburton
d. (*c.*) 1657

John Anderson
b. (*c.*) 1610   d (*c.*) 1690
m. 1634 Anne Gordon
d. 19.11.1670

Alexander Anderson
Advocate in Edinburgh
fl. 1641

James Anderson
b. (*c.*) 1635   d. (*c.*) 1704
m. (1) 1657 Katharine
Leslie
b. 1628   d. 9.3.1667

m. (2) 1667 Isobel Douglas

Alexander Anderson
b. (*c.*) 1636   d. (*c.*) 1685

John Anderson   Mary Anderson
               m. William Smithwick

Arthur Anderson (Rev.)
b. 1648   dsp. 1714

Susannah Anderson
m. William
Smithwick

William Smithwick
m. Mary Anderson

Alexander Smithwick

Margaret Anders
m. Angus
McPherson

John
McPherson
xd. 25.4.1689

Aeneas
McPherso
m. Kather
Field

Elizabeth Anderson
b. (*c.*) 1658
m. 16.10.1675 John Gordon   d. 1701

John Gordon
d. (*c.*) 1737

Robert Gordon   William Gordon   Katherine Gordon   Elizabeth Gor

Hugh Gordon   John Gordon

James Anderson
xd. 26.3.1684
d. (*c.*) 1737
m. 10.10.1721
Jane Brewster
d. 1754

Katherine Anderson
xd. 19.5.1685
d (*c.*) 1704

John Anderson
xd. 30.9.1686

Alexander Ander
xd. 4.7.1688
d. 1737

James Anderson
b. (*c.*) 1722
m. (1) Henrietta Boyd   d. before 1762
m. (2) 26.12.1764 Susanna Paul
b. 1748   d. 1816

contd. overleaf

KEY TO ABBREVIATIONS

a.	adopted
b.	born
bd.	buried
c.	circa — approximately
d.	died
dsp.	died without issue
dspm.	died without male issue
dvp.	died before his father
fl.	living
kia.	killed in action
m.	married
m.dis.	divorced
ob.coel.	died a bachelor
ob.inf.	died in infancy
ob.inn.	died a spinster
ob.juv.	died in childhood
s.	a son
xd.	baptised
DL	Deputy Lieutenant
JP	Justice of the Peace

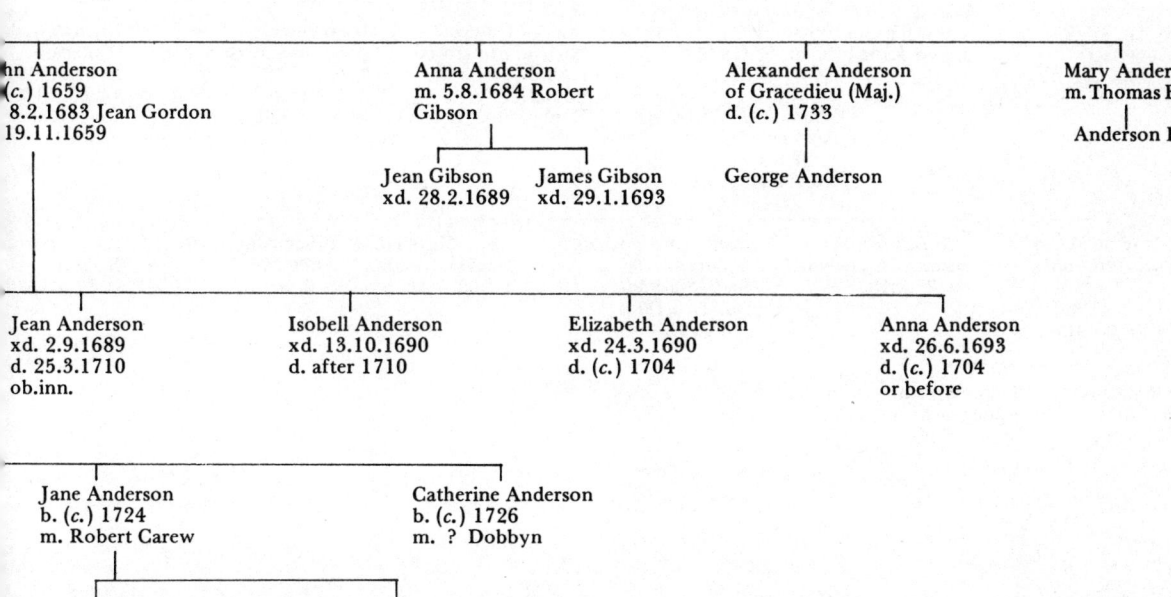

George Anderson
fl. 1641   d. after 1700
m. Jean Stewart

John Anderson
b. (c.) 1680

Thomas Anderson
b. 1682

Marjorie Anderson
b. 1687

hn Anderson
(c.) 1659
8.2.1683 Jean Gordon
19.11.1659

Anna Anderson
m. 5.8.1684 Robert
Gibson

Alexander Anderson
of Gracedieu (Maj.)
d. (c.) 1733

Mary Anderson
m. Thomas Baker

Anderson Baker

Jean Gibson
xd. 28.2.1689

James Gibson
xd. 29.1.1693

George Anderson

Jean Anderson
xd. 2.9.1689
d. 25.3.1710
ob.inn.

Isobell Anderson
xd. 13.10.1690
d. after 1710

Elizabeth Anderson
xd. 24.3.1690
d. (c.) 1704

Anna Anderson
xd. 26.6.1693
d. (c.) 1704
or before

Jane Anderson
b. (c.) 1724
m. Robert Carew

Catherine Anderson
b. (c.) 1726
m. ? Dobbyn

Robert Carew
m. ? Robins

Jane Carew
m. ? Wogan

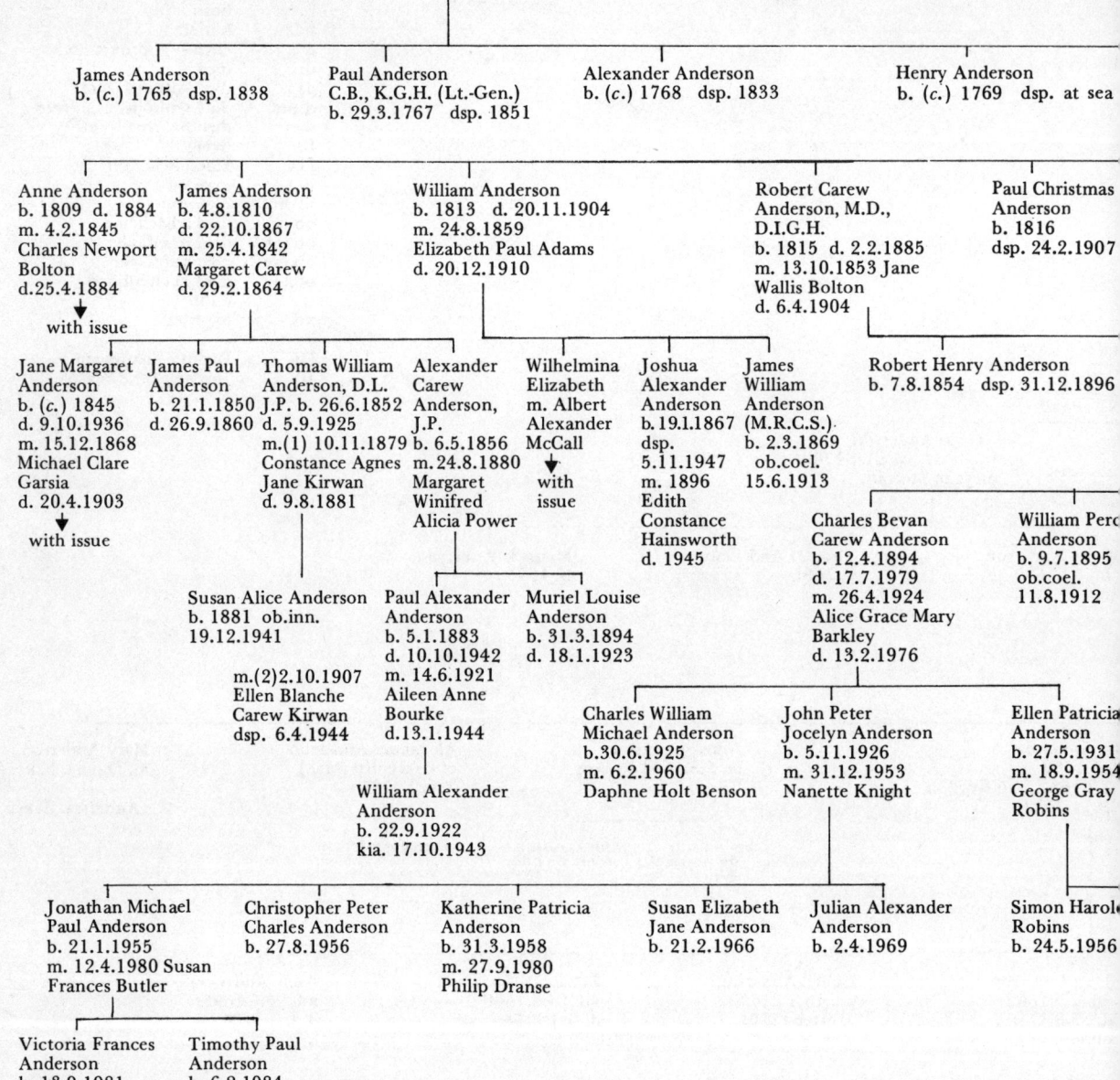

James Anderson
b. (c.) 1765 dsp. 1838

Paul Anderson
C.B., K.G.H. (Lt.-Gen.)
b. 29.3.1767 dsp. 1851

Alexander Anderson
b. (c.) 1768 dsp. 1833

Henry Anderson
b. (c.) 1769 dsp. at sea

Anne Anderson
b. 1809 d. 1884
m. 4.2.1845
Charles Newport
Bolton
d.25.4.1884

with issue

James Anderson
b. 4.8.1810
d. 22.10.1867
m. 25.4.1842
Margaret Carew
d. 29.2.1864

William Anderson
b. 1813 d. 20.11.1904
m. 24.8.1859
Elizabeth Paul Adams
d. 20.12.1910

Robert Carew
Anderson, M.D.,
D.I.G.H.
b. 1815 d. 2.2.1885
m. 13.10.1853 Jane
Wallis Bolton
d. 6.4.1904

Paul Christmas
Anderson
b. 1816
dsp. 24.2.1907

Jane Margaret
Anderson
b. (c.) 1845
d. 9.10.1936
m. 15.12.1868
Michael Clare
Garsia
d. 20.4.1903

with issue

James Paul
Anderson
b. 21.1.1850
d. 26.9.1860

Thomas William
Anderson, D.L.
J.P. b. 26.6.1852
d. 5.9.1925
m.(1) 10.11.1879
Constance Agnes
Jane Kirwan
d. 9.8.1881

Alexander
Carew
Anderson,
J.P.
b. 6.5.1856
m. 24.8.1880
Margaret
Winifred
Alicia Power

Wilhelmina
Elizabeth
m. Albert
Alexander
McCall

with
issue

Joshua
Alexander
Anderson
b.19.1.1867
dsp.
5.11.1947
m. 1896
Edith
Constance
Hainsworth
d. 1945

James
William
Anderson
(M.R.C.S.)
b. 2.3.1869
ob.coel.
15.6.1913

Robert Henry Anderson
b. 7.8.1854 dsp. 31.12.1896

Susan Alice Anderson
b. 1881 ob.inn.
19.12.1941

m.(2)2.10.1907
Ellen Blanche
Carew Kirwan
dsp. 6.4.1944

Paul Alexander
Anderson
b. 5.1.1883
d. 10.10.1942
m. 14.6.1921
Aileen Anne
Bourke
d.13.1.1944

William Alexander
Anderson
b. 22.9.1922
kia. 17.10.1943

Muriel Louise
Anderson
b. 31.3.1894
d. 18.1.1923

Charles William
Michael Anderson
b.30.6.1925
m. 6.2.1960
Daphne Holt Benson

John Peter
Jocelyn Anderson
b. 5.11.1926
m. 31.12.1953
Nanette Knight

Charles Bevan
Carew Anderson
b. 12.4.1894
d. 17.7.1979
m. 26.4.1924
Alice Grace Mary
Barkley
d. 13.2.1976

William Perc
Anderson
b. 9.7.1895
ob.coel.
11.8.1912

Ellen Patricia
Anderson
b. 27.5.1931
m. 18.9.1954
George Gray
Robins

Jonathan Michael
Paul Anderson
b. 21.1.1955
m. 12.4.1980 Susan
Frances Butler

Christopher Peter
Charles Anderson
b. 27.8.1956

Katherine Patricia
Anderson
b. 31.3.1958
m. 27.9.1980
Philip Dranse

Susan Elizabeth
Jane Anderson
b. 21.2.1966

Julian Alexander
Anderson
b. 2.4.1969

Simon Harol
Robins
b. 24.5.1956

Victoria Frances
Anderson
b. 13.9.1981

Timothy Paul
Anderson
b. 6.2.1984

Compiled by Michael A. Anderson,
based on research by Sir Francis
James Anderson

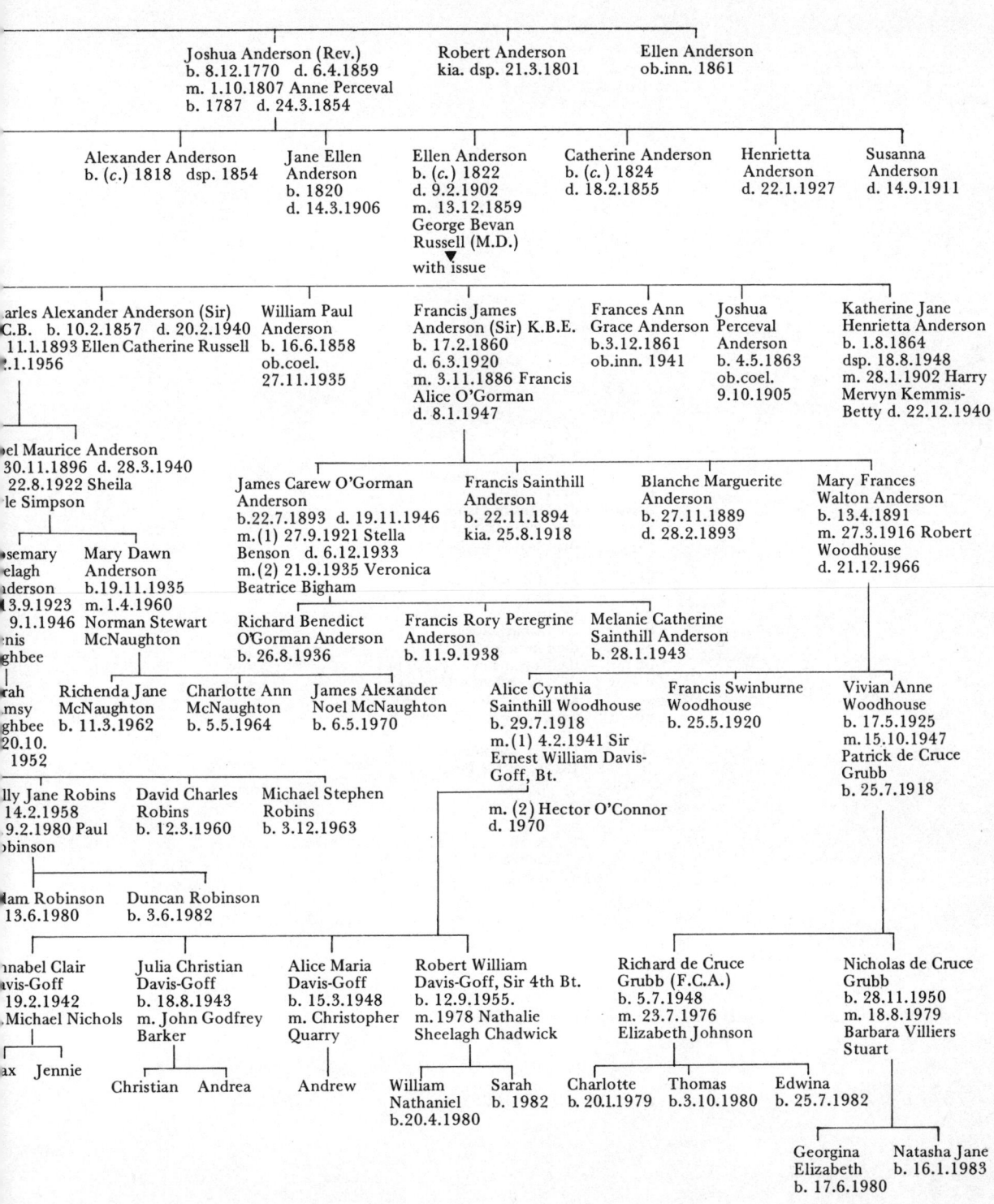

Joshua Anderson (Rev.)
b. 8.12.1770 d. 6.4.1859
m. 1.10.1807 Anne Perceval
b. 1787 d. 24.3.1854

Robert Anderson
kia. dsp. 21.3.1801

Ellen Anderson
ob.inn. 1861

Alexander Anderson
b. (c.) 1818 dsp. 1854

Jane Ellen
Anderson
b. 1820
d. 14.3.1906

Ellen Anderson
b. (c.) 1822
d. 9.2.1902
m. 13.12.1859
George Bevan
Russell (M.D.)
▼
with issue

Catherine Anderson
b. (c.) 1824
d. 18.2.1855

Henrietta
Anderson
d. 22.1.1927

Susanna
Anderson
d. 14.9.1911

arles Alexander Anderson (Sir)
C.B. b. 10.2.1857 d. 20.2.1940
11.1.1893 Ellen Catherine Russell
2.1.1956

William Paul
Anderson
b. 16.6.1858
ob.coel.
27.11.1935

Francis James
Anderson (Sir) K.B.E.
b. 17.2.1860
d. 6.3.1920
m. 3.11.1886 Francis
Alice O'Gorman
d. 8.1.1947

Frances Ann
Grace Anderson
b.3.12.1861
ob.inn. 1941

Joshua
Perceval
Anderson
b. 4.5.1863
ob.coel.
9.10.1905

Katherine Jane
Henrietta Anderson
b. 1.8.1864
dsp. 18.8.1948
m. 28.1.1902 Harry
Mervyn Kemmis-
Betty d. 22.12.1940

el Maurice Anderson
30.11.1896 d. 28.3.1940
22.8.1922 Sheila
le Simpson

James Carew O'Gorman
Anderson
b.22.7.1893 d. 19.11.1946
m.(1) 27.9.1921 Stella
Benson d. 6.12.1933
m.(2) 21.9.1935 Veronica
Beatrice Bigham

Francis Sainthill
Anderson
b. 22.11.1894
kia. 25.8.1918

Blanche Marguerite
Anderson
b. 27.11.1889
d. 28.2.1893

Mary Frances
Walton Anderson
b. 13.4.1891
m. 27.3.1916 Robert
Woodhouse
d. 21.12.1966

semary
elagh
derson
3.9.1923
m.1.4.1960
9.1.1946 Norman Stewart
nis McNaughton
ghbee

Mary Dawn
Anderson
b.19.11.1935

Richard Benedict
O'Gorman Anderson
b. 26.8.1936

Francis Rory Peregrine
Anderson
b. 11.9.1938

Melanie Catherine
Sainthill Anderson
b. 28.1.1943

rah
msy
ghbee
20.10.
1952

Richenda Jane
McNaughton
b. 11.3.1962

Charlotte Ann
McNaughton
b. 5.5.1964

James Alexander
Noel McNaughton
b. 6.5.1970

Alice Cynthia
Sainthill Woodhouse
b. 29.7.1918
m.(1) 4.2.1941 Sir
Ernest William Davis-
Goff, Bt.

m.(2) Hector O'Connor
d. 1970

Francis Swinburne
Woodhouse
b. 25.5.1920

Vivian Anne
Woodhouse
b. 17.5.1925
m.15.10.1947
Patrick de Cruce
Grubb
b. 25.7.1918

ly Jane Robins
14.2.1958
9.2.1980 Paul
binson

David Charles
Robins
b. 12.3.1960

Michael Stephen
Robins
b. 3.12.1963

am Robinson
13.6.1980

Duncan Robinson
b. 3.6.1982

nabel Clair
avis-Goff
19.2.1942
Michael Nichols

Julia Christian
Davis-Goff
b. 18.8.1943
m. John Godfrey
Barker

Alice Maria
Davis-Goff
b. 15.3.1948
m. Christopher
Quarry

Robert William
Davis-Goff, Sir 4th Bt.
b. 12.9.1955.
m.1978 Nathalie
Sheelagh Chadwick

Richard de Cruce
Grubb (F.C.A.)
b. 5.7.1948
m. 23.7.1976
Elizabeth Johnson

Nicholas de Cruce
Grubb
b. 28.11.1950
m. 18.8.1979
Barbara Villiers
Stuart

ax   Jennie

Christian   Andrea

Andrew

William
Nathaniel
b.20.4.1980

Sarah
b. 1982

Charlotte
b. 20.1.1979

Thomas
b.3.10.1980

Edwina
b. 25.7.1982

Georgina
Elizabeth
b. 17.6.1980

Natasha Jane
b. 16.1.1983

KEY TO ABBREVIATIONS

a.	adopted
b.	born
bd.	buried
c.	circa — approximately
d.	died
dsp.	died without issue
dspm.	died without male issue
dvp.	died before his father
fl.	living
kia.	killed in action
m.	married
m.dis.	divorced
ob.coel.	died a bachelor
ob.inf.	died in infancy
ob.inn.	died a spinster
ob.juv.	died in childhood
s.	a son
xd.	baptised
DL	Deputy Lieutenant
JP	Justice of the Peace

LINDSAY

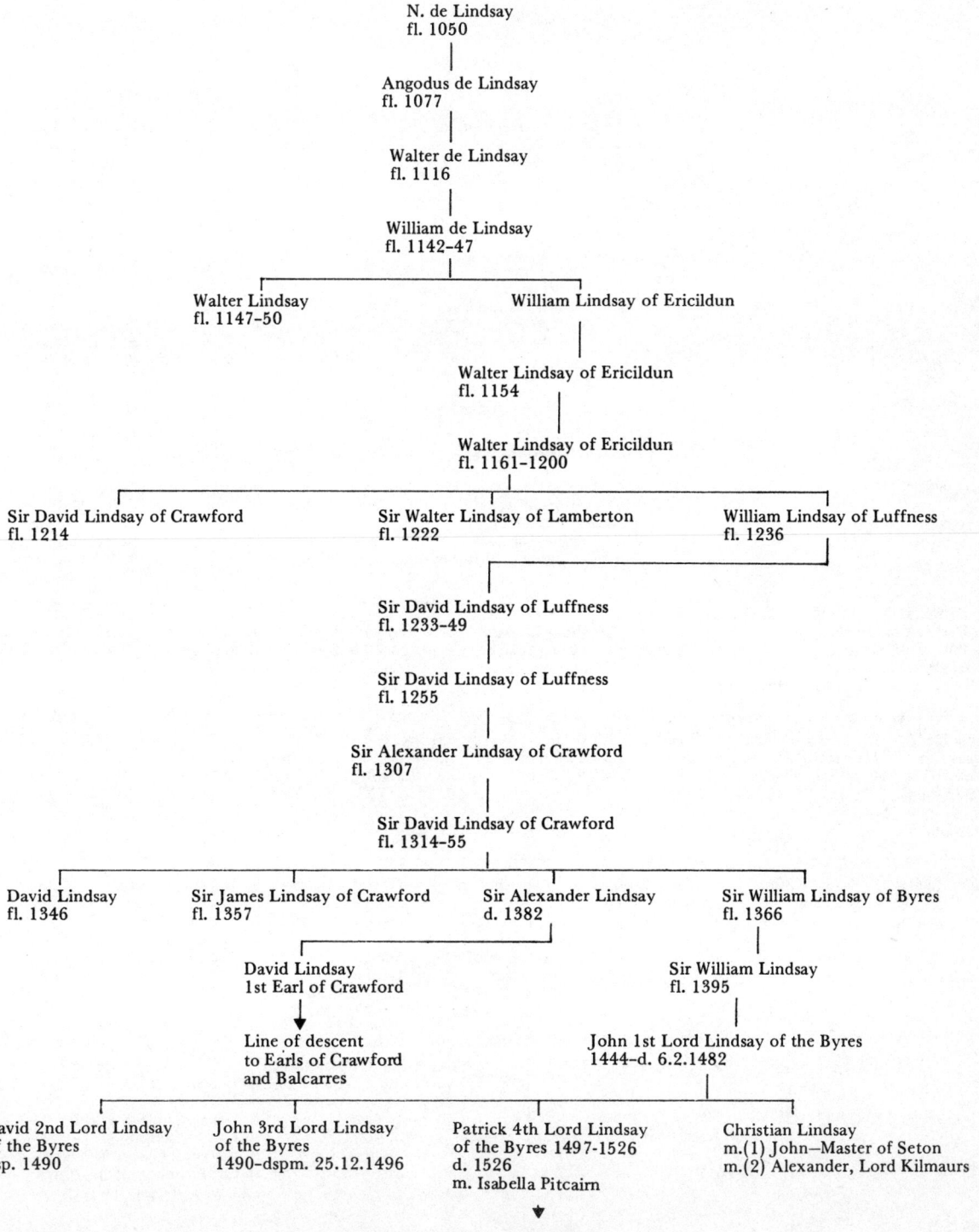

N. de Lindsay
fl. 1050

Angodus de Lindsay
fl. 1077

Walter de Lindsay
fl. 1116

William de Lindsay
fl. 1142–47

Walter Lindsay
fl. 1147–50

William Lindsay of Ericildun

Walter Lindsay of Ericildun
fl. 1154

Walter Lindsay of Ericildun
fl. 1161–1200

Sir David Lindsay of Crawford
fl. 1214

Sir Walter Lindsay of Lamberton
fl. 1222

William Lindsay of Luffness
fl. 1236

Sir David Lindsay of Luffness
fl. 1233–49

Sir David Lindsay of Luffness
fl. 1255

Sir Alexander Lindsay of Crawford
fl. 1307

Sir David Lindsay of Crawford
fl. 1314–55

David Lindsay
fl. 1346

Sir James Lindsay of Crawford
fl. 1357

Sir Alexander Lindsay
d. 1382

Sir William Lindsay of Byres
fl. 1366

David Lindsay
1st Earl of Crawford

Sir William Lindsay
fl. 1395

Line of descent
to Earls of Crawford
and Balcarres

John 1st Lord Lindsay of the Byres
1444–d. 6.2.1482

David 2nd Lord Lindsay
of the Byres
dsp. 1490

John 3rd Lord Lindsay
of the Byres
1490–dspm. 25.12.1496

Patrick 4th Lord Lindsay
of the Byres 1497-1526
d. 1526
m. Isabella Pitcairn

Christian Lindsay
m.(1) John—Master of Seton
m.(2) Alexander, Lord Kilmaurs

contd. overleaf

Descended from David Lindsay
1st Earl of Crawford

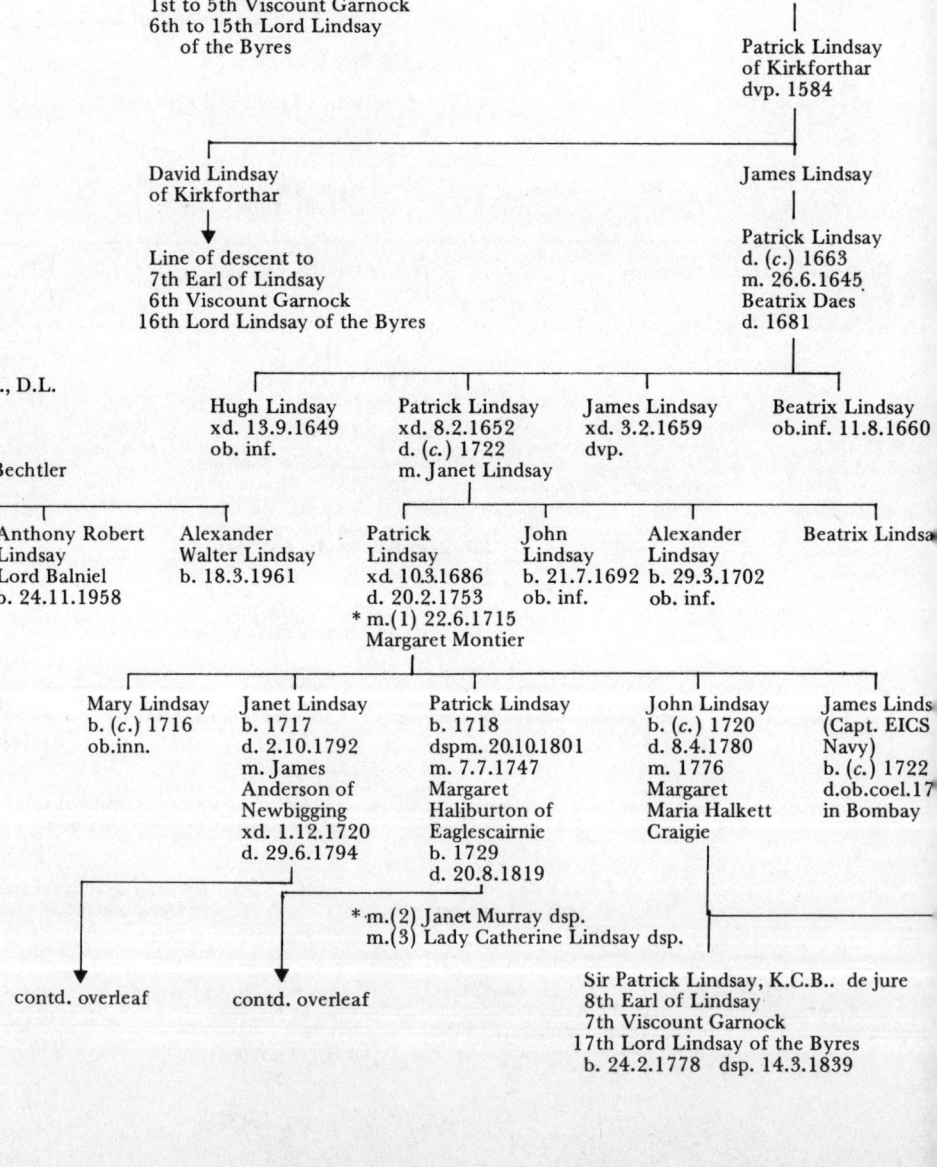

Sir John Lindsay
dvp. 1525

John 5th Lord Lindsay
of the Byres
d. 13.12.1563

Patrick Lindsay
of Kirkforthar
dsp.

David Lindsay
of Kirkforthar
d. 1592
m. Helen Crichton

Line of descent to
1st to 6th Earl of Lindsay
17th to 22nd Earl of Crawford
1st to 5th Viscount Garnock
6th to 15th Lord Lindsay
of the Byres

John Lindsay
of Kirkforthar
d. 4.12.1599

Patrick Lindsay
of Kirkforthar
dvp. 1584

David Lindsay
of Kirkforthar

James Lindsay

Line of descent to
7th Earl of Lindsay
6th Viscount Garnock
16th Lord Lindsay of the Byres

Patrick Lindsay
d. (c.) 1663
m. 26.6.1645
Beatrix Daes
d. 1681

Robert Alexander Lindsay, P.C., D.L.
29th Earl of Crawford
12th Earl of Balcarres
b. 5.3.1927
m. 1949 Ruth Beatrice Meyer-Bechtler

Hugh Lindsay
xd. 13.9.1649
ob. inf.

Patrick Lindsay
xd. 8.2.1652
d. (c.) 1722
m. Janet Lindsay

James Lindsay
xd. 3.2.1659
dvp.

Beatrix Lindsay
ob.inf. 11.8.1660

Bettina Mary
Lindsay
b. 26.6.1950
m. 1975 Peter
Charles
Drummond-Hay

Iona Sina
Lindsay
b. 10.8.1957

Anthony Robert
Lindsay
Lord Balniel
b. 24.11.1958

Alexander
Walter Lindsay
b. 18.3.1961

Patrick
Lindsay
xd. 10.3.1686
d. 20.2.1753
* m.(1) 22.6.1715
Margaret Montier

John
Lindsay
b. 21.7.1692
ob. inf.

Alexander
Lindsay
b. 29.3.1702
ob. inf.

Beatrix Lindsa

Tamsin Rachel
b. 1977

Alice Ruth
b. 1980

Mary Lindsay
b. (c.) 1716
ob.inn.

Janet Lindsay
b. 1717
d. 2.10.1792
m. James
Anderson of
Newbigging
xd. 1.12.1720
d. 29.6.1794

Patrick Lindsay
b. 1718
dspm. 20.10.1801
m. 7.7.1747
Margaret
Haliburton of
Eaglescairnie
b. 1729
d. 20.8.1819

John Lindsay
b. (c.) 1720
d. 8.4.1780
m. 1776
Margaret
Maria Halkett
Craigie

James Linds
(Capt. EICS
Navy)
b. (c.) 1722
d.ob.coel.17
in Bombay

* m.(2) Janet Murray dsp.
m.(3) Lady Catherine Lindsay dsp.

contd. overleaf

contd. overleaf

Sir Patrick Lindsay, K.C.B., de jure
8th Earl of Lindsay
7th Viscount Garnock
17th Lord Lindsay of the Byres
b. 24.2.1778   dsp. 14.3.1839

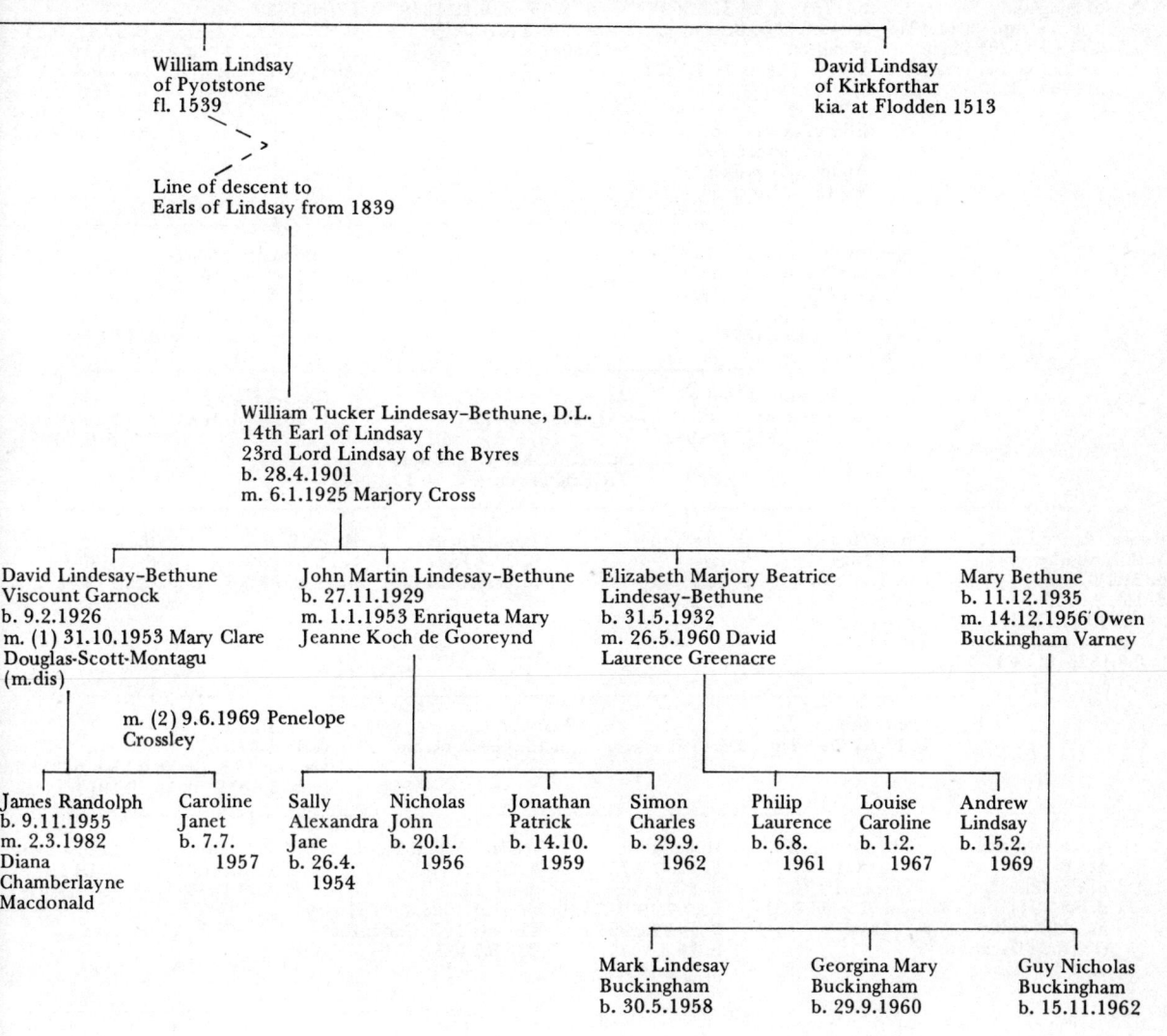

William Lindsay
of Pyotstone
fl. 1539

David Lindsay
of Kirkforthar
kia. at Flodden 1513

Line of descent to
Earls of Lindsay from 1839

William Tucker Lindesay–Bethune, D.L.
14th Earl of Lindsay
23rd Lord Lindsay of the Byres
b. 28.4.1901
m. 6.1.1925 Marjory Cross

David Lindsay-Bethune
Viscount Garnock
b. 9.2.1926
m. (1) 31.10.1953 Mary Clare
Douglas-Scott-Montagu
(m.dis)

m. (2) 9.6.1969 Penelope
Crossley

John Martin Lindesay-Bethune
b. 27.11.1929
m. 1.1.1953 Enriqueta Mary
Jeanne Koch de Gooreynd

Elizabeth Marjory Beatrice
Lindesay-Bethune
b. 31.5.1932
m. 26.5.1960 David
Laurence Greenacre

Mary Bethune
b. 11.12.1935
m. 14.12.1956 Owen
Buckingham Varney

James Randolph
b. 9.11.1955
m. 2.3.1982
Diana
Chamberlayne
Macdonald

Caroline
Janet
b. 7.7.
1957

Sally
Alexandra
Jane
b. 26.4.
1954

Nicholas
John
b. 20.1.
1956

Jonathan
Patrick
b. 14.10.
1959

Simon
Charles
b. 29.9.
1962

Philip
Laurence
b. 6.8.
1961

Louise
Caroline
b. 1.2.
1967

Andrew
Lindsay
b. 15.2.
1969

Mark Lindsay
Buckingham
b. 30.5.1958

Georgina Mary
Buckingham
b. 29.9.1960

Guy Nicholas
Buckingham
b. 15.11.1962

Anne Lindsay
b. (c.) 1780
ob.inn. 7.1.1851

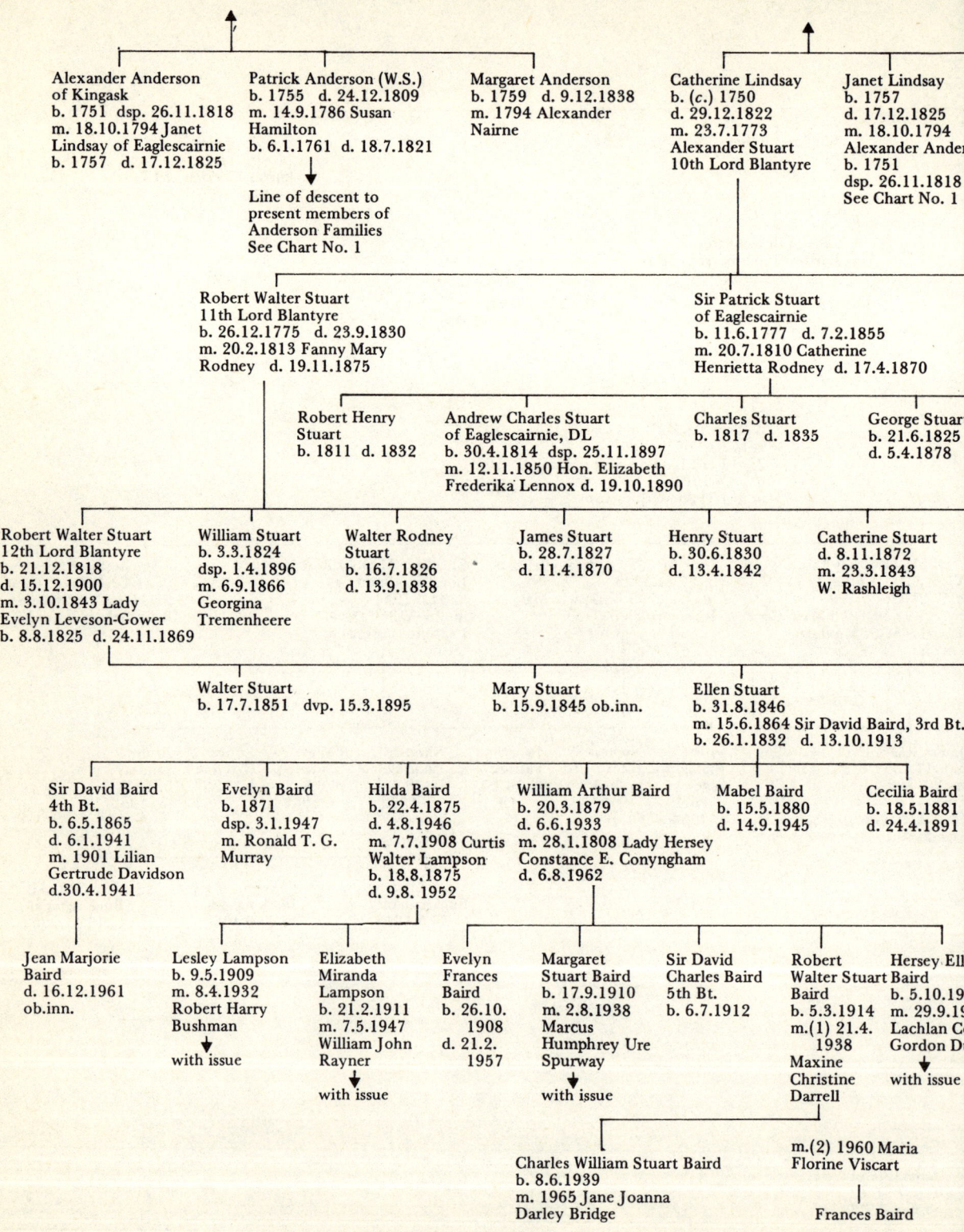

Alexander Anderson
of Kingask
b. 1751 dsp. 26.11.1818
m. 18.10.1794 Janet
Lindsay of Eaglescairnie
b. 1757 d. 17.12.1825

Patrick Anderson (W.S.)
b. 1755 d. 24.12.1809
m. 14.9.1786 Susan
Hamilton
b. 6.1.1761 d. 18.7.1821

Line of descent to
present members of
Anderson Families
See Chart No. 1

Margaret Anderson
b. 1759 d. 9.12.1838
m. 1794 Alexander
Nairne

Catherine Lindsay
b. (c.) 1750
d. 29.12.1822
m. 23.7.1773
Alexander Stuart
10th Lord Blantyre

Janet Lindsay
b. 1757
d. 17.12.1825
m. 18.10.1794
Alexander Anders
b. 1751
dsp. 26.11.1818
See Chart No. 1

Robert Walter Stuart
11th Lord Blantyre
b. 26.12.1775 d. 23.9.1830
m. 20.2.1813 Fanny Mary
Rodney d. 19.11.1875

Sir Patrick Stuart
of Eaglescairnie
b. 11.6.1777 d. 7.2.1855
m. 20.7.1810 Catherine
Henrietta Rodney d. 17.4.1870

Robert Henry
Stuart
b. 1811 d. 1832

Andrew Charles Stuart
of Eaglescairnie, DL
b. 30.4.1814 dsp. 25.11.1897
m. 12.11.1850 Hon. Elizabeth
Frederika Lennox d. 19.10.1890

Charles Stuart
b. 1817 d. 1835

George Stuart
b. 21.6.1825
d. 5.4.1878

Robert Walter Stuart
12th Lord Blantyre
b. 21.12.1818
d. 15.12.1900
m. 3.10.1843 Lady
Evelyn Leveson-Gower
b. 8.8.1825 d. 24.11.1869

William Stuart
b. 3.3.1824
dsp. 1.4.1896
m. 6.9.1866
Georgina
Tremenheere

Walter Rodney
Stuart
b. 16.7.1826
d. 13.9.1838

James Stuart
b. 28.7.1827
d. 11.4.1870

Henry Stuart
b. 30.6.1830
d. 13.4.1842

Catherine Stuart
d. 8.11.1872
m. 23.3.1843
W. Rashleigh

Walter Stuart
b. 17.7.1851 dvp. 15.3.1895

Mary Stuart
b. 15.9.1845 ob.inn.

Ellen Stuart
b. 31.8.1846
m. 15.6.1864 Sir David Baird, 3rd Bt.
b. 26.1.1832 d. 13.10.1913

Sir David Baird
4th Bt.
b. 6.5.1865
d. 6.1.1941
m. 1901 Lilian
Gertrude Davidson
d.30.4.1941

Evelyn Baird
b. 1871
dsp. 3.1.1947
m. Ronald T. G.
Murray

Hilda Baird
b. 22.4.1875
d. 4.8.1946
m. 7.7.1908 Curtis
Walter Lampson
b. 18.8.1875
d. 9.8. 1952

William Arthur Baird
b. 20.3.1879
d. 6.6.1933
m. 28.1.1808 Lady Hersey
Constance E. Conyngham
d. 6.8.1962

Mabel Baird
b. 15.5.1880
d. 14.9.1945

Cecilia Baird
b. 18.5.1881
d. 24.4.1891

Jean Marjorie
Baird
d. 16.12.1961
ob.inn.

Lesley Lampson
b. 9.5.1909
m. 8.4.1932
Robert Harry
Bushman

with issue

Elizabeth
Miranda
Lampson
b. 21.2.1911
m. 7.5.1947
William John
Rayner

with issue

Evelyn
Frances
Baird
b. 26.10.
1908
d. 21.2.
1957

Margaret
Stuart Baird
b. 17.9.1910
m. 2.8.1938
Marcus
Humphrey Ure
Spurway

with issue

Sir David
Charles Baird
5th Bt.
b. 6.7.1912

Robert
Walter Stuart
Baird
b. 5.3.1914
m.(1) 21.4.
1938
Maxine
Christine
Darrell

m.(2) 1960 Maria
Florine Viscart

Hersey Elle
Baird
b. 5.10.19
m. 29.9.19
Lachlan Ce
Gordon Du

with issue

Charles William Stuart Baird
b. 8.6.1939
m. 1965 Jane Joanna
Darley Bridge

Frances Baird

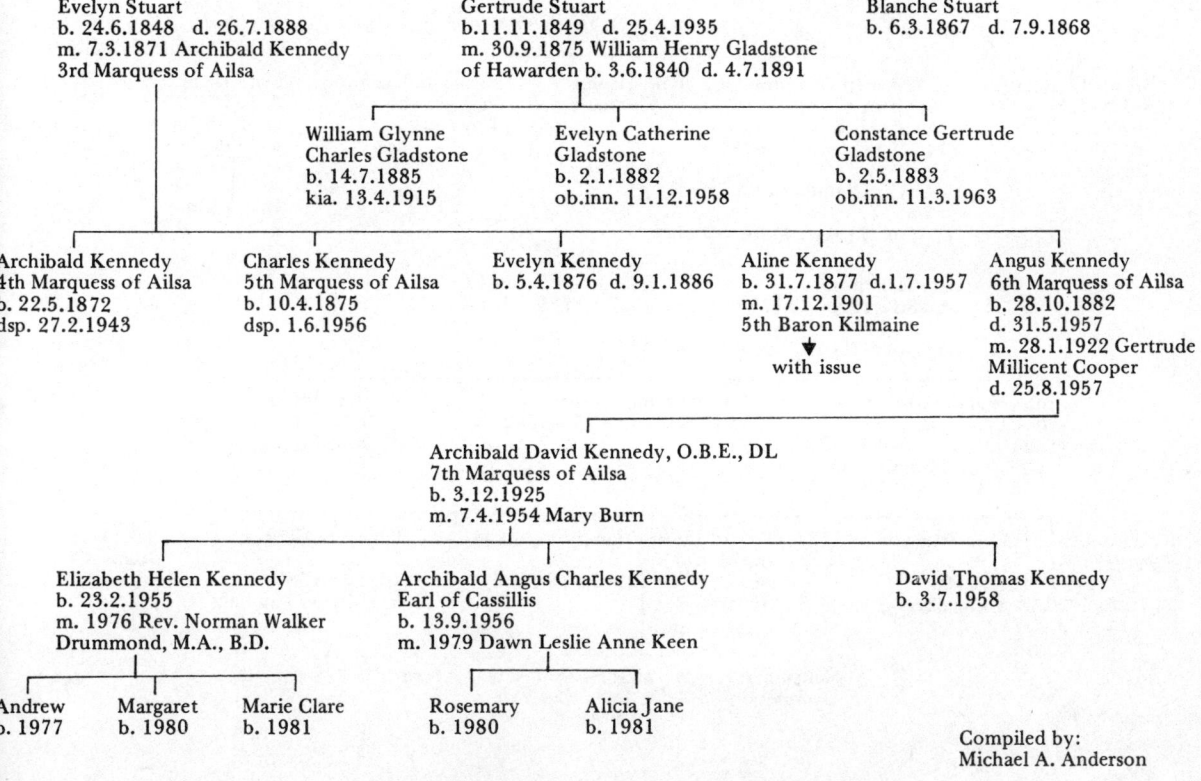

Lindsay
:.) 1758
nn. 14.9.1821

William Stuart
b. 1778 dsp. 1837

Charles Francis Stuart
b. 1780 d. 2.12.1858

Margaret Stuart
dsp. 20.10.1839
m. 5.10.1809
Rev. Andrew Stuart

herine Margaret
art d. 15.1.1887
6.9.1847 Bryan
me Holme

ing issue

Louisa Stuart
dsp. 15.9.1850
m. 21.11.1848 Rt.
Rev. George
Tomlinson
d. 6.2.1863

Patrick
Lindsay Stuart
b. 11.2.1832
dsp. 19.9.1893

William
Stuart
b. 1834
d. 1840

Jane Frances
Stuart d. 13.11.1872
m. 20.6.1845 Adm.
Hon. George Grey
R.N. d. 3.10.1891

Mary Janet
Stuart
d. 7.2.1891
m. 8.7.1869
William Bligh
O'Connell

Emily
Henrietta
Stuart

Helen Elizabeth
Stuart
dsp. 26.5.1879
m. 24.9.1856 Rev.
Thomas Huntley
Greene

Fanny Mary Stuart
d. 18.12.1896
m. 10.8.1847
W. B. Ferrand

with issue

Georgina Eliza Stuart
m. 27.5.1857 Rt. Hon.
Sir Andrew Buchanan

Caroline Henrietta Stuart
m. 12.8.1850 John Charles
7th Earl of Seafield

with issue

Evelyn Stuart
b. 24.6.1848 d. 26.7.1888
m. 7.3.1871 Archibald Kennedy
3rd Marquess of Ailsa

Gertrude Stuart
b.11.11.1849 d. 25.4.1935
m. 30.9.1875 William Henry Gladstone
of Hawarden b. 3.6.1840 d. 4.7.1891

Blanche Stuart
b. 6.3.1867 d. 7.9.1868

William Glynne
Charles Gladstone
b. 14.7.1885
kia. 13.4.1915

Evelyn Catherine
Gladstone
b. 2.1.1882
ob.inn. 11.12.1958

Constance Gertrude
Gladstone
b. 2.5.1883
ob.inn. 11.3.1963

Archibald Kennedy
4th Marquess of Ailsa
b. 22.5.1872
dsp. 27.2.1943

Charles Kennedy
5th Marquess of Ailsa
b. 10.4.1875
dsp. 1.6.1956

Evelyn Kennedy
b. 5.4.1876 d. 9.1.1886

Aline Kennedy
b. 31.7.1877 d.1.7.1957
m. 17.12.1901
5th Baron Kilmaine

with issue

Angus Kennedy
6th Marquess of Ailsa
b. 28.10.1882
d. 31.5.1957
m. 28.1.1922 Gertrude
Millicent Cooper
d. 25.8.1957

Archibald David Kennedy, O.B.E., DL
7th Marquess of Ailsa
b. 3.12.1925
m. 7.4.1954 Mary Burn

Elizabeth Helen Kennedy
b. 23.2.1955
m. 1976 Rev. Norman Walker
Drummond, M.A., B.D.

Archibald Angus Charles Kennedy
Earl of Cassillis
b. 13.9.1956
m. 1979 Dawn Leslie Anne Keen

David Thomas Kennedy
b. 3.7.1958

Andrew
b. 1977

Margaret
b. 1980

Marie Clare
b. 1981

Rosemary
b. 1980

Alicia Jane
b. 1981

Compiled by:
Michael A. Anderson

HAMPTON AND HAMPTON-LEWIS

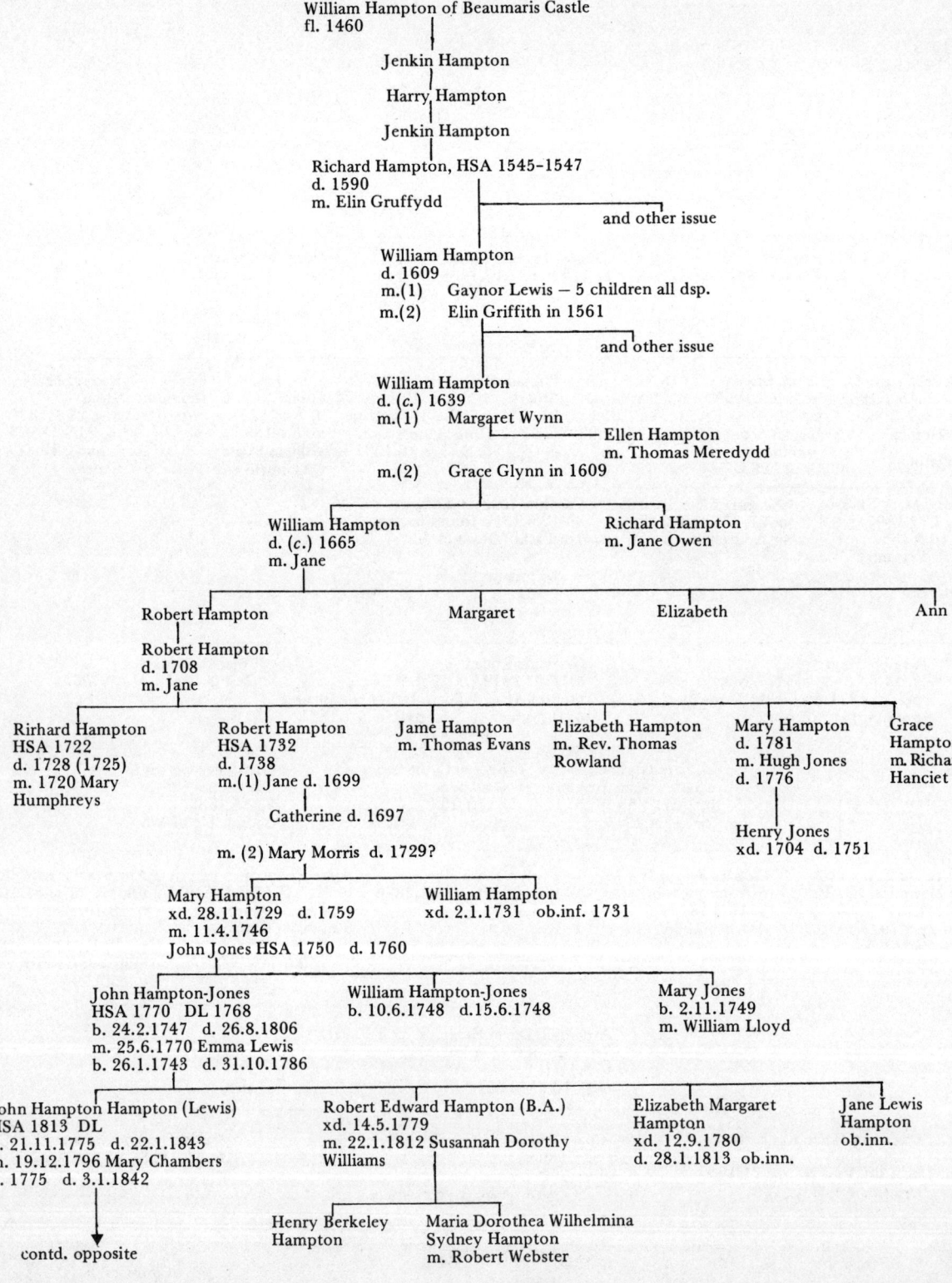

William Hampton of Beaumaris Castle
fl. 1460

Jenkin Hampton

Harry Hampton

Jenkin Hampton

Richard Hampton, HSA 1545–1547
d. 1590
m. Elin Gruffydd

and other issue

William Hampton
d. 1609
m.(1) Gaynor Lewis — 5 children all dsp.
m.(2) Elin Griffith in 1561

and other issue

William Hampton
d. (c.) 1639
m.(1) Margaret Wynn

Ellen Hampton
m. Thomas Meredydd

m.(2) Grace Glynn in 1609

William Hampton
d. (c.) 1665
m. Jane

Richard Hampton
m. Jane Owen

Robert Hampton   Margaret   Elizabeth   Ann

Robert Hampton
d. 1708
m. Jane

Rirhard Hampton
HSA 1722
d. 1728 (1725)
m. 1720 Mary
Humphreys

Robert Hampton
HSA 1732
d. 1738
m.(1) Jane d. 1699

Jame Hampton
m. Thomas Evans

Elizabeth Hampton
m. Rev. Thomas
Rowland

Mary Hampton
d. 1781
m. Hugh Jones
d. 1776

Grace
Hampton
m. Richard
Hanciet

Catherine d. 1697

Henry Jones
xd. 1704 d. 1751

m. (2) Mary Morris d. 1729?

Mary Hampton
xd. 28.11.1729 d. 1759
m. 11.4.1746
John Jones HSA 1750 d. 1760

William Hampton
xd. 2.1.1731 ob.inf. 1731

John Hampton-Jones
HSA 1770 DL 1768
b. 24.2.1747 d. 26.8.1806
m. 25.6.1770 Emma Lewis
b. 26.1.1743 d. 31.10.1786

William Hampton-Jones
b. 10.6.1748 d.15.6.1748

Mary Jones
b. 2.11.1749
m. William Lloyd

John Hampton Hampton (Lewis)
HSA 1813 DL
b. 21.11.1775 d. 22.1.1843
m. 19.12.1796 Mary Chambers
b. 1775 d. 3.1.1842

Robert Edward Hampton (B.A.)
xd. 14.5.1779
m. 22.1.1812 Susannah Dorothy
Williams

Elizabeth Margaret
Hampton
xd. 12.9.1780
d. 28.1.1813 ob.inn.

Jane Lewis
Hampton
ob.inn.

Henry Berkeley
Hampton

Maria Dorothea Wilhelmina
Sydney Hampton
m. Robert Webster

contd. opposite

John Hampton Hampton (Lewis) etc.

John Lewis Hampton-Lewis HSA 1846 JP, DL
b. 18.10.1798
d. 5.9.1871
m. 2.9.1833 Frances
Elizabeth l'Anson
b. 1806   d. 30.1.1878

Joseph Hampton Hampton (Col. HEICS)
b. 2.2.1800
d. 5.10.1878
m. 21.4.1824
Ellen Hall

Emma Hampton
b. 2.2.1801
d. 5.8.1819
ob.inf.

Anna Maria Hampton
b. 27.4.1802

Mary Margaret Hampton
b. 7.9.1803 d. 13.9.1856
m. 22.11.1825 Alexander
Anderson (Maj. HEICS)
b. 17.3.1794 d. 25.6.1855
See Chart No. 1 for issue.

Anna Maria Surman
b. 4.1.1811
m. 8.6.1835
Charles Longman

John Lewis Hampton

Thomas Lewis Hampton-Lewis HSA 1869 JP, DL (Col.)
b. 9.8.1834   d. 10.3.1912
m. 20.2.1872 Lettice Martha
Pritchard

John Vivian Hampton
b. 18.6.1835   d. 18.5.1890
m. 2.6.1868 Lady Laura
Elizabeth Phipps

Fanny Mary Hampton
b. 4.4.1838   d. 26.6.1908
m. William G. Griffith

with issue

Mary Freeman Grace Hampton
b. 11.6.1842   d. 20.10.1927

Constance Laura Hampton
m. 1892 George Warren Biddulph

with issue

John Arthur Lewis
b. 26.3.1874
d. 2.8.1875

Mary Gwendolen Hampton
b. 1.4.1875   dsp. 1946
m. 3.10.1914 Bertie
Cunynghame Dwyer
(Dwyer–Hampton)
HSA 1929, JP, DL
b. 1872   d. 9.6.1967

John Lewis Hampton-Lewis
b. 1.10.1876
d. 6.6.1906

Dorothy Lettice Lewis
b. 14.4.1880
d. 16.8.1923
m. 2.8.1913
Randal –
Lord Louth

Sisili Myfanwy Lewis
b. 11.3.1883 dsp. 2.2.1968
m.(1) 26.2.1908 Arthur
Charles Davies, kia. 1915
m.(2) 2.8.1921 Cyril Panton
Vivian (Vivian-Hampton)
b. 12.9.1885 d. 23.11.1960

Thomas Herbert Richard Hampton-Lewis
b. 2.4.1885
d. 29.10.1911

Randal Patrick Ralph Oliver
b. 9.12.1914   d. 14.7.1936
m. 13.2.1936 Gwendoline
Mary Cowling

KEY TO ABBREVIATIONS

a.	adopted
b.	born
bd.	buried
c.	circa — approximately
d.	died
dsp.	died without issue
dspm.	died without male issue
dvp.	died before his father
fl.	living
kia.	killed in action
m.	married
m.dis.	divorced
ob.coel.	died a bachelor
ob.inf.	died in infancy
ob.inn.	died a spinster
ob.juv.	died in childhood
s.	a son
xd.	baptised
DL	Deputy Lieutenant
JP	Justice of the Peace
HSA	High Sheriff of Anglesey
HEICS	Honourable East India Company Service

Compiled by:
Michael A. Anderson

INDEX TO PLACES AND EVENTS

INDEX TO NAMES OF PEOPLE

having some connection
with the families detailed
in the text.

Dates shown are for guidance to assist when tracing a reference to a particular person. They mainly indicate the approximate date of birth or marriage or, where this is not known, an indication of a year when the individual concerned was probably living. Most married women are listed under both their maiden and married names, where this is known.